LUCIAN

The central detail from *The Marriage of Alexander and Roxane* by Giovanni
Bazzi *dit* Il Sodoma. This painting closely reproduces Lucian's description in
his *Herodotus*, of a supposed work by the Greek artist Aetion. Such Lucianic
transpositions d'art were a favourite source of inspiration for many Italian
Renaissance painters.

LUCIAN

AND HIS INFLUENCE IN EUROPE

Christopher Robinson

The University of North Carolina Press
Chapel Hill

Published in 1979 by
Gerald Duckworth & Company Limited
The Old Piano Factory
43 Gloucester Crescent, London NW1

Library of Congress Cataloging in Publication Data
Robinson, Christopher

Lucian and his influence in Europe
Includes index
1. Lucianus Samosatensis.   2. Lucianus
Samosatensis – Influence.   3. European literature –
History and criticism.   I. Title
PA4236.R6   887'.01   79–16580
ISBN 0–8078–1404–0

Printed in Great Britain by
Western Printing Services Ltd, Bristol

Contents

Preface

MY object in this book has been to identify the main literary characteristics of Lucian's work, and to give some idea of the major facets of his influence on European literature. It is not practicable for such a book to be exhaustive in its coverage. My analysis of Lucian is a literary one, and does not concern itself primarily with the many technical problems of a historical and linguistic kind which the text raises. Similarly, my account of later authors is selective, intended to offer examples of how and why Lucian's influence was important. I have not attempted to compile a general bibliography: the scope of the material handled precludes it. Works which I have found particularly useful (or sometimes the reverse) are listed in the footnotes. There is a brief bibliographical note on Lucian himself in the Appendix.

I wish to thank Dr G. Anderson, Mrs P. Currie, Dr R. W. Truman, Mrs Y. de Henseler and Mrs H. Bering-Jensen for their kind help. I am particularly indebted to Mr C. W. Macleod, who patiently read part of the manuscript and offered several invaluable suggestions. I am also grateful to the General Editor for his constant encouragement and assistance.

Christ Church, Oxford   C.R.

I

Lucian: the Man and the Work

I. THE AGE AND THE MAN

THE period from A.D. 117 to 167, covering the reigns of Hadrian and
Antoninus Pius, and the early years of the reign of Marcus Aurelius,
is traditionally regarded as the material golden age of the Roman
empire. The frontiers had reached their maximum point of expansion,
no major wars were undertaken, and prosperity reached a new height.
Admittedly the root causes of later economic and social disorders were
already to be found, particularly in the process of continuing industrial
decentralization which shortages of man-power and raw materials
forced upon the commercial system of the empire.[1] But superficially
nothing much seemed wrong for the upper and middle classes. New
cities were being built, methods of trading and banking improved,
more artefacts were available. The sense of satisfaction was nowhere
more keenly felt than among the educated provincials, for the emperors, of provincial birth themselves, made significant changes in the
status of the provinces, allowing them particularly to feel the benefit
of the current prosperity. No longer regarded as estates of the Roman
people, but represented in both the senatorial and the equestrian
classes by men descended from their own municipal aristocracies, the
separate provinces were able to deal with their own problems as individual social units within the consolidated structure of the united
empire. Private fortunes, local centres of culture, even a sense of
meritocratic opportunity within the imperial bureaucracy are all hallmarks of provincial urban society of the period. The Greek-speaking
east acquiesced in the material benefits of the Roman system just as
much as the western provinces. Aelius Aristides' speech *On Rome,*
though marked with the characteristic exaggerations of a rhetorical
prose poem, probably represents the consensus of educated opinion in
Greece and Asia Minor when it dwells on the advantages to society in

[1] See F. W. Walbank, *The Awful Revolution: the decline of the Roman Empire
n the West*, Liverpool 1969.

general of constitution, emperor and army, and of the values which they uphold.[1] The keynote is one of peace, a peace within which 'cities gleam with radiance and charm and the whole earth has been beautified like a garden'. And alongside the prosperity there is also a sense of security, of law and order:

Now indeed it is possible for Hellene or non-Hellene, with or without his property, to travel wherever he will, easily, just as if every country through which he passes were his own land.

Yet, for all this satisfaction with the new material order, Greek society continued to be backward-looking. Economic independence was not a complete counterbalance to political dependence. In the face of the political domination of Rome, the Greek-speaking upper class asserted its superiority by cultural concentration on a broad range of activities which exploited the past as an alternative to the present.[2] It is the age of archaism, in form and theme as much as in language, in history and philosophy as much as in lighter branches of literature. In this respect it is the sophists, and the rhetorical education which bred them, that best represent the intellectual atmosphere of the period. As early as the second half of the first century rhetorical declamation on topics drawn from myth and history had become forms of public entertainment. A typical example that survives is Aristides' *Speech for an Embassy to Achilles*, but a brief glance through Philostratus' *Lives of the Sophists* would uncover countless other such themes drawn from Trojan, Persian or Peloponnesian wars. This is not to say that contemporary events and conditions are never brought into art. They merely have a secondary status, or are seen through the distorting glass of past traditions. In day-to-day material existence the Greek aristocracies were subjects of the empire. In their cultural lives they remained firmly part of worlds that had vanished four hundred years and more previously.

This, then, is the age into which Lucian was born and under which he lived the greater part of his life. He was born around 120 in the province of Syria, or, to be more exact, in Commagene, an ex-client kingdom annexed by Vespasian fifty years earlier and incorporated

[1] See J. H. Oliver 'The ruling power: a study of the Roman Empire in the second century after Christ through the Roman Oration of Aelius Aristides', *Transactions of the American Philosophical Society* 43.4 (1953) 873–1003. The quotations are from Oliver's translation.

[2] See E. L. Bowie 'The Greeks and their past in the Second Sophistic', *Past and Present* 46 (1970) 1–41.

into the northern corner of Syria, with which its natural geographical connexions lay. It is a mountainous area straddling the Euphrates; Samosata, the town of Lucian's birth and the old royal capital, was what passed for its metropolis. The population, Iranian with Semitic traces, had acquired a certain Hellenization as early as the first century B.C. It may sound like a backwater, but this would be not altogether a fair judgment. River and land routes kept it in direct contact with Mesopotamia, Persia and India. There were adequate roads to Cilicia and Cappadocia, but better communications—three roads and the river—southward to Syria. Moreover, despite its altitude, the area was very rich, so Strabo tells us, because of the mountain streams that watered it: it was known for its fruit trees, its timber exports, its guinea-fowl, its herbal medicines. Above all, Samosata itself was on a direct trade route from Ephesus to India, and earned a certain privileged political status as the site of a legionary camp merited, doubtless, by its virtual military impregnability and its potential usefulness to the Parthians. However, Roman occupation of Commagene has left few traces. It was a policing exercise conducted for the benefit of Rome, not part of a process of cultural proselytization. The principal social institutions remained Greco-Iranian even where Roman material alterations—bridges, roads, public monuments—were made. As late as 110 on the Philopappus monument, in Athens, inscribed to aristocrats of the old Commagenian royal house, two nobles are called 'king', which suggests that even the imperial image impinged only marginally on the consciousness of the inhabitants.

Such, then, is the period of Lucian's life, and such the place of his birth and childhood. But of the man himself little is known. No contemporary or near-contemporary mentions him. He himself makes few overt references to events or people in the world about him, and those few are not entirely to be trusted. It seems he was trained in public speaking, which was in any case the basis of all contemporary education. He then earned his living by giving lectures, first in Asia Minor, later in Athens. This probably brought him no more than a modest success, for, though he himself claims in *The Double Indictment* that oratory made him famous, the silence of his contemporaries goes against him. And the internal evidence which indicates that various of his speeches were delivered in Gaul, Macedonia, and the Pô valley suggests that many of his lecture tours took him into what were, for a Greek-speaking orator, hardly the most fashionable parts of the empire. An Aristides, a Pollux, a Polemon made their name in Asia

Minor, in Athens, or in Rome. On the other hand, Lucian was not strictly a sophist in their sense, a virtuoso extemporizer on historical and mythical themes. He could turn his hand to many standard rhetorical exercises, but his speciality was the satirical dialogue, the techniques of which he claims, perhaps this time truthfully, to have developed himself, towards the middle of his life. All that is known for certain is that he gave up lecturing temporarily to take up a minor post in the imperial bureaucracy in Egypt, probably around 170, and in turn abandoned this for reasons unknown, returning to the provincial lecture scene. His life then fades into final obscurity sometime shortly after the death of Marcus Aurelius in 180.[1]

2. THE WORK: TRADITIONALISM

This absence of biographical evidence is neither surprising nor disturbing as far as Lucian's works themselves go. For Lucian himself is a prime example of the traditionalism that permeates all literature of his period. The world around him occurs incidentally in his work, and the events of his own life equally peripherally, because he is wholly taken up with the task of making out of the imitation of traditional themes and forms works which have themselves independent artistic validity. It is the theory of *mimesis*, or imitation, which gives the clue to what Lucian's audiences looked for, and enjoyed, in his work. What, then, does imitation mean in this context?[2]

Imitation is the principle that underlies the educational curriculum in the Roman empire. To learn about life is to learn about life as codified, analysed and exemplified in great works of art. To write about life is to reproduce the picture of life as presented in the same works of art. Education was intended to train pupils how to choose authors for their appropriateness, read carefully, and transfer what was read into their own writings. Whether the branch of study was grammar or rhetoric made no difference to the pattern of learning, for both referred in the same way to a corpus of accepted masters, both to philosophers, historians, playwrights and poets, who provided the authority on matters of theme and form. Ancient theorists either

[1] For an elaborate but speculative attempt at biographical reconstruction, see J. Schwartz, *Biographie de Lucien de Samosate*, Brussels 1965.

[2] Throughout my account of Lucian's work I have drawn heavily upon J. Bompaire, *Lucien écrivain, imitation et création*, Paris 1958. I have also been much helped by B. Reardon's excellent general study, *Courants littéraires grecs des IIe et IIIe siècles après J-C*, Paris 1971.

recommend this double imitation of theme and form, or accept it as inevitable, so that the whole post-Romantic notion of originality is irrelevant to their concept of literary creation. This does not mean that imagination is excluded. 'Longinus' *On the Sublime* XIII. 2–14 lyrically expresses his view of the inspiration necessary to creative imitation, e.g.:

For many are carried away by the inspiration of another, just as the story runs that the Pythian priestess on approaching the tripod where there is, they say, 'a rift in the earth upbreathing steam divine', becomes thereby impregnated with the divine power and is at once inspired to utter oracles; so, too, from the natural genius of those old writers there flows into the hearts of their admirers as it were an emanation from the mouth of holiness . . . Such borrowing is not theft; it is rather like taking an impression from fine characters, as one does from moulded figures or other works of art. (2–4)[1]

Longinus' enthusiasm was by no means entirely misplaced. The doctrine of imitation did produce very great works of art in antiquity, notably the *Aeneid*. This does not alter the fact that in the rhetorical tradition, novelty is merely the illusion of the new, achieved by the novel combination of old elements. In the words of Isocrates (*Paneg.* 8): 'One should not avoid the subjects of which others have spoken before one; one should try to do better than they did.'

The sophists of Lucian's day underwent precisely this sort of training at school.[2] They were men who had a particular aptitude for oratory, took up careers as lecturers and teachers of rhetoric, and whose highest ambition was probably to fill one of the new state-financed chairs of rhetoric. They were possessors of distinguished libraries and had read widely. Many of them, interestingly enough, were, like Lucian, not Hellenes by blood, and were perhaps particularly drawn to a profession devoted to the imitation of the Greek past by some personal compulsive need for thorough self-hellenization. For if some sophists were accused of modernism, this seems to have meant no more than that, instead of the standard models, they imitated Alexandrian and even occasionally later literature, or that they mixed genres or otherwise transgressed the strict rules of the classic theorists on the subject. It was almost unthinkable for a writer to invent a subject out of his own head,

[1] Trans. W. Hamilton Fyfe, Loeb Aristotle *Poetics* and 'Longinus' *On the Sublime*, 167.
[2] The fullest account of what is known about the sophists of the period can be found in G. W. Bowersock, *Greek Sophists in the Roman Empire*, Oxford 1969.

or express an idea in a form that owed nothing to tradition. But imagination was not excluded, for the distinction between good and bad imitation lies in the fact that true imitation is the recreation of the total experience of the work imitated, or the creation of a new literary experience out of material carefully culled from the best elements of several models. As the reader acquainted with any of the major works of the Renaissance will know, imagination and artistic sensibility are fully as necessary for this level of imitation as for any other creative act.

As far as imitation is concerned, Lucian, though not strictly a sophist, adheres to the same cultural principles as his contemporaries, and much of his work can be fitted into similar rhetorical categories. The art of sophists such as Aelius Aristides and Polemon has been entertainingly and profitably compared by one modern critic with that of the jazz performer: an intricate but ephemeral act, embroidering in virtuoso fashion on a few stock elements, for the entertainment of an 'informed' audience. The thematic range of the art was in a significant sense decidedly narrow. The distinctive functions of the three branches of oratory as defined by Aristotle, *logos sumbouleutikos* (parliamentary oratory), *logos dikanikos* (forensic oratory) and *logos epideiktikos* (occasional oratory) had been elided into one, in that the first two categories, having had their raison d'être whittled away by Roman occupation, now existed for their form, rather than their content. In other words, though the three genres continued to exist independently, the first two came to look very much like the third. The important thing for the sophist was not what you said, but the way you said it.

Lucian's extant work[1] contains certain formal exercises which fall directly into Aristotelian categories. As examples of fictitious forensic rhetoric there are *The Tyrannicide* and *Disowned*. In the former a man claims the reward for killing a tyrant on the grounds that by killing the tyrant's son he caused the tyrant himself to commit suicide from grief. The second contains a complex argument about disinheritance and the moral responsibilities of a doctor. Both works are conducted strictly according to traditional precepts; e.g. in *The Tyrannicide* an exordium setting out the essence of the defence case is followed by a narrative of events relevant to the case which contains the main proofs on which the defence will rely; the prosecution's arguments are then refuted

---

[1] I have not concerned myself with the problems of the authenticity of various works traditionally attributed to Lucian. In the present section I have largely concentrated discussion around works over which no doubts have been raised. In sections two and three the issue is irrelevant, for all that matters is that a later author should have *thought* a work to be by Lucian.

and a summing up is attempted. In similar fashion *In Praise of my Country* and *The Fly* belong to the category *logos epideiktikos*, in its strict original function of a formal speech apportioning praise or blame.

None of these works seems more than at best ingenious. It has been fairly said indeed of *In Praise of my Country* that if it had not been handed down to us among the works of Lucian, no one would have thought of attributing it to him. Yet it would be a mistake to dismiss all Lucian's more traditional works as mere school exercises. He has the virtue of taking elements which had previously been considered only as preparation towards proficiency in the three divisions of formal oratory, and raising them to the status of art forms in themselves. In this, it is true, he is following a tendency of the age. After him Philostratus would do the same for the *ecphrasis* (formal description), and in his *Letters of Courtesans* Alciphron the same for the epistle (not technically a *progumnasma* but probably practised as such at this period). Like them, Lucian sometimes develops a particular exercise for its own sake, as with the *ecphrasis Hippias*. More significantly, he uses a wide range of exercises, notably *diēgēma* (narrative), *chreia* (characteristic moral saying), *sunkrisis* (comparison), and *ecphrasis*, as the basis for a special literary form, the *prolalia*, or introduction.

This is a short piece evidently used as a curtain-raiser at a public performance. Eleven such works by Lucian survive: *Bacchus*, *The Dipsads*, *Amber*, *Harmonides*, *Hercules*, *Herodotus*, *The Scythian*, *Zeuxis*, *Lucian's Career*, *The Hall*, and *A Prometheus in Words*. The aim of the work is always to commend the speaker to his audience in some way. A typical tactic is to build up to some modesty topos:

> So I am giving you warning that when you have taken the water away and revealed what fish I have to offer, do not expect anything big in your haul or you'll only have yourself to blame for your disappointment. (*Amber* 6)[1]

Another function is to prepare the audience for the novelty to be found in the speaker's works, as in *Zeuxis* and *A Prometheus in Words*, by disparaging the value of novelty as a quality in itself:

> I wouldn't be at all happy to be thought an innovator, creator of a work for which no pedigree could be found. I should be deeply ashamed, I can tell you, if my work weren't thought elegant as well; I should trample it to pieces. The originality would be no grounds, as far as I'm concerned, for not tearing it up. (*A Prometheus in Words* 3)

[1] All quotations from Lucian are given in my own translation unless otherwise indicated.

What is interesting about the *prolalia* as a genre is that although it was sufficiently popular in the second century A.D. to command recognition by the theorists, who tentatively included it under the heading *logos epideiktikos*, it appears to have no formal rhetorical structure at all. Yet it can have a very precise *literary* structure, as is the case with *Zeuxis*. This is built around a *diēgēma*, the story of Zeuxis and his painting of a female Hippocentaur, and this narrative itself contains an *ecphrasis*, the account of the painting. The choice of the hybrid figure of the Hippocentaur is peculiarly happy as a symbol for the hybrid novelties of Lucian's literary forms. On each side of this central block is another narrative, the first decked out with proverbial sayings, the second a full-blown *diēgēma* in its own right, illustrating the theme of novelty yet again, this time with the historical example of Antiochos using his elephants against the Galatian troops. The structure is thematically impeccable. It starts with the idea of the inadequacy of novelty as an artistic criterion in itself, illustrates this in two quite different ways, and closes by restating the idea in terms of the two narrative examples used:

> It's time for me to consider whether I am not just like Antiochus: not up to the fight in most ways, but putting on show a few elephants and strange trolls, performing a little sleight of hand. At least, these are the aspects of my work that get universal praise. Not a word is said about the qualities I myself have faith in. People are merely astonished at the very fact of painting a Hippocentaur. They find it, as indeed it is, novel and monstrous. Did the rest of Zeuxis' work go for nothing then? No, surely not for nothing. For you are all artists, you see everything with an expert eye. All I hope is that I can offer a display worthy of my audience. (*Zeuxis* 12)

One can reasonably say of this very neat and economic structure that Lucian has exploited his formal training with great skill to produce something other than a formal rhetorical exercise.

3. INNOVATION

In fact, for the inventive mind it was the very redivision of the genres of oratory, or rather the simplification of their function, that offered in itself an opening for literary ingenuity. The true sophist continued to distinguish with care the rules appropriate to each type of speech, but he might, like Aelius Aristides in the *Pro quattuor*, present an apparent panegyric in such a way as to incorporate an historical argument previously more common in parliamentary oratory, or, like Polemon, he might disguise under a historical subject—which was the braver man at the battle of Marathon: Cynegirus or Callimachus?—the formal procedures of a courtroom exchange. Lucian was a far more inventive writer than Aristides or Polemon. The main interest of his work lies in the extent to which he has not merely used an extant genre, or even, like contemporary sophists, disguised one genre as another, but created a series of new forms whose literary merit lies essentially in the skill with which traditional elements have been combined for new comic effects. To achieve this he has used exactly the same rhetorical elements as the sophists, with one notable addition, dialogue.

Before Lucian's day the use of dialogue in prose literature had been associated mainly with philosophical works, notably in the form of the Socratic dialogue, developed by Plato and imitated in more recent times by Plutarch. In the comic court-room scene of *The Double Indictment* Lucian himself promotes the idea that his own use of dialogue is philosophical in origin, when he claims that, at the age of about 40, he switched from the meretricious charms of rhetoric to the sober attractions of 'Dialogue, who is said to be the son of Philosophy' (28). Later in the same work he sets out the way in which he sees himself as having adapted the form of the philosophical dialogue by blending other elements into it. The words are put into the mouth of Dialogue himself, as he puts the plaintiff's case to the jury:

Here is how I have been wronged and maltreated by this fellow. I used to be immensely serious. I would ponder upon the gods and nature and the universe, building castles in the air high o'er the clouds where, as Plato put it, great Zeus in heaven is borne along upon his winged chariot. Then, just as I was soaring through the celestial vault and about to mount upon 'the very back of heaven', this fellow dragged me down, clipped my wings, and put me on the level of the average man. He took away my sober tragic mask, and gave me another, a mask for comedy or farce, that is all but absurd. Then he shut me up with Epigram and Lampoon and Cynicism and Eupolis and Aristophanes, great ones for making fun of all that is sacred and ridiculing all that is right. Finally he even dug up Menippus, one of the old Cynics, whose bark is bad and whose bite is worse, and set this dog on me, a really terrible creature with a sneaky bite. He smiles as he sinks his teeth in.

The mention of Eupolis and Aristophanes properly highlights Lucian's debt to Old Comedy. The claim that he has been influenced by Menippean satire is unfortunately less easy to judge, as we know very little about the genre. Possible indications of influence are the mixing of dialogue, monologue and narrative within the same work, and the use of certain themes: the aerial journey, the visit to the underworld, the sale of souls, the comic banquet, the assembly of the gods, and the exchange of letters between gods and men. None of these elements can be said to prove the influence of Menippus on Lucian, and none of them really affect the question of the *form* of dialogue in Lucian. Even so, we must accept that, however stylized the context, Lucian is making a coherent claim to have adapted three kinds of dialogue.

It would be a mistake, however, to suppose that the explanation provides an exhaustive account of the sources of Lucian's inspiration, or of the nature of the product they inspired. Apart from any other considerations, dialogue as a form cannot be held wholly foreign to rhetoric. At least one schoolroom exercise, the *chreia*, contains the germ of a dramatic situation, of which dialogue is a natural extension. In it the maxim of a famous character is delivered and commented upon, sometimes with the creation of an appropriate physical context, and often with a brief exchange between speakers. Plutarch's *Sayings of Kings and Generals* are largely a collection of *chreiai*, some of them with a sketchy 'dialogue', e.g.

(on Cleomenes, no 17) When someone said, 'Why have you not killed off the people of Argos who wage war against you so often?' he said, 'Oh, we would not kill them off, for we want to have some trainers for our young men.'[1]

For a straightforward example of the genre in Lucian's work one can go to *Dialogues of the Dead* 26, where Antilochus questions Achilles on his saying 'Better a poor man's servant, and alive, than king among the dead', and offers a moral commentary on both Achilles and his words. There are also numerous examples of the extended use of the *chreia* within a longer work which is itself in dialogue form, as with the conversation between Solon and Croesus in *Charon* 12. Of course, Lucian's use of dialogue goes well beyond the potential scope of a *progumnasma*, but that is no reason to ignore the potential rôle of the *chreia* in the development of a particular variety of Lucianic dialogue.

Variety is, in fact, a key word. For, if Lucian does not, as he himself admits in *The Double Indictment*, adhere to the conventions of the philosophical dialogue, neither does he create a uniform blend of elements to be used in all contexts. In some works there is argument conducted wholly or mainly after a Platonic pattern, as in *Hermotimus*,

[1] Trans. F. C. Babbitt, Loeb *Moralia* vol. III, 341.

Anacharsis, The Ship and *The Parasite*. In other works the manner of
the dialogue is entirely dramatic—*Timon, Charon, Zeus Rants, The
Cock*. Even where the philosophical or dramatic form predominates,
the classifications are not clear ones. There is a substantial difference of
type between the form of dialogue in *Hermotimus* and in *Anacharsis*.
Hermotimus is, at least superficially, a serious exploration of the claims
made for the discipline of philosophy by the eponymous hero, a somewhat elderly student, who is encouraged to explain his motives and
expectations by the apparently anodyne approach of his interlocutor,
Lycinus, only to find them systematically and ruthlessly undermined.
The development of the dialogue is Socratic in the sense that the argument itself is conducted after the manner of question and answer in,
say, *Protagoras*, or *Gorgias*. In *Anacharsis*, on the other hand, the
central theme of the right nature of physical education is really only an
excuse for a formally elaborated *sunkrisis* or comparison of the two
points of view. The Platonic element derives from conventions of
presentation: the scene is clearly located (in a gymnasium), the characters are walking as they speak, the two speakers are clearly characterized by what they say. There is no attempt to reproduce the Socratic
method of argument. Much the same can be said of *The Ship*, where the
focus is on the entertaining quality of the stories told, representing as
they do a satire on the folly of human wishes. There is no parading of
reductive logic. The Platonic element lies, again, in the setting—like
the *Republic*, it opens with a visit to the Piraeus—and the use of the
talk-as-you-walk theme. As for *The Parasite*, it is different again,
since the Socratic method becomes in part the subject while the bulk
of the structure is purely rhetorical. The work is on one level a paradoxical encomium, on another a parody, using the false conducting of
a Socratic argument to the comic end of proving a demonstrably
absurd thesis, that the art of the scrounger is superior to that of philosopher or rhetorician.

The diversity to be found in Lucian's use of dialogue on a philosophical pattern is fully matched by the diversity of his dramatic dialogue, though here it is as much a diversity of matter as of manner.
There is a clear difference in manner and purpose between the *Dialogues
of the Courtesans*, on the one hand, and dialogues such as *Timon* or
The Dead Come to Life. In the former, types and situations are plainly
drawn, for the most part, from New Comedy. Each dialogue is the
transposition of a scene or scenes, with the familiar range of characters
and situations: lovers' quarrel and misunderstanding put right (*Dial.*

2 and 12), rivals in love quarrel (*Dial.* 9), the madam instructs the young courtesan (*Dial.* 6), the courtesan confessing her love for a penniless young man (*Dial.* 7). In *Timon* and *The Dead Come to Life* the material is drawn from Old Comedy, and is much more loosely knit. The borrowing consists less in detailed transposition than in the use of certain structures (e.g. the comic *agōn*) and the appearance of familiar Aristophanic motifs amid elements of non-dramatic provenance. As with *Philosophers for Sale* both *Timon* and *The Dead Come to Life* use the technique of presenting a succession of types in collision with the hero or heroes, and each destined to meet the same fate. In *Timon* this motif is combined with another, the violent expulsion of the villain. Timon chases off the succession of parasites who come to batten on his new-found riches. In *The Dead Come to Life* the dialogue opens with a variant of this, as Socrates urges the band of philosophers on to stone Parrhesiades. Both motifs are found in Aristophanes: e.g. violent expulsion of unwanted guests occurs in *Clouds* and *Acharnians*, a succession of types plague the hero in *Acharnians* and *Birds*. In Lucian the themes are still exploited for their comic potential, but not specifically so as to evoke the experience of Old Comedy as such. The difference in use of the two types of dramatic material is evident. In the one case Lucian is recreating the essence of the genre from which he has borrowed: a sort of modified pastiche. In the other, he is incorporating themes, types and structures into works whose primary effect is not pastiche at all.

This classification of dialogue forms in Lucian according to their source is, of course, far from providing a complete account of the range of his dialogue. *Prometheus*, for example, transposes from tragedy, using Aeschylus' *Prometheus Bound* as its base; but it cannot be called pastiche, for Lucian has transferred everything into a comic mode. It is perfectly plausible that there are also transpositions from works of which we know very little, such as satyr plays, and where, therefore, the effect of the transposition cannot be judged. It is, in fact, neither possible nor useful to attempt a monolithic definition of the form and function of dialogue in Lucian's works. What is clear is that the element of dialogue, whatever its source, because it is so varied in manner and effect, combines with the traditional rhetorical structures to create a new series of literary forms.

4. UNITY IN DIVERSITY

The phrase 'new series of literary forms' highlights the problem of quite what it is that Lucian is writing. How are his works to be grouped? Traditional classifications tend to use loose terms such as 'satirical dialogues'. Some of the satires contain no dialogue, and some of the dialogues are not satirical. Alternatively they apply over-inclusive categories such as 'rhetorical works'. Which of Lucian's works is not, in some important respect, rhetorical? Occasionally a precise grouping seems possible, as in the case of the *psogoi* or pamphlets *Alexander, Peregrinus, A Professor of Public Speaking, The Ignorant Book-collector, The Mistaken Critic, On Salaried Posts* (all of which fulfill the conditions (such as they are) for arousing 'indignation' set out in Aristotle *Rhetoric* II. 9. 6–11). The question then arises: are there features which these works have in common with other non-pamphlets and which are as significant as the features which they share with one another? The answer, we shall see, is probably yes. Another problem with traditional classifications is that they group some works according to function, some to form, some to content. Again this can serve to disguise more affinities than it reveals. The *prolaliai*, or introductions, can be classified together on the grounds of their function. But, perhaps because of the imprecise conventions of the *logos epideiktikos* to which they belong, in other respects they have little enough in common. *Lucian's Career*, for example, uses a modified form of forensic rhetoric in the debate between Sculpture and Education. *The Dipsads* is a comic fantasy developing from reminiscences of Herodotus and Nicander, and possibly parodying a genre of traveller's tale (the fifth oration of Dio is a bravura piece of a similar kind, but with a moral purpose). *The Scythian*, on the other hand, is a straight-forward example of epideictic oratory, an elogium of patrons (father and son, but unnamed—perhaps Lucian used it wherever appropriate), based on a *narration* and a *comparison*. And if function were considered a suitable basis for grouping these works, it is of no use elsewhere. The rest of Lucian's works do not have a definable function in common beyond that of entertainment, and therefore cannot be grouped according to such a principle. Form is, if anything, a still less helpful criterion. Apart from the few works that fall exclusively within one of the categories of formal rhetoric, there are works which combine dramatic dialogue with forensic oratory (*The Double Indictment, Zeus Rants*), works which combine philosophical dialogue with techniques of

occasional oratory (*Anacharsis, The Parasite, On the Dance*), works
that are wholly narrative (*A True Story, The Ignorant Book-collector*),
works that are principally narrative within a barely characterized dialogue framework (*The Lover of Lies*). *Alexander* and *Peregrinus* are
narratives disguised as letters; *Nigrinus* uses letter and dialogue as a
double framework for a rhetorical centrepiece contrasting Athens and
Rome. The combinations are endless.

If the manner of composition is not a useful criterion for dividing
up the works, what of their content? Here the striking feature is not
variety but unity. The same characters, the same settings, the same
themes, the same examples recur in works whose compositional features are quite unalike. The literary origins of the burlesque mythological characters one takes for granted; the stereotyped presentation
of human types is less obviously necessary. At the first hint of art,
Lucian will adduce Phidias or Zeuxis. If a ruler appears or is mentioned, he will be Alexander, Philip, Croesus, Cyrus, Cambyses,
Xerxes or Sardanapalus; tyrants are Phalaris, the two Dionysioi of
Syracuse, Gelon, Hieron, Dion, Polycrates, Peisistratus. The sage is
usually represented by Solon (*Charon, Anacharsis, The Scythian,
Dialogues of the Dead* 6), the philosopher by Pythagoras, Heraclitus,
Socrates, Menippus, Diogenes (other philosophers are rarely more than
cyphers). In each case a small number of traits and anecdotes is associated with the figure concerned, without any necessary coherence
between the traditions invoked. This is particularly true of Socrates,
who is presented, according to the exigencies of the moment, in a
positive light:

Socrates, who was unjustly represented to the Athenians as impious and
treacherous (*Slander* 29),

in a negative light (as in *Dialogues of the Dead* 4, where his famous indifference in the face of death is made out to have been a total sham),
or simply as a physically, morally, and intellectually absurd figure:

Men. But Socrates, Aeacus, where is he, then?
Aeac. He'll be babbling away to Nestor and Palamedes.
Men. Still, I'd like to see him, if he's somewhere around.
Aeac. Do you see the bald one?
Men. They're all bald. That would be a way of recognizing any of them.
Aeac. I mean the one with the snub nose. (*Dialogues of the Dead* 6)

A bald, snub-nosed, hypocritical, pederastic lecher, who swore by dogs and plane trees, held a dotty theory of 'ideas', was (or was not) brave on military campaigns, was (or was not) brave in the face of death: this meagre list of traditional features provides the recipe for almost all the references in Lucian's works to the most famous of all the Greek philosophers!

What Lucian is plainly doing is to follow the *topoi* of the rhetoricians. *In utramque partem disputare* was a basic feature of rhetorical training, so that an advocate should be in a position to prosecute *or* defend a client. Hence the co-existence of a positive and a negative way of presenting a character; in the case of Socrates, an orator could draw on Plato and Xenophon for the 'pro' elements, on Aristophanes' *Clouds*, Middle comedy and the anti-philosophical tradition for the 'anti' elements. This reliance on *topoi* leads at times to Lucian's characters being entirely interchangeable. The Cynic philosophers who take the stage to debunk the pretensions of their fellow men are all a single type, to whom a label is attached, sometimes historical (Menippus, Diogenes, Crates, Antisthenes, even Peregrinus), sometimes invented (Cyniscus, Alcidamas). Lucian deals, in fact, entirely in stock types, drawing his social and psychological portraits either from the schoolroom, or directly from comedy or from Cynic diatribe. The artist, ruler, tyrant and philosopher, to whom historical labels happen to be attached, are no different in kind from the miser, the misanthrope, the sycophant, the parasite, the slanderer, the superstitious man, who receive invented names. For any of his types Lucian will choose at random aspects from whatever tradition best suits the comic needs of a particular context. Doctors, for example, are either the mouthpiece of honesty and scientific good sense (Sopolis, who helps Lycinus to purge Lexiphanes of his 'archaïtis', *Lexiphanes* 18ff.), or charlatans (like Paetus, one of the impostors around Alexander of Abonutichus. Lucian calls him 'a doctor by trade, but doing things unworthy of a doctor or a man of his years'). The latter trait is one of the rare references to contemporary mores: the combination of medicine and an interest in the occult was a common one in the second century, as we know from Galen and indirectly from Aelius Aristides. *The Ignorant Book-collector* 29 contrasts these two types, while Antigonos in *The Lover of Lies* is an example of the confusion of traditions, for he is shown as representing both. At the beginning of the dialogue he is clearly anxious to protect his patient against the mumbo-jumbo being put about by his friends, and to give him sensible advice on diet. But later (26) he joins in the lie-spinning with a tall tale of his own, which purports to be a case history. This makes sense as a form of malicious characterization. Even if it were a slip, however, it is of a kind not likely to be noticed in public performance, for the simple reason that characterization is not an aspect of the work to which the audience's attention would be directed.

What is true of the representatives of humanity is equally true of the ambience in which they move, though here the literary preoccupation would, perhaps, not be surprising, given the stylized nature of most ancient geography. Lucian's map starts in the inherently comic fantasy world of the barbarian, focuses upon a Greece neatly divided into states each with its traditional occupation, dress and mores, and has at its centre—providing the décor for a considerable number of works—an impeccably fifth-cum-fourth century Athens and Attica. Nothing is mentioned that gives a hint of privately observed local colour or of contemporary period. Where detailed itineraries are given, the effect of reality is only an illusion. The good ship Isis in *The Ship*, for example, could not have followed the route described in 9 in the time and manner suggested. Indeed, it would be amazing enough if the ship as Lucian describes it ever floated, let alone put to sea.

If the characters and settings come from the stock-in-trade of the rhetorician, it is all the more natural that the activities and problems with which they concern themselves should do so too. How far, if at all, Lucian does reflect the events and concerns of the world around him is a problem for separate consideration. What is interesting about his themes is that Lucian seems to have relied as much on the moral commonplaces of Cynic diatribe as upon lists of *topoi* in manuals. In practice, however, it is difficult to distinguish the two types of material from one another. For one thing, they are used in conjunction. For another, the part played by rhetoric in the diatribe itself seems to have been substantial. The theme of inheritance is a good example of the blending of the two traditions. In origin it is a stock theme of forensic rhetoric (cf. Seneca, *Controversiae*, passim, notably IV extr. 5). As such it is formally expounded and embroidered upon in *Disowned*. However, aspects of it are also used as the subject of *Dialogues of the Dead* 15–19, and are incorporated into *Dialogues of the Dead* 14, 21, 22. In these little dialogues, inheritance is treated not as a legal topic but as one of the numerous variants on the general Cynic theme of the vanity of human activities. Its treatment in the *Dialogues of the Dead* is itself not monolithic, but represents a series of variations on its own stock types and motifs. The principal types are the rich man who lives on into an apparently indefinite hale old age, the legacy hunter, and the unexpected heir, of whom a sub-species is the young male slave who inherits in recompense for 'services rendered'. The main motifs are the death of the would-be heir before his intended benefactor, and the administering of poison to help the benefactor on. None of this is unique to this group of dialogues, or to the truism on which they embroider, for the many passing references to inheritance in other works show the continued reappearance of precisely the same elements in quite different contexts—e.g. the lucky slave in *Timon* 22, the use of poison to speed up an inheritance in *A Professor of Public Speaking* 24. In turn the poison motif links inheritance with another stock theme of forensic rhetoric, adultery (again see Seneca, *Controversiae*, passim) with its own pyramid of motifs and types. Adultery is used by Lucian less as a central theme (though see *Toxaris* 13ff.) than as an incidental one. It often illustrates the Cynic commonplace of the disproportion between appearance and reality, either in a purely comic sense, as with adulterous philosophers of *The Banquet*, or as part of the traditional invective against an 'enemy' (*Alexander, Peregrinus*), where it is usually part of a series of charges that include the corruption of boys and murder.

In this way the moral themes of the diatribe and the examples of rhetoric meet and cross throughout Lucian's work. Starting from the basic commonplaces it is possible to trace a network of motifs, each with its attendant types and classic illustrations, but not limited to any one genre of work since they are as adaptable to pure pastiche as to the pamphlet. A good illustration of this adaptability is Lucian's attitude to athletics. One of the main motifs illustrating the vanity of human activities is that of Death the Leveller, which provides the key image for *Dialogues of the Dead, The Downward Journey, Menippus* and *Charon*. This in turn is generally illustrated by one or more of four items: the ephemerality of wealth, of power, of beauty and of physical strength. The last is embodied in the 'type' of the athlete—in *Charon* 8 Milo of Croton, in *Dialogues of the Dead* 20 one Damasias, in *Dialogues of the Dead* 2 Damoxenus the wrestler. The implicit critique of the value of athletics can, however, just as well be developed as a theme in its own right, as it is in *Anacharsis*, where the arguments are presented quite without reference to any consistent moral issue, as part of a formal rhetorical comparison, with no resolution for or against. The same motif occurs in the two quite different types of work, merely being modified or developed to suit the particular context and purpose.

What has to be stressed is that this uniformity of literary technique extends throughout Lucian's writings, embracing works with apparently personal and contemporary subjects just as much as the overtly artificial dialogues set in Hades or on Olympus. The 'pamphlets', *Alexander, Peregrinus, A Professor of Public Speaking, The Mistaken Critic* and *The Ignorant Book-collector*, are a useful case in point.[1] In them character and theme are fused, for the focus of the satire is to undermine the central character. If it can be shown that all the central characters are variants on a stock type, this must alter our response to the nature of the satire. The simplest way to discover the relationship between the various works is to draw up a portrait of the villain.

Alexander: he is in a general sense characterized as impudent and daring (4). From the outset his career depends on his laying claim to skills which he does not possess (6 and passim). He is a debauchee with a wide range of vices: male prostitution (5), pederasty (41), adultery (39, 42). He is quite prepared to commit murder (56).

Peregrinus: his total motivation is proposed as a love of notoriety (1 and passim), his career depends on his laying claim to skills which he does not possess (11–12 and passim). He is a debauchee with a wide range of vices, notably pederasty (9, 43) and adultery (9). He is quite prepared to commit murder (10—parricide).

A Professor of Public Speaking: he is motivated by a desire for notoriety (22). He is of low birth (24). He is notable for his impudence and daring (24; cf. 15). His career depends on his laying claim to skills which he does not possess (passim). He is a debauchee, who refers to his own prostitution (24, as a gigolo) and effeminacy (15), and recommends homosexual practices (23) and heavy drinking (23). He is quite prepared to commit murder (24). He champions ignorance (15, 24 and passim), and linguistic incompetence (16–17).

The Mistaken Critic: he is impudent and daring (3, 18). He is motivated by a desire for notoriety (18). He is of low birth (18). His career depends on his laying claim to skills which he does not possess (3, 5, 6 and passim). He is a debauchee with a wide range of vices: drunkenness (2), male prostitution (18), effeminacy (23, 31), homosexual practices (17, 18, 25, 27, 28), pederasty (20–1). He is marked by his ignorance (2 and passim) and particularly by his linguistic incompetence (24).

The Ignorant Book-collector: His principal motivation is a desire for

[1] Excluding *On Salaried Posts*, because it is not directed against a single figure.

notoriety (1). He is marked by his impudence and boldness (3). His career depends on the absence of certain skills (2 and passim). He is a debauchee with a wide range of vices: drunkenness (23), effeminacy (3), homosexuality (23). He is marked by his ignorance (2 and passim).[1]

No two of these figures are identical, but each of the traits listed is shared by two or more of them. Of course, the particular examples of a given quality may differ. Alexander's charlatanism manifests itself in a different area from that of the professor of public speaking. The root character flaw is none the less the same. Lucian is drawing on a stock of *topoi* of vilification to create a negative character-type. In fact, the type is recognizable. He is a variant on the *parvenu* as he appears elsewhere in Lucian, notably in *The Cock, The Ship, Timon* and *On Salaried Posts*. A figure of dubious origins, the parvenu rises by dishonest means, is notorious for his immorality, and positively profits by his ignorance. Exactly the same can be said of the villains of the pamphlets (with the proviso that Alexander is the very opposite of ignorant). There are some further variants, of course. In *The Mistaken Critic* (30) the dishonesty is theft, as well as charlatanism. *The Ignorant Book-collector* (19) and *A Professor of Public Speaking* (25) both add legacy-hunting to the list of crimes. *The Mistaken Critic* (19) and *The Ignorant Book-collector* (22) make connexion with dancers an additional source of moral opprobrium. But the essence of Lucian's method is to make the same type the focus of each pamphlet and to develop certain aspects of it in such a way as to provide the illusion of a variety of themes. In *The Mistaken Critic* he expands the motifs of ignorance and homosexuality, and constructs the invective around these. In *Alexander* he concentrates on charlatanism and moral depravity in general, in *Peregrinus* on charlatanism and the desire for notoriety. *A Professor of Public Speaking* parades all these motifs in about equal proportions. Possibly the type is not confined to the pamphlets. *Lexiphanes* and *The Sham Sophist* could be regarded as extremely simplified variants of the same figure. In them Lucian takes a single aspect of the tradition, linguistic incompetence, and performs a set of virtuoso variations on it. However, since both works differ from the pamphlets by being in dialogue form, and since *Lexiphanes* is also in certain respects a parody, this may not be a significant relationship. What is clear is that there is a much closer relationship than might be supposed between the

[1] For a list of references to similar charges in the works of Aeschines and Demosthenes, see M. Caster, *Études sur Alexandre ou le faux prophète de Lucien* Paris 1938, 84 n.2.

superficially particular satire of the pamphlets and the overtly general moral satire of much of the dialogues. Clearly content is no more satisfactory a base on which to distinguish works than is form.

5. INGENUITY AND HUMOUR

If there is one relatively clear-cut division between the works, it is quite simply between those whose principal effect is humour, and those whose principal effect is ingenuity. The second category contains the eleven *prolaliai* and the pieces which can be assigned to one rhetorical genre, *Disowned*, *The Tyrannicide*, *Phalaris I* and *II*, *In Praise of my Country*, *The Fly* (whose paradoxes are clever, not funny) and *The Consonants at Law*, where the fantasy of the situation is subordinate in interest to the linguistic display. With these can be classed *Anacharsis*, *Toxaris*, *Essays in Portraiture*, *Essays in Portraiture Defended*, *Slander*, *On the Dance*, *Hippias*, *A Slip of the Tongue in Greeting* and *Apology for 'On Salaried Posts'*, all of which are exercises in the skilful combination of a number of traditional forms. Some of these works have amusing elements, especially in their anecdotes, but they are clearly intended to be admired for their artistry rather than their humour. The first and larger category, comic works, falls into two groups: pastiches, transpositions and parodies, where the humour derives from the nature of the material imitated or from the skill of the parody, and what may loosely be called satires, including pamphlets, dialogues and the mock treatises. In making such a subdivision the criterion has to be that of principal effect, for many of the satirical works use both parody and pastiche among their comic techniques.

To analyse what makes a work funny is almost impossible, humour being a decidedly fragile commodity, apt to vanish into dust at the first probing touch. At most one can isolate within a work those structures, themes and stylistic devices which are clearly designed to amuse. Lucian's comic techniques are particularly complex, but with the exception of transposition and pastiche, they are all designed to play upon the gap between a concept of normality which writer and audience share, and what passes for normality within the text. Since pastiche and transposition fall partly outside this definition, let us look at them first.

A true pastiche is an almost evenly matched exhibition of verbal dexterity and humour. The ingenuity lies in the ability of the writer to recreate the flavour of his model in theme, structure and style, without merely copying it. The comic element derives in part from the fact that the audience is constantly aware that the text is not what it purports to be. An additional source of comedy is frequently that the imitation is modified by touches of burlesque or parody. Closely allied to the pastiche proper is the transposition, where the essence of a work or of a genre is transferred into another genre. The technique doubtless derives from the rhetorical exercise of paraphrase, in which verse is re-expressed in prose and vice-versa. Transposition is not an inherently comic form. It results in comedy if the material transposed is comic, or if, as with pastiche, elements of parody or burlesque are allowed to creep in.

Three of Lucian's collections of short dialogues, *Dialogues of the Gods, Dialogues of the Sea Gods* and *Dialogues of the Courtesans*, are all essentially pastiches or transpositions. Most of the *Dialogues of the Courtesans* are pastiches of New Comedy, but some recreate in a comic light themes from Hellenistic love poetry (e.g. the complaint of the lover shut out by his mistress in *Dial.* 14). A rare example of a dialogue modelled on a particular poem is *Dial.* 4, which has the same thematic structure as Theocritus *Idylls* 2. The humour in these works is less an additive of Lucian's than a quality inherent in the types and situations of the source material. The *Dialogues of the Gods* and of the *Sea Gods* are slightly different. They transpose elements from Homer, the *Homeric Hymns* and Alexandrian poetry. (The sources are not exclusively literary. At least two dialogues, *Dialogues of the Sea Gods* 14 and 15, may well represent transpositions from pictures, of Perseus and Andromeda and of Europa and the bull respectively.) In these two sets of dialogues the burlesque potential of humanizing the gods, so evident in dialogues such as *Zeus Rants*, is uniformly played down in favour of picturesque detail, and of ingenuity in the rethinking of the poetic material. A good example of the manner is *Dialogues of the Sea Gods* 2, which reworks the material of *Odyssey* ix. 216–525. The Cyclops is complaining to Poseidon about the behaviour of Odysseus. Within the short space of some forty lines of prose, the major events of the episode are all presented. Odysseus and the companions are trapped in the cave; Polyphemus devours some of them; he is drugged with wine and blinded with a red-hot, sharpened stake; the 'No-man' ploy deceives the other Cyclopses; the prisoners escape beneath the sheep when the Cyclops removes the rock in the entrance; Odysseus taunts his former captor. Poseidon's final words suggest the Homeric sequel, with the threat of punishment at sea. But not only are the major events there. All the details are culled from Homer too. The Cyclops' suggestion that the companions 'obviously had designs on my flocks' develops the image 'as sea-robbers over the brine' from his first question to Odysseus (*Od.* ix. 254). His description of relighting his fire, 'kindling it with a tree I had brought from the mountain', elaborates Homer's first image of the Cyclops as he enters the cave:

He bore a huge load of dry wood for the preparation of his supper. (233–4)

At times a detail suffers deliberate reduction. Homer's Polyphemus, who is very much an epic figure, says of the drugged wine: 'This is a rill of very nectar and ambrosia.' Lucian's Cyclops, who has the air of a plaintive child, can only manage: 'It was sweet and smelled nice.' In general the most important feature of the presentation in Lucian is clearly his ingenuity in recasting the Homeric narrative in as much detail as possible into a retrospective dialogue, put mostly into the mouth of the victim. The comic element, deriving almost exclusively from the contrast between grand subject and domestic presentation, is merely a spin-off from the traditions to which the dialogues have been attached, for the portraiture of the gods as having the manners and problems of ordinary men is a standard feature of Homer and one favoured by Alexandrian poets.

Outside the short dialogues, pastiche as an extended form occurs largely as linguistic pastiche, in *Lexiphanes* and *The Syrian Goddess*. The two cases are widely different. *The Syrian Goddess* is a pastiche of the language and manner of Herodotus, particularly with reference to his account of Egypt in bk. 2. The description of the temple and cult, with its naive acceptance of the most implausible tales and its delight in erotic anecdote, is well within the Herodotean manner, as are certain themes: the borrowings made by other peoples from Egyptian mythology, the parallels between Greek and barbarian gods, the taboos relating to various animals. There are also typical formulae of presentation, of the type 'I saw it myself', 'I am only recounting what I have been told', 'This seems probable but I also heard another version'. If the work is read as a tongue-in-cheek imitation of a well-known writer, the difference between the credulity of the religious attitudes put forward in it and the dismissal of such stuff elsewhere in Lucian becomes irrelevant. The aim is to out-Herodotus Herodotus, and the comedy lies therein. *Lexiphanes*, on the other hand, very plainly combines pastiche of hyperatticism with a mild parody of Plato's *Symposium*, as Lexiphanes himself informs us when he defines the theme of his latest work as 'counter-banqueting the son of Ariston'. Over half the text is devoted to reading the extract from the supposed new work. It is a comic reduction of Plato's dialogue to all its extraneous details: minute description of the preparations for the banquet, the paraphernalia of the feast, entertainments, the uninvited guest, the guest who is unwell. Nothing serious is said at all. The linguistic pastiche for which the parody is the vehicle depends mainly on the profusion of words from Old Comedy, mostly concrete nouns for items long disappeared, intermingled with a few Platonic formulae and the occasional syntactic oddity. Wherever possible Lucian has sought to make the archaizing diction funnier by playing on the differences between obsolete and current uses of words. Unlike *The Syrian Goddess*, this pastiche-parody does not provide the entire structure of the work, however. It is set within a dialogue framework which allows the linguistic theme to be expressed in two quite different ways. First the recitation is followed by a farcical scene, doubtless modelled on Old Comedy, in which a doctor, Sopolis, literally purges Lexiphanes of his archaisms. Secondly, Lycinus, the author's mouthpiece, rounds off with a short homily on true learning and its contrast with the excesses of Lexiphanes. Though the pastiche is the main comic device of the work, it is integrated into a schema of other such devices. In this it is more typical of Lucian's work as a whole than is *The Syrian Goddess*.

Parody forms a bridge between the verbal ingenuities of pastiche or transposition, and the content-oriented humour of satire. It shares the technical preoccupations of the former, but, like the latter, it depends ultimately on the gap between accepted norm and what is presented in the text. Extended parody is relatively uncommon as a self-sufficient literary form in Lucian's work. However, the two examples of it, *The Parasite* and *A True Story*, are both works of substance. (There are three in all if *Gout* is accepted as a genuine work.)*A True Story* is too elaborate a work in its variety of comedy to be seen exclusively as a parody, but that is certainly the major element in its structure. Lucian himself says so in his opening paragraph:

> Each detail of the story is a veiled allusion, not without a touch of satire, to the old poets, historians and philosophers whose writings are full of wonders and tall tales. I would name names, but you will surely recognize them for yourself from your reading.

The Byzantine patriarch Photius (*c.* 820–891) indicates the main source for Lucian's work as a novel by Antonius Diogenes, *The*

Wonders beyond Thule, of which he possessed a copy. According to his very complicated résumé, the main features of the plot seem to have been a double voyage whose action was of less interest to the author than the opportunity it provided to elaborate a series of 'strange but true' anecdotes about men, animals, plants, the moon and the sun, with a suitable admixture of plain magic. It is obviously difficult to estimate the degree to which *A True Story* parodies a work we do not have, though some of the details provided by Photius, the voyage to the moon, for example, and the description of its inhabitants, confirm the parallel. Into the framework of the mock traveller's tale Lucian has inserted an immense variety of short pastiches and parodies. In certain instances the parody is simply that of a traditional theme. The 'perfect island', for example, for which the prototype is Phaeacia in the *Odyssey* but which occurs particularly as a series of utopias in various philosophers and historians, appears here as the Isle of the Blest, with every possible traditional aspect exaggerated to its uttermost, but recorded with the apparent precision of a *Guide Bleu*. In the traditional picture of the Isle of the Blest there are two springs; in Lucian's island there are no less than 365 springs of water, 365 springs of honey, 500 springs of myrrh ('but those are smaller') seven rivers of milk and eight of wine—not to mention the river of finest myrrh one hundred royal cubits wide which surrounds the city. The technique is to pile up detail, each element more absurd than the last, while retaining total gravity of presentation.

As well as the parody of traditional themes there is considerable specific parody of individual authors. Lucian himself names Ctesias and Iambulus, snatches of whose work we know through Diodorus and Photius. The formal disclaimer of truth at the outset of the story is already an inversion of the protestations of Ctesias and Antonius Diogenes: 'I am writing about things which I haven't seen, haven't experienced and haven't heard about from anyone else. In fact, they are things which don't exist at all and couldn't possibly exist. So those who happen to read this account of them should certainly not believe in them.' There are more immediately recognizable parodies of Herodotus and Thucydides. In the first case it is, as in *The Syrian Goddess*, the author's naive delight in the supernatural which Lucian picks upon. The 'divine footprint' theme is a good example. Lucian and companions not only find an inscribed bronze plaque recording the visit of the gods (an early example of 'Queen Elizabeth slept here'), but 'near at hand there were also two footprints in the rock, one a hundred feet long, the other shorter. I think the smaller one belonged to Dionysus, the other one to Herakles.' This is a typical comic exaggeration of Herodotus' account (IV. 82) of the wonders of Exampaios in Scythia: 'They show you a rock with the imprint of Herakles' foot; it looks like a human footprint, but it is three feet long.' Twice the number of gods, and thirty times the length of the footprint. Thucydides provides the pattern for the descriptions of armies and military engagements. Particular battles in *A True Story* may reflect the tactics of particular episodes in the Peloponnesian Wars. The first phase of the battle between Heliots and Selenites (I. 17–18) bears some resemblance to the pattern of the engagement between Boeotians and Athenians in Thucydides IV. 96. More often the parallel is a general one depending on the vocabulary and upon the kind of detail selected. In this sense the confusion and brutality of the fight between the floating islands recalls the encounter between Corinthian and Corcyrean fleets in Thuc. I. 48. Sometimes it is not really necessary to assign a specific source. The whole Heliot–Selenite war, with its disputed colonies and the building of a Long Wall, is meant to suggest the Peloponnesian Wars, so what more natural than that the account of it should be concluded by a pastiche treaty, using appropriate official language, just as Thucydides records the terms of the Athens-Sparta treaty in V. 18? There is no need for verbal echoes here; the imitation is thematic.

The comedy of the Thucydidean references does not lie in the multiplication and exaggeration of elements, but in the straightforward application of the historian's techniques to a totally absurd topic. Much the same is true of the borrowing from Homer. That there should be borrowings from Homer in a tall tale is only natural. His reputation as the greatest of all liars, and the authority of the *Odyssey* as the original *roman de voyage* made him an obvious target. Lucian in fact lists Odysseus as the original charlatan 'telling tales to Alcinoos about winds enslaved, one-eyed men, cannibals and savages, and about animals with many heads, too, and magic potions that metamorphosed his companions' (I. 3). The Homeric touches are less thematic, however, than this reference might suggest. The most extensive thematic borrowing is the reference to the Isle of Dreams, and this is not really comic at all. Lucian goes out of his way to pinpoint his source: 'Only Homer mentioned it, and he did not describe it entirely accurately' (II. 32). He then takes Penelope's simple statement 'Twain are the Gates of shadowy dreams; the one is fashioned of horn, the other of ivory', and elaborates a whole fantasy landscape, in which the element of exaggeration, 'there are not two gates in it, as Homer says, but four', is less important than the imaginative ornamentation. This example is exceptional, however. The bulk of the Homeric reference could loosely be called stylistic. It serves to parallel Lucian himself, as narrator, with Odysseus, by associating the style of his voyage, his landfalls, his adventures, with certain Homeric narrative mannerisms. Just as Odysseus and his companions, reaching Aeaea, 'stepped ashore and for two days and two nights lay there consuming their own hearts for weariness and pain' (*Od.* x. 142–3), so Lucian and his companions, after the tribulations of their (79 day!) voyage, 'putting in and going ashore . . . lay upon the ground for a long time because of their long misery'. When Lucian wants to seek out the lie of the land, he leaves a detachment of men to guard the ships and takes the rest to explore (I. 7; cf. *Od.* IX. 193–6) or climbs a vantage point (II. 42; cf. *Od.* x. 148, 194). When leaving a place he camps out on the beach, feasts, and leaves at dawn, like Odysseus and his men after their encounter with the Cyclops. All of which makes it the funnier that when something actually happens to some of his companions—the sexual encounter with the seductive tree-women, an incident with undertones of Circe and the Lotus-eaters combined—Lucian shows no Odyssean heroics, or even noble lament. Not for him the risks of outfacing Circe, or leading his men weeping back to safety (*Od.* IX. 98). Instead, 'We left them in the lurch and beat it back to the boats' (I. 9). The Homeric references provide an epic flavour whose inappropriateness to the narrative is a useful comic additive.

The purpose of the tissue of parody and pastiche in *A True Story* is quite clear. It is to amuse, to dazzle, and to tease the audience by keeping them alert for stylistic and thematic allusions to well-known works. Just how well-read they must have been can be judged from the fact that they were expected not only to know their Homer and their Ctesias, but also to be capable of spotting that the description of the halcyon's nest in II. 40 is a humorous exaggeration of the account of the bird in Aristotle *History of Animals* v. 8 (542b) and IX. 14 (616a). The nature of the parody in *The Parasite* is very different, but the purpose is hardly more serious. As with *Lexiphanes*, the work is built up from two separate elements. One theme is purely rhetorical, the paradoxical encomium of the art of the sponger. A substantial part of the work accordingly follows the standard school-room formulae for the genre. The encomium of the *soi-disant* art is put into the mouth of its practitioner; a formal comparison is made between 'Spongery' and the other arts (here, rhetoric and philosophy); the sponger in peacetime is compared with the sponger in war, thus introducing the enunciation of the physical and moral qualities natural to the sponger. This aspect of *The Parasite* is marked more by its skilful use of traditional motifs and structures than by its humour, though there is something inherently funny about the fact that Simon the sponger, in demonstrating the superiority of his art to rhetoric and philosophy, uses precisely the literary methods of his opponents. This is where the parody proper comes in. For not only is the centre of his defence a rhetorician's, but its framework is a philosopher's. The lengthy reasoning by which spongery is defined as an art echoes the process of defining sophistry as an art in Plato's *Sophist*, and Simon's style of argument is in more general terms a caricature of the Socratic method. He professes great modesty as to his own skills, he leads Tychiades on with immense patience, he uses the reductive method to compel his companion's assent. All that is missing is the logic of the ideas, for which Simon substitutes the quotations, examples, and paradoxes of rhetorical display. At one point, the actual conduct of the argument is made to suffer a comic hiccough. Tychiades is allowed to ask a question that Simon cannot answer. So he simply ignores it, and passes swiftly on to another topic:

Tych. Don't you think that it is wrong to take things that belong to other people?
Sim. Certainly.
Tych. Then why should the sponger be the only person for whom it is wrong to take other people's things?
Sim. I couldn't say.—Then again, in the other arts (etc.).

The proper effect here can only be judged if one imagines the piece performed: split-second facial dismay, covered by Simon hurrying loudly on to his next point. This is the way, Lucian seems to suggest, that Socrates must have dealt with those tricky questions that Plato didn't tell us about. This particular instance of humour is at Socrates' expense. In general, however, the humour derives quite simply from the incongruity of associating a serious philosophical method with an entirely frivolous subject. It does not constitute any kind of critique of philosophy. Like the pastiche-parody in *Lexiphanes*, it is merely amusing.

Lucian's comedy is not usually so overtly *l'art pour l'art*, for the remaining works all give the illusion of having a butt for their humour,

be it institution, value or individual. Lucian's satires divide sharply
into two groups: those which are presented as an aspect of reality, and
those whose circumstances belong largely or entirely to a fantasy world.
In practice this division does not mark any important thematic differences, but it does constitute a basic stylistic dichotomy. The
realistic approach itself offers a variety of forms of presentation. The
simplest is the treatise—*On Funerals, On Sacrifices, How to Write
History,* where the author directly denounces the shortcomings of
what can loosely be called institutions. Allied to the treatise is the
pamphlet (see above, pp. 18ff.), where the satire is focussed on an individual, or, in the case of *On Salaried Posts,* a particular section of
society. Again, direct denunciation of vices is the most natural (though
by no means the only) method of criticism. More complicated in form
are the dialogues. These fall into two main groups. In the first the
dialogue is a disguised narrative; Lycinus recounts to Pamphilus the
details of the lawsuit between the two philosophers (*The Eunuch*),
Lycinus describes for the benefit of Philo the unedifying events at the
wedding feast of Aristaenetus' daughter (*The Banquet*). In this sort of
dialogue the listener has an almost passive rôle, though he does contribute a limited amount of moral commentary. In the second group,
the dialogue forms the framework for a series of short narratives (*The
Lover of Lies, The Ship*). *The Lover of Lies* retains the disguised narrative element, in that Philocles' rôle is to listen to the account given
by Tychiades, and to reinforce Tychiades' moral position. Tychiades'
narrative, on the other hand, is a *Ship* in reported speech, with each
character contributing his own story or stories. In *The Ship* all the
characters contribute to the dialogue and to the narrative, and hence
are all active expressions of the moral argument of the work. The
distinction between an authorial voice, as in treatises and most pamphlets, and the genuinely dramatic presentation of *The Ship* is a
substantial one. For one thing, the more a character is allowed to speak
for himself, the greater the opportunity for ironic self-betrayal. The
extreme example of this is *A Professor of Public Speaking,* where the
values proposed by the speaker, and by the rhetorician himself, are
(for most of the dialogue) plainly the opposite of what a rational man
would suppose. For another thing, the less a character is allowed to
stand outside the action of an event, the less he becomes the *porte-
parole* of the author. The moral criteria of *The Banquet,* conveyed for
us by Lycinus, are as clear as those put forward explicitly by the author
in *The Ignorant Book-collector,* whereas it is a great deal less plain

where the satirical emphasis lies in *The Ship*, for Lycinus to some extent puts himself in the wrong by taking the game of wishes seriously.

Despite this variety of presentation, there is a notable uniformity, in the 'realistic' dialogues, about the way in which Lucian creates his satirical effect. If the gap between the world as it is shown in the text and the world as it ought to be is to be properly appreciated by the audience, there must exist a common moral standpoint between writer and audience. Lucian has chosen (for reasons which I shall discuss later) the most neutral of all standards, the appeal to practicality. In *The Banquet* Lycinus contrasts the behaviour of the ordinary people present at the banquet with that of their supposed betters (34–5), pointing the moral that actions speak louder than words: 'While all this was happening, Philo, I was privately thinking a number of things—among them the obvious point that knowledge is useless if you do not try to improve the way you conduct your life.' In *The Eunuch*, 6, Pamphilus opines that a philosopher should be judged by his *mores*, not by his doctrinal competence. In *Hermotimus* the climax of the dialectic is the 'proof' that philosophy is unnecessary to sensible living. Even in *The Ship*, though we may not thank him for it, Lycinus recalls us to reality from the extravagances of Samippus' dreams of power:

Sam. My dear chap, do you think you're still in Athens? This is Babylon. You're one of a host of soldiers camped on the plain outside the city walls, planning tactics.
Lyc. Thanks. You did well to remind me. I thought I was sober and talking about reality.

In *The Lover of Lies* the appeal is directed toward a specific, necessary aspect of practicality: common-sense. Philocles and Tychiades open with a discussion that assumes truthfulness, in a limited and strictly pragmatic sense, to be a social norm, and Tychiades restates the idea at the close of the work by assuming the value of rationality. What is, perhaps, very significant is not the repetition of the same moral standpoint in each dialogue, but the fact that in almost every case it is merely touched upon, as if to remind the audience, not to convince it. This leaves the focus of the works on the *alazones*, the characters who create the gap by pretending, or believing themselves to be, or trying to be something more than they are.

The *alazones* in the realistic dialogues are almost all philosophers; in *The Eunuch* the two Aristotelians, in *The Banquet* representatives of

all the major sects, in *The Lover of Lies* a Stoic, an Aristotelian, a
Platonist and a Pythagorean. The importance of this professional
identity is to allow the author to exploit the difference between
theoretician and practitioner. He can, and does, use other professions:
grammarian and rhetorician in *The Banquet*, doctor in *The Lover of
Lies*. But philosophy has the advantage of claiming to deal with life
as a whole, rather than a single aspect of it. The difference between
philosopher as theoretician and the actions of a philosopher as man
can be varied into three types of contrast. The tenets of particular
philosophies can be contrasted with an abstract concept of philosophy.
Philosophers as they are can be contrasted with an abstract concept of
what a philosopher should be. Philosophers as they are can be contrasted with what the tenets of their particular philosophies say they
should be. Lucian appears to take as his definition of perfect philosophy and the perfect philosopher the rather vague notion of moral
superiority to the ordinary man. He then uses the incidents of his
narratives to show particular philosophies and their followers as clearly
morally inferior to the ordinary man. The opening of *The Eunuch*
neatly illustrates how the different motifs can be fitted together. On
his entrance, Lycinus explains his hilarity as the effect of a court case
between philosophers which he has been watching. Pamphilus responds
initially on an abstract plane:

> You are indeed right to call it absurd that men professing philosophy
> should take one another to court when they ought to settle the matters in
> dispute peacefully between themselves.

This sets the particular conduct of the philosophers against what
Pamphilus sees as the standards appropriate to philosophy as a discipline. When Lycinus goes on to describe the abuse which characterized the case (i.e. these philosophers were actually *more* contentious
than ordinary men in the same situation), Pamphilus returns:

> I suppose, Lycinus, they were adherents of different sects disagreeing over
> doctrine as usual.

The 'as usual' changes the ground, showing that there is a permanent
contrast between the adherents of particular philosophies and what
Pamphilus expects of a philosopher. The audience has thus been
encouraged to accept the philosopher as an *alazōn* by definition. This
leaves the rest of the dialogue free to concentrate on the contrast
which has the greatest comic potential, the contrast between the private

lives of philosophers and what they profess to be. This has the greatest potential because it is the least abstract and the least technical of the possible contrasts. Lucian wastes little effort on ridiculing doctrines, except in *Hermotimus*, a work whose tediousness proves how wise he was to avoid such an approach elsewhere. In general the characterization of his philosophers by sect is minimal. A Stoic may mention one or two of the classic fallacies, or be associated with indifference to pain. A Platonist will probably invoke the theory of ideas. Rarely is there any deeper representation of doctrinal differences. By concentrating on the problem of the private man and his human failings, Lucian has given himself almost endless scope for comic disparities.

Endless in theory, that is. In practice Lucian sticks to a very specific range of vices. *The Lover of Lies* deals with charlatanry; Lycinus ridicules the various philosophers as they recount their supposed mystic experiences and lay claim to supernatural powers. *The Eunuch* is principally about sexual misdemeanours, the paradox of Bagoas the eunuch taken in adultery, and secondarily about quarrelsomeness and material greed. *The Banquet* offers examples of greed (food and money), sexual misdemeanours (hetero- and homosexual, including adultery and attempted rape), quarrelsomeness, physical violence and egocentricity. We are back in the realm of stock types, a fact emphasized by the use of two names (Cleodemus and Ion) in both *The Banquet* and *The Lover of Lies*. What is more the range of vices is quite close to those picked out in the pamphlets (see pp. 18–19 above), so that the philosopher appears as merely a variant of the *villain*. Accordingly, the contrast between the possession of vices and the profession of virtue depends for its satirical interest not on the individuality of the vice, but on the variety of techniques which Lucian uses to describe and ridicule it.

The Ship offers an immediate contrast with the other realistic dialogues, in that its satire is nominally exercised at the expense of an abstraction, human aspiration and the material goals which it proposes for itself. I say nominally, because although the fantasies of the three proponents, Adimantus (riches), Samippus (power) and Timolaus (magical powers), are in many ways inherently absurd, so is the flat refusal of Lycinus to join in the fun, especially given his declaration (17): 'I'm not going to be disparaging amid the general good-fortune.' As I said earlier, Lycinus does not have the privileged position, here, of retrospectively reporting and commenting upon a completed action, as he does in *The Eunuch, The Banquet* and *The Lover of Lies*. The audience is thus freer to reject his position, at least in part, and with it the moral basis of the dialogue. When one looks at the three wishes themselves, however, and the arguments used against them, the dialogue falls more into line with the other three. Instead of concentrating on a single comic type, Lucian has taken three themes, two of them— the triviality of material possessions and the vanity of human power— themes of Cynic diatribe, the third—the non-existence of magical powers—being a rephrasing of the magician motif which provides half the portrait of charlatanry in *The Lover of Lies*. Each theme is embodied in a stock figure: the rich man (with overtones of the parvenu, for Adimantus' wealth, and some of the use to which he puts it, is extremely vulgar), the king-cum-military commander, and the wizard. Clearly, as with the other dialogues discussed above, the satirical interest cannot derive from the novelty of the subjects, but is dependent on the comic skill with which the wishes are built up and deflated.

Although the comic interest derives in part from purely humorous elements, such as puns, misused or adapted quotations and parodies, it relies in the main on three satirical manners which are common to all the realistic satires, whether pamphlets, treatises or dialogues: invective, verbal irony and burlesque. Invective is the direct denunciation of vices, irony rejects the claims of the *alazōn* by contrasting them with his reality, and burlesque is reduction to the ridiculous by singling out and exaggerating certain salient characteristics. Of these categories, irony is the most complex. At its most transparent, it is sarcasm, where the difference between what the words superficially mean and what they actually mean is intended to be understood by the victim. Slightly more opaque is the technique whereby the author or his *porte-parole* begins by adopting the persona of an innocent, who accepts the *alazōn* at face value and then gradually casts off his mask. (Ingénu irony, which is a variety of the same technique in which the criticism is transmitted via the observation of a genuine innocent, is not used in the realistic satires, although it forms an important subsection of the fantastic ones.) Finally, there is the irony of self-betrayal, where the author allows the *alazōn* unwittingly to expose himself, the irony being perceptible only to the audience.

The mock treatises, *On Funerals* and *On Sacrifices*,[1] are the simplest

---

[1] *How to Write History* is difficult to classify. It is a genuine treatise, but its raison d'être is a string of faintly absurd anecdotes and parodies of contemporary historians, coupled with sarcasm and a little mild invective. Perhaps the work is more remarkable for its ingenuity than its humour, and should be thought of as a rhetorical display, rather than as even the semblance of satire.

in their satirical approach. In each case, the first paragraph is used to establish the author's standpoint, just as the 'morality' of *The Eunuch* or *The Lover of Lies* is established in the opening dialogue. In *On Funerals* this takes the form of a plain statement rejecting that common view of death which is essential to the attitudes about to be ridiculed. In *On Sacrifices* it is a piece of mild invective attacking religious practices. Thereafter the main weapon in both works is sarcasm. This can be confined to a word or phrase slipped into an apparently neutral description. For example, in *On Funerals* 9 Lucian explains the custom of pouring libations and making offerings of food at the tomb of the deceased, by the need to nourish them '. . . so that if there is anyone without friend or relative left on earth, he lives out his life an unfed and starving corpse.' The custom had been one of the greatest importance: Orestes in Aeschylus' *The Libation Bearers* (484–6) says in complete seriousness to the dead Agamemnon that if he helps his children avenge his death, he will get his due share of the funeral feasts, 'but otherwise at the rich and savoury banquet of burnt offerings made to earth thou shalt be portionless of honour.' In Lucian's version, the absurd image of a starving corpse, reinforced by the peculiarly inappropriate technical precision of the verb *politeuetai*, stressing that the corpse lives as a free citizen, make it transparent that the speaker finds the whole suggestion nonsensical. At other times, the sarcasm orders the structure of an entire paragraph, as when Lucian treats seriously the details of a custom which he considers ridiculous in its entirety. Of the custom of placing an obol in the mouth of the dead man to pay his passage across the Styx he says:

They do not give any forethought to the problem of what currency is in use in the underworld, of whether Athenian or Macedonian or Aeginetan coins are legal tender there. Nor have they considered the fact that it would be better not to have any money to pay the fare with. For then the ferryman would not accept them, and they would have to be brought back to the world of the living again.

The whole centrepiece of *On Funerals*, in which the corpse of a young man is imagined as commenting upon his father's behaviour at his funeral, is devoted to sarcastic developments of this kind. The youth, substituting the Cynic view of the world for the common one, pretends to suppose that what his father regrets is his son's inability to experience life's deprivations. This kind of technique in unbroken sequence risks becoming extremely monotonous. Accordingly Lucian

seeks to vary it. Whereas the insistence of the sarcasm is alleviated in
On Funerals by the device of making father and son speak for themselves, *On Sacrifices* achieves a lightening of tone by an admixture of
burlesque. Of its three objects for attack—beliefs about the gods,
concepts of heaven and religious rites—the first, which occupies about
half the work, readily admits the downgrading of myths by (i) reducing
the gods to human status, with Artemis sulking at home because
Oeneus has not invited her to the sacrifice, and Apollo and Poseidon
working as bricklayers for Laomedon, and (ii) by stripping the myths
to their least credible or creditable details and then piling them up in
rapid succession (two dozen and more in seven paragraphs). Essentially,
however, the technique of the two treatises is the same. Like the Cynic
diatribe from which they derive both their form and their sentiments,
they depend principally on a single satirical manner.

A similar narrowness of manner is found in the pamphlets. But there
the weapon is invective. *Alexander, Peregrinus, The Ignorant Book-
collector* and *The Mistaken Critic* all concentrate on exposing the vices
of a single figure drawn according to a particular set of conventions
(see above p. 18ff.). In addition to a certain amount of abstract denunciation, each vice is allowed to emerge as vividly as possible from the
details of a series of scabrous anecdotes. The verbal variety of the
invective ranges accordingly from the simple insult, 'But the so-and-
so also dreamed up a smart fiddle, not the sort of thing just any old
crook would come up with', to the technicolour description of a
particular enormity. The insults are sharpened by a limited amount of
sarcasm, and at the same time made funny by the selecting of absurd
(frequently obscene) detail:

When this work of art shaped by nature's own hand, this example of
Polyclitan perfection, crossed the threshold of manhood, he was promptly
caught in the act of adultery in Armenia, was soundly beaten, and finally
got away by jumping off the roof with a radish stuffed up his arse. (*Peregrinus* 9)

Variety is also achieved in other ways. Where the *alazōn* is a charlatan
the scope of the invective is widened to include those who are taken in
by him (particularly the Paphlagonians in *Alexander*) and those who
are associated with him, such as the Cynic Theagenes in *Peregrinus*.
The delivery of the invective can be partly allotted to a figure other
than the author but either a barely disguised *alter ego*, like the 'other
man' in *Peregrinus*, or even an openly fictional projection, as with

'Damning evidence', the personified figure, apparently from a Menander prologue, who takes over the attack in *The Mistaken Critic*. But the most sophisticated variant is to place the attack in the mouth of the *alazōn* himself, making him deliver a mock-encomium of his own vices. This is the case with *A Professor of Public Speaking*.

The possibilities of such a technique are played with in *The Mistaken Critic* where Lucian gives the conduct of the attack to the personification of the victim's tongue. This allows him to couple the charges of professional (i.e. linguistic) incompetence and moral degeneracy (fellatio) within the activity of the one organ, symbolizing its owner. However the presentation is still that of invective, because the tongue, though physically a part of its master, is set up in opposition to him. There is still a distinction between speaker and victim. For the second part of *A Professor of Public Speaking* this distinction has disappeared. The Professor's assumption of the rightness of his own professional and personal conduct is total, an assumption apparently supported by the case proposed by the speaker. Yet the bulk of what the professor says is easily recognized as false, because it offends against commonsense. It is the vocabulary of attack posing as that of eulogy:

Bring with you ignorance as your most important weapon, then impudence, and recklessness and brazenness as well. A sense of shame, of fair play, of moderation, a tendency to blush, all those you can leave at home. (15)

It seems strange that the authorial voice of the first part of the pamphlet should appear to accept the validity of what is to follow. A closer reading shows that the speaker inserts into his introductory encomium certain asides which do not in fact quite fit with the case he is presenting. Rhetoric is, note *en passant*, to be 'a great deal below the inflated style of poetry', which is hardly complimentary to poetry but a great deal less so to rhetoric. The guide whom we are to reject is given an attractive physical presence; the professor, though described as 'very clever and very handsome', is attributed with 'a swaying walk, a gawky neck, an effeminate glance'. So that when, in the closing phrases of the work, the speaker finally dissociates himself from the position he initially supported, there is no change of view involved, no inconsistency. The moral stance of the work merely becomes explicit. Such a form of irony is hardly subtle, but it is a great deal subtler than pure invective.

The satirical manner of the dialogues takes a similar form of simple irony, and combines it with burlesque. The philosophers of *The*

Banquet, The Eunuch, The Lover of Lies, are as much condemned by their own words and actions as by the commentary of Lycinus or Tychiades. At the same time, they have been deliberately reduced in stature so that they are nothing more than the sum of their vices. Caricature makes them subhuman, yet they lay claim to superhuman status. In *The Banquet,* for example, Lycinus describes the arrival of Ion the Platonist thus:

> When he appeared, they all got to their feet and greeted him as if he were one of the higher powers. It was just like a visitation from a god, when the wonderful Ion joined us.

But when we see Ion in action, he is making an inconsequential and quite inappropriate little speech (a rigmarole of Platonic jargon), and swapping abuse with the rhetorician (39–40).

Self-revelation through action and dialogue is a very varied medium of irony. However, Lucian evidently appreciates that any single satirical device will eventually lose its effect. Ion's set speech is just one of the ways of varying the technique. Where the ridicule is aimed at intellectual qualities, the speech or extended narration by the *alazōn* is the most common device (e.g. *Lover of Lies*); where the moral qualities are the focus of attack, then action and dialogue are equally appropriate. One of the most sophisticated variants is the petulant letter in *The Banquet* sent by the Stoic Hetoemocles to the giver of the banquet, Aristaenetus. It succeeds in fulfilling two separate satirical functions. Following the rhetorical rules for the genre, it reveals the character of the sender; but what is revealed is the opposite of what is said. Hetoemocles parades his indifference to rich living, and his humility. What we see is his pique at not having been invited, his greed, and his bitchiness. At the same time the letter is a piece of comic invective against the philosophers actually present, notably in exposing Diphilus as a pederast.

As long as the balance between irony and caricature is sufficient to remind the audience that the dialogue has (or purports to have) a moral point, the cumulative effect is genuinely satirical. But when, as in *The Eunuch,* the burlesque reduces the philosophers to the embodiment of no more than two or three characteristics, in the case of Bagoas virtually to the single one of sexual impropriety, the satirical manner hardly seems more than the peg on which purely comic elements are hung. *The Eunuch* has the air of an after-dinner story, moving relentlessly towards a single joke. The absurd definition 'a philosopher is a man who has normal sexual powers', which Lucian deduces from the arguments of the case, leads in the final paragraph to lewd *double-entendre*—Bagoas is 'practising his masculinity and keeping the thing in hand'—and closes on the punch line, 'I could wish my son . . . may be well-tooled up for philosophy'. In *The Lover of Lies*, the effect of the imbalance is to make one forget the identity of the story-tellers and simply to enjoy the stories told, an effect Lucian seems conscious of when he makes even Tychiades and Philocles agree about the enjoyable aspect of the romancing. In both cases it is clear that the reduction of the satirical aspect to a subsidiary rôle, and the promotion of purely comic aims to the main rôle, alters the reader's response to the work as satire.

The dialogues which portray a self-consciously unreal world present a surprisingly large number of characteristics in common with those that purport to represent reality. These fantasy dialogues fall into two categories: (i) underworld visits (and variations on that form), as in *The Downward Journey, Menippus, Charon* and *Icaromenippus,* and (ii) works where the action takes place in heaven (*The Parliament of the Gods, Zeus Rants*), or in which non-human characters intervene in human affairs. The 'underworld visit' dialogues are the most homogeneous of all Lucian's works. They are among the earliest extant examples of ingénu satire, demonstrating its three major types. In *Charon* a member of another society comes to visit the earth. In *Icaromenippus* a member of our own society gains the perspective of an outsider by seeing the world from above. In *Menippus* a member of our own society visits another, and compares it with our own. *The Downward Journey* and certain of the *Dialogues of the Dead* (e.g. nos 2–10) present a variation on the latter where the ingénu is a recent 'immigrant' to another society. The phrase 'other society' needs qualification here, because the society that Lucian chooses, hell, is a consequence of, and not a utopian alternative to, our world. This leads to a greater similarity between the types of ingénu satire, since the lower world is much concerned with actually rehearsing the crimes of the upper, and does not merely serve to show them up by implied comparison. There are, obviously, distinctions of motif that accompany the choice of this world or the next as primary focus. Those dialogues set in hell use, for example, the ferryboat across the river Styx and the judgment of the dead by Rhadamanthus as their stock situations; whereas *Icaromenippus* and *Charon* have as initial motif the idea of attaining a great height and then employing magical means to obtain the sharp sight necessary for perceiving the insignificant doings of man. But all these elements are really only questions of décor, and do not mark any essential difference between types of satire. A more important distinction is that of audience perspective, how far our view of the two worlds is defined for us from within the dialogue. The significant factor here is the narrative form, which can either be dramatic (*Charon, The Downward Journey, Dialogues of the Dead* 20), or retrospective narrative (*Menippus, Icaromenippus*). In the latter Menippus functions more or less like Lycinus or Tychiades in the realistic dialogues, formulating our criticism for us. In the former, he, or his substitutes (Diogenes, Cyniscus, Micyllus the cobbler) perform a rôle closer to that of the strict ingénu.

Whatever the décor and whichever of the narrative structures is used, the themes are the same. The moral norm is again that of the common man, personified, as by Micyllus in *The Downward Journey*, or propounded, as by Menippus in *Menippus*. As the latter puts it (4):

> They swiftly proved to me that the way ordinary men live is the golden one.

This championing of commonsense is reinforced by the Cynic theme of the vanity of human endeavour, and its variant, the mutability of fortune. These, too, are in part preached direct; thus Menippus (*Menippus* 16):

> When I saw all this, I felt that man's life is like a parade for which Fortune has furnished the costumes and organized all the details. . . . Often, in the middle of the pageant, she swaps round the costumes of some of those taking part, and will not let them follow the parade through to its end in their original rôles.

For the most part, however, the themes are embodied in the usual stock types and human institutions. The range is neatly summed up by Charon at the end of the eponymous dialogue: 'kings, gold bars, sacrifices, battles.' The dreams of Adimantus and Samippus (*The Ship*) and their deflation by Lycinus are here re-expressed in terms of the contrast between famous kings, generals, outstanding examples of wealth (sometimes, as with Croesus, the categories overlap) as they were in life, and as they are now in the featureless equality of Hades (vice-versa in *Charon*). Similarly, human beliefs about the dead are ridiculed after the manner of *On Sacrifices*, and the usual run of vices with which philosophers and charlatans are pilloried in the realistic works are now liberally distributed throughout humanity. Adultery, corruption, theft and murder cease to be the monopoly of one type, as society in general takes on the rôle of the *alazōn*. Coupled with all this material there is also, in *Menippus* and *Icaromenippus*, the theme of the vanity of human knowledge, inevitably expressed through the contrast between what philosophy, in the abstract, purports to teach, and the jumble of contradictory theories which specific philosophies actually put forward. As in *Philosophers for Sale*, and rather more randomly in *The Dead Come to Life*, stylized examples of ethical (*Menippus*) and scientific (*Icaromenippus*) doctrines are piled one upon another, but here a moral is drawn. The authors are 'presumptuous charlatans'. In *Icaromenippus*, this satire of systems is complemented by the stock portrait of the moral and physical shortcomings of the philosophers themselves, which Zeus paints to the hastily assembled gods. This juxtaposition of attacks on wealth and power with ridicule of philosophy and its adherents is not as incoherent as some critics have maintained. It merely extends the range of human futility by adding another of Lucian's stock topics, viewed principally from the more abstract angle that is the norm for that particular topic in the fantastic dialogues.

Clearly, in the ingénu satires, as in the realistic works, it is not the themes and characters, stock types all, which maintain the satirical interest. More important is the skill with which Lucian varies their presentation. In *Charon* the two main themes are the vanity of human values and the innate corruption of man. The first of these is embodied in the type of the tyrant, Megapenthes, who reveals the emptiness of his values as he attempts to persuade Clotho to let him go back to earth again. In contrast to this ironic self-exposure, the cobbler Micyllus directly denounces the same gap between Megapenthes' values and mortal realities, as he contrasts the tyrant's life with his own for Clotho's benefit. Finally Cyniscus, using stronger invective, accuses Megapenthes before Rhadamanthus. But this time Lucian has moved to the second theme of the dialogue. The emphasis is on the man's vices, not his illusions. The two strands are then brought together by the punishment that is devised: to pay for the sins of his life by eternally yearning for life's illusory pleasures. Two stock themes and one stock type, by judicious variation of dialogue and set speech, irony and invective, have been neatly brought together to reinforce one another. A comparable blending of elements is used in *Icaromenippus* to give variety to the attack on philosophy. In the first place, as was said above, the gap between philosophy and *philosophies* is coupled with the gap between philosophy and *philosophers*. The attack on the first is given to Menippus, in an account seasoned with little ironies that prepare us for the later introduction of the second motif:

... so I selected the best of them, which I was able to judge by the grimness of their faces, the pallor of their complexions and the length of their beards ...

The ridicule of Menippus' tirade is given variation by the fact that the person he is addressing, characterized merely as 'companion' is made a genuine naif (cf. Pamphilus in *The Eunuch*), expressing his astonishment at the dissensions between the sects. When the subject occurs again it is put into the mouth of the moon, who reiterates Menippus' theme of the divergency of scientific doctrines, this time about herself, and then switches, via the conceit of 'deeds that do make the moon to draw her veil', to an attack on the mores of the philosophers themselves. This then becomes the topic of Zeus' oration to the gods. There, within the invective manner already used by Menippus and the moon, Lucian inserts the little variation of self-irony. A philosopher's supposed definition of his profession reveals his own faults:

I bawl, go unwashed, take cold baths, go around barefoot in winter, wrap myself up in a dirty old cloak and slander everything other people do (31).

Through the dialogue the theme remains essentially the same, but there are three variations of manner and motif.

The second group of fantasy dialogues are obviously a fairly disparate group, but share significant characteristics. The characters they stage are principally gods, personified abstractions and philosophers. Other human types—spongers in *Timon*, the rich in *Saturnalia*—may be substituted for the philosophers, and in one case, *The Cock*, the non-human element is supplied by a magic bird. The admixture of these types varies considerably, ranging from *The Parliament of the Gods*, set exclusively in heaven, to *The Dead Come to Life*, where there are no gods at all. Thematically, the dialogues share much of their material with the realistic dialogues. *The Runaways*, *Philosophers for Sale*, and *The Dead Come to Life* deal with the claims of philosophy and its reality, or the shortcomings of those who profess it. *Saturnalia*, *The Cock* and *Timon* deal with wealth in the Cynic manner (cf. Adimantus' wish in *The Ship*), but with the emphasis, particularly in the first two, on the contrast between rich and poor. There are, however, new themes, notably relating to the nature and power of the gods, variants of which are essential to *Zeus Rants*, *Zeus Catechized*, and

The Parliament of the Gods. In terms of structural techniques there is an even greater homogeneity. A dramatic action, sometimes with change of scene, is widely used, the only exceptions being *Zeus Catechized*, which uses a catechism format, and *Saturnalia*, which is a series of letters. The dramatic sequence may be the only structure (*The Parliament of the Gods*), or it may provide the framework for a separate structure, such as the exchange of Damis and Timocles in *Zeus Rants*. It involves its own special motifs, e.g. the gods descending to involve themselves actively in the doings of men, as in *The Runaways*, *Timon*, and *The Double Indictment*. The retrospective narrative so widely used in the realistic dialogues is not excluded—Zeus' account of the initial debate between Damis and Timocles is an example of it— but it is never a major structural device, even where Lucian assumes a direct rôle in the piece (*The Double Indictment, Saturnalia*).

Invective and irony play their part in the satirical manner of these dialogues as much as elsewhere in Lucian's work. Momus is a handy character for open critique of the gods, while men, especially philosophers, are handled here much as they are in *The Banquet* or the pamphlets, the rôle of censor being assumed by the personified abstracts, particularly philosophy herself, or by the author's *porteparole*, where there is one, e.g. Parrhesiades. The dramatic presentation of most of the dialogues provides a good opportunity for characters to condemn themselves, too: either in action, the philosopher-fish swallowing the bait of gold in *The Dead Come to Life*, or verbally, like the Cynic in *Philosophers for Sale*. But the most striking feature of these dialogues is the importance of burlesque in them. It can, of course, be said of the *alazones* in all Lucian's satires that caricature is an important way of diminishing them in the eyes of the audience. But in this group of works, not only are the gods consistently reduced to human status and men, especially philosophers, to sub-human status, but the audience is also frequently made aware of the caricature as a literary game. In *Zeus Rants*, the satirical function of the scenes in heaven is to portray the disarray of the gods, their inability to counteract the threat posed by Damis' attack on them: in other words, the demonstration of that very powerlessness which Damis is ridiculing. The ironic potential of the situation is expressed *en passant*, as when (25) Jupiter condemns himself out of his own mouth in reminding Poseidon of the limitations placed on the gods by Fate:

If the matter were in my power, do you suppose I would have allowed those temple-robbers to get out of Olympia without a blow from my thunderbolt the other day, after they had cut off two of my gold curls weighing almost six pounds each?

In fact, this satirical function and ironic potential are largely ignored in favour of the purely humorous possibilities which the scene offers in terms of parody, cento and the general use of literary reference in an amusingly out-of-context way. Within the opening seventeen lines of dialogue, all in iambics or hexameters, Hermes, Athena and Zeus contrive a cento of lines from New Comedy, a loose parody of Homer, a precise parody of the opening lines of Euripides *Orestes*, and a quotation from Euripides' *Hercules Mad*. For the uninitiated Hera is made to underline what is going on:

> Calm your wrath, Zeus. We can't put on a comedy or sing an epic lay like this lot, and we haven't swallowed Euripides whole, so as to be able to play supporting parts to your tragic lead.

At times the literary borrowing is made the very subject of conversation. When Zeus complains that Hermes has not got the right style for a proclamation, Hermes pleads in defence that high style is for minstrels and that he himself is not a poetic sort of chap. Zeus' advice is to put in a lot of material from Homeric proclamations. The proclamation that results is, indeed, a patchwork of Homeric lines and formulae. Similarly, when Zeus begins to address the gods, himself borrowing from Homer, Hermes advises him to change his material, and points to the source for the new *à la manière de* . . . :

> If you like, unload your metrics, and string together any old one of Demosthenes' speeches against Philip, changing a few details.

Zeus promptly obliges with a version of the opening of the first Olynthiac. This flood of borrowings continues throughout the scenes in heaven: Apollo's absurd oracle, Hermagoras' speech with its references to Euripides' *Orestes*, and a host of Homeric quotations. The parodic atmosphere has in its turn a considerable effect on the tone of the confrontation between Damis and Timocles, for so much of the Epicurean's damaging documentation (40) against the gods is also borrowed from Homer that the entire work becomes a bravura exercise in using literary classics for a variety of comic effect. The seriousness of the topic which the philosophers debate becomes submerged in the cleverness of the inter-reference between the illustrations of the argument and the style of its framework.

The device is not confined to scenes in heaven. The opening of *The Dead Come to Life* is a slanging match of Homeric and tragic quotations between Parrhesiades and the philosophers. At the climax of *The Runaways*, Philosophy and the gods locate the runaway Cynics when they hear the abducted woman lamenting and declaiming invective in a series of four short Homeric parodies. There is, too, a comparable use of literary burlesque in the 'underworld visit' dialogues. Menippus in *Menippus* opens with a series of lines of Euripides, and one from the *Odyssey*, emphasizing this literary game by his costume—a felt cap, for Odysseus and his descent into hell, a lyre for Orpheus and a lion-skin for Herakles (as in Euripides' *Alcestis*), the whole reminiscent of Dionysus got up in fancy dress for his descent into the underworld in Aristophanes' *Frogs*. Doubtless the rest of Menippus' adventures owe much to the Menippean satire *Nekuia*, though the surviving evidence is too slight to allow profitable theorizing; but the audience's attention is already sufficiently drawn to the game of literary reference for them to be alert both to the many Homeric references in the description of hell, and to other references no longer accessible to us (the magician Mithrobarzanes, similar in type to the sorceresses of Alexandrian verse, may be a figure from New Comedy). In all these instances the effect is much that of *Zeus Rants*. The burlesque passes from being an adjunct of satirical criticism to being the main comic purpose in itself.

This overt use of parody in the framework to a piece, thus distracting the audience in some measure from the apparent seriousness of the theme, is in fact the tip of a literary iceberg in both groups of fantasy dialogues. I have had occasion to mention earlier (p. 12) the presence of motifs and structure typical of Old Comedy in *The Dead Come to Life*, *Timon*, and *Philosophers for Sale*. There are set-piece parodies of non-literary conventions too (unless they were among the stock-in-trade of Menippean satire), such as mock decrees (*The Parliament of the Gods* 14–18, *Timon* 50–1, *Menippus* 20). Another completely different approach to the use of literary material is that of *Zeus Catechized*, where the method is to take as many contradictory references as possible out of Homer, Hesiod and the Homeric Hymns, and for Cyniscus to embarrass Zeus with them. The result is not strictly satire, either on the gods or on the authority of the poets. It is an ingenious network of familiar but mutually incompatible traditions, given added literary respectability by its links with anti-stoic polemic.

Clearly Lucian's satires, wheather realistic or fantastic, are satires of a very specific kind. They draw heavily on the prevailing rhetorical tradition and on previous literature for their themes and types, they consciously play with the audience's awareness of their literary ante- cedents, and in certain cases they openly give pride of place to comic techniques, which eclipse rather than enhance the critical element of what they are saying. In fact, what we are dealing with is an excellent example of *literary irony*. A Lucianic satire relies on the previous existence of myth, romance, tragedy, comedy, the novella, all of which it absorbs into its own pattern. It belongs to an esoteric tradition, in that only the cognoscenti—those who can identify the ingredients and thus appreciate the assimilation—will fully appreciate the art. To take a simple example of the process in the popular arts, Ken Russell's film *The Boy Friend* required of its audience the ability to appreciate not merely its relationship with the musical comedy on which it was based (itself a pastiche), but also with the general traditions of English musical comedy in the 1920s, the American musical extravaganza of the 1930s (including broad reference to the films of Busby Berkeley and visual 'quotations' of famous scenes from films like the Rogers and Astaire *Flying Down to Rio*), plus the conventions of the Hollywood 'drama of backstage life'. All these elements, whether pastiched or parodied, were blended into a new self-contained fantasy. Lucian is presenting a much subtler, more complex and more intellectually demanding version of the same game. The theme of the satires is not, in a sense, their ostensible subject matter, but the fact of imitation itself. It is not 'the immorality of philosophers' but 'the presentation of the immorality of philosophers in Old Comedy'. It is not 'the absurdity of the Olympian gods', but 'the presentation of paradoxical traditions about the gods in epic and tragedy'. This is an extreme and self-aware form of a phenomenon that is true of all literature. As Northrop Frye puts it:

Literature may have life, reality, experience, nature, imaginative truth, social conditions or what you will for its *content*; but literature itself is not made out of these things. Poetry can only be made out of other poems; novels out of other novels. Literature shapes itself, and is not shaped extern- ally.[1]

And why not poems out of novels, novels out of plays etc.? It can be shown that whole families of character types and associative clusters of themes and images connect together works by different authors and of different periods. In most modern authors this is unconscious accept-

[1] *The Anatomy of Criticism*, Princeton 1957, 97.

ance of tradition. In Lucian it is conscious exploitation of the relationships in different ways for the purpose of entertainment.

6. THE ROLE OF THE CONTEMPORARY WORLD

Is this the same as saying that Lucian's works have no contemporary reference and no coherent intellectual content? Not necessarily. What it means is that such factors cannot be assumed. The satire, just as much as the purely ingenious rhetorical works, has an artistic justification in itself. It does not require to be related to the outside world. Contemporary reference and intellectual system would have to be separately demonstrated, and the evidence would need to be substantial.

There are two obvious areas in which to look for intellectual system in Lucian: religion and philosophy. Can a sustained philosophical position be deduced from his many references to philosophy and her adherents? Can a sustained critique of contemporary religious beliefs and practices be found in his many references to supernatural forces and human superstitions? To answer this question we must look at his work in its historical context. The condition of religion and philosophy in the second century is a complex one which can only be properly understood in relation to the past.[1] In a sense, philosophy in Greece had always fulfilled one of the major functions elsewhere supplied by the dogma of theology. It was its function to attempt to discover a straightforward explanation of the universe, particularly of man's place in the order of things. Long before the end of the first century it had become plain to many people that the processes of reason, on which almost all philosophies relied, were not leading to any significant results. The various systems, logically deduced but on the basis of very rudimentary attention to physical phenomena, were fixed, codified and institutionalized. For those who continued to adhere to the different sects, philosophy provided topics for study, but did not promote new forms of thought. It was in danger, indeed, of becoming a sub-form of rhetoric, as when Maximus of Tyre cheerfully propounds the arguments for and against a serious philosophical proposition in different speeches (*Orat.* v and vii). Such development as there is takes the form of a narrowing of aims to the purely ethical. At the same

[1] In what follows I have drawn upon the following works in particular: A. D. Nock, *Conversion*, Oxford 1933; M. Caster, *Lucien et la pensée religieuse de son temps*, Paris 1937; A. J. Festugière, *La révélation d'Hermès Trismégiste*, vol. 1, Paris 1944; E. R. Dodds, *Pagan and Christian in an Age of Anxiety*, Cambridge 1965.

time, there is a move towards eclecticism. Even Marcus Aurelius, whose Stoicism has been called relatively pure, concentrates on those aspects of the creed which most fulfil his personal need to relate individual and universe. Equally, he is not afraid to accept, via Epictetus admittedly, the influence of the Cynic code of conduct, and he shows himself accessible to the non-rational currents of his time in such matters as his belief in the power of dream-revelations to relieve him of physical illness. Given the distrust in the further potential of reason to unlock the secrets of the universe, it is natural that the more overtly rationalist a philosophy was, e.g. Aristotelianism, the more its popularity declined. Total scepticism had its vogue, but it was a manner of argument, not an alternative approach to life. If anything, the Sceptics had a frivolous air of caring little what happened to you when they had demolished your certainties. The growth areas were precisely in those philosophies most adaptable to non-rational trends, neo-Platonism and neo-Pythagoreanism. Neo-Pythagoreanism was a ragout of Platonic, Peripatetic and Stoic elements, mixed with a small amount of early Pythagorean tradition. Pythagoreanism itself had never been a coherent system of thought; its successor had no definable body of philosophical doctrine, but gained an aura of tradition from spurious works attributed to early Pythagoreans such as Ocellus of Lucania and Philolaus of Croton. Ultimately it relied on revelation by the inspired. 'The master has spoken' was the formula that ended all speculation. As for neo-Platonism, it took for granted the truth of the Platonic vision, and prepared for what Bréhier has called, *à propos* of the philosophy of the third century, 'a description of the metaphysical landscapes through which the soul is transported as it undergoes what might be described as spiritual training'.[1] Both these philosophies were thus peculiarly adaptable to the needs of an age which could not find solutions to its problems in reason alone.

Why the second century should still have cared so much, despite its material contentment, for metaphysical guarantees, is an interesting question in itself. The reaction against rationalism is an explanation that will only hold good for the intelligentsia (cf. the Catholic revival in France in the late nineteenth century). The broader influences were social. In an important sense the *pax romana* had a destabilizing influence on men's private lives. The implications of the founding of the empire, and its expansion to its maximum extent under Trajan, are

[1] E. Bréhier, *The History of Philosophy: the Hellenistic and Roman Age*, trans. W. Baskin, Chicago 1965, 182.

more than merely political. The Olympian deities had provided a tradition designed to serve a small social unit. Their power to ensure the good fortune of that unit was assumed as an essential aspect of its continued existence. The paying of respects to them via ritual was thus always in part a question of public order and well-being. Faith was not a significant criterion, since there was no theology and no real religious organization. In accepting myths and traditional observances the citizen demonstrated his solidarity with the other members of his social unit. The conquests of Alexander had removed from those social units their political significance. The city as such could no longer fully protect the well-being of its citizens. Accordingly, the real function of the Greek gods in their local aspect disappeared too. Instead the Greeks were exposed to creeds which attempted a universal explanation for a human condition that politically had now to be seen in universal terms. The Roman conquest confirmed that situation. The first universalist doctrine, astrology, supplied a fatalistic explanation which, like philosophical scepticism, was arid and uncomforting. At the same time the social unit no longer gave the individual a sense of protection, since it was so large as to be invisible. The only solution seemed to be to seek for meaning in life through personal revelation.

The consequences for the Olympian cult were various. By the beginning of the second century it continued at one level to have an official and symbolic significance, no more metaphysically persuasive then the purely political imperial cult. It was a formal demonstration of links with a past culture. At another level, there was renewal of the manner of the cult to give it what Festugière calls 'une liturgie paienne analogue par certains traits à la chrétienne'[1] but this was designed to appeal to the masses, not to the kind of people for whom Lucian was writing. And at a third level, the various deities became synthesized with oriental figures whose traditions admitted of a more personal approach. So Statius, at the end of the first book of the *Thebaid*, can make the equivalence Apollo = Titan = Osiris = Mithras. These eastern deities were also imported in their own right. They had obvious advantages: they were definitively held to be superior to fate, and they were borrowed from 'barbarian' societies which, because uncorrupted by the processes of reason, were thought to have retained purer notions of the divine. This assumption of new cults is not a process of *conversion*. Nock convincingly argues that conversion to paganism is only possible much later, when Christianity has become so powerful that its

[1] Quoted in Bompaire, op. cit., 496 n. 1.

otherwise elusive rival is defined by opposition and contrast. The synthesis of traditional and new elements in paganism was a process by which men saw in a new cult 'the original and best expression of a devotion voiced by all men in their several ways'.[1]

By the middle of the second century the dominant forms of religion and philosophy were no longer complementary, but had become parallel, in their attempt to answer the same needs. The emphasis in religion was on individual revelation, symbolic mysteries and initiation. Isis, Cybele, Sabazios, Sarapis, Mithras commanded substantial numbers of adherents, and had affected local cults of more traditional figures. Judaism, and more particularly Christianity, offered appropriate mystical attractions. Theurgy, which acquired prestige from its association with neo-Platonism, used animated statues to utter prophecies. Human mediums communicated with the divine for you. Oracles flourished as never before. But not, significantly, the traditional ones. Plutarch *Moralia* 408B–409A gives evidence for the decline of Delphi. If other Apolline centres such as Claros and Didyma prospered, it was in great measure because they responded to the times in such ways as the extension of their traditional services by initiation rites and mysteries. The importance of the oracles in general is attested both by the attack on them by the Cynic Oenomaus of Gadara (*flor.* early second century), parts of whose work *A Detection of Frauds* is preserved for us by Eutropius, and by the paramount importance attributed to oracular revelation as a proof of the validity of paganism by Celsus in his *True Word* (*c.* 180). Another less institutionalized manifestation of this craving for supernatural relevation is the obsession with miracles attested by Aelian in *On Divine Manifestations* and *On Providence,* and more especially by the sub-literary evidence provided by papyri on the popularity of magic. How far conscious chicanery and material exploitation dictated the growth of a magic 'industry' is impossible to estimate. The testimony of such figures as Aelius Aristides proves the spiritual efficacy of the irrational beliefs even on apparently intelligent believers. Everything points to a climate of opinion which would have bred the same form of conviction in the priests and exponents of revelation themselves. It was an age of compulsive emotional communication with the supernatural in ways that the rationalist criticism of the post-Enlightenment has found impossible to swallow, but which the rebirth of mysticism in the second half of our own century may yet make more accessible to us.

[1] Nock, op. cit., 15.

To what extent does Lucian's picture of gods and philosophers mirror such an age? Plainly in many ways not at all. The review of the gods in *The Parliament of the Gods* is an excellent example. There could hardly be a better opportunity for satirizing the importance of mystic cults, in particular the cult-dramas associated with their divinities. Who does Momus begin by attacking? Dionysus! Lucian continues with a host of minor divinities of the old regime: Pan, Silenus, satyrs. Some space is given to the old Egyptian gods, Anubis and Apis, long a target for comedy. The Scythians, we are told, 'deify and elect anyone they fancy as gods': the example given is Zalmoxis, so recent that he gets into Herodotus (IV. 95). The only instance of syncretism, Zeus Ammon, had become famous centuries earlier when Alexander the Great paid his respects to him. Isis, Osiris, Sarapis are not mentioned, Sabazius is merely listed, Mithras gets a brief joke about his appearance, Asclepius warrants only the most perfunctory traditional comments about his medical capacities. Only when Lucian reaches oracles does he offer a piece of information with undoubted potential contemporary application (12):

You are, therefore, no longer popular, Apollo: oracles are now given by every stone and every altar that has had oil liberally poured over it, garlands put round it, and is equipped with a fake magician, of whom there are plenty.

Yet the terms of the image are only a literary cliché. Lucian uses it elsewhere to demonstrate the credulity of Rutilianus (*Alexander* 30), and its paradigm is given in Theophrastus' picture of the superstitious man, *Characters* XVI. To distract one still further from any effect of contemporary reference, the examples of theurgy that Lucian takes, the statues of Polydamas and Theagenes, are by no means up-to-date; they belong to the stock-in-trade of Cynic invective against miracle-mongers.

The Parliament of the Gods offers a picture of Lucian's presentation of religion which is confirmed in every detail in other works. Not only are Lucian's gods the Olympians, but they are portrayed in Homeric terms, with at most reference to Euripides and the Cynic tradition for variety. The renewal of the old cults by new ceremonial, or by their association with the manner and functions of new deities—compare Jupiter Dolichenus with Mithras, for example—is not reflected in *Dialogues of the Gods, Zeus Rants* or *Zeus Catechized*. The silence on the great new cults is almost total. Sarapis is nowhere mentioned, Mithras only fleetingly, the Egyptians get the appropriate Herodotean pastiching in *The Syrian Goddess* but no serious treatment elsewhere. The fleeting mentions of Christianity in *Peregrinus* show a kindly indifference to a sect that could have furnished so much satirical ammunition, but lacked a literary pedigree. The same is true of what might be called the theological issues of the day. Astrology is ignored, even when the subject is fate, as in *Zeus Rants* and *Zeus Catechized;* for his account of Providence Lucian sticks to the commonplaces of the Cynic tradition. Oracles are usually those in their prime in the fifth century B.C., though Claros and Didyma get some mention (*Dialogues of the Gods* 18. 1: *Alexander* 8, 29, 43). Only when we come to *Alexander* is the contemporary reference undeniable, both in the broad reference to the development of minor cults offering methods of personal revelation, and in the specific reference to mysteries and initiation ceremonies (38–40) and to aspects of neo-Pythagoreanism. The documentary value of the work on these matters is, however, as Caster effectively proved, highly suspect.[1]

What is perhaps most fascinating about Lucian's presentation of religion is that while it can almost all be accounted for in terms of literary traditions and Cynic motifs, there are tantalizing ways in which it does suggest the burning issues of the day without ever directly handling them. What better evidence of this than the existence of two dialogues on the relationship of the gods to fate, another about the credentials of interloping cults, and another devoted to the fashion for superstition and magic among the intelligentsia (*The Lover of Lies*)? The most subtle examples of this insubstantial 'relevance' come in the allied field of philosophy. This may seem surprising, for in general nothing could be more clichéd than Lucian's portrait of the sects. There is, as we have seen, a type underlying all Lucian's philosophers, regardless of sect, which is constructed simply around the comic potential of the contrast between speech and action: *The Runaways* 19, 'You could not find two things so different from one another as what they say and what they do.' Most of this moral portrait is built on the twin topics of sexual immorality and financial greed, which Lucian applies elsewhere in the same measure to all his other stock types, tyrants, rhetoricians, parvenus. Along with this goes the physical cliché: serious countenance, pale complexion, long beard (e.g. *Icaromenippus* 5). The specifically philosophical references are no less traditional in character, whether it be general accusations of ignorance of doctrine (e.g. *The Banquet* 36) or the guying of particular doctrines

[1] See below, pp. 59–61.

or fashions in argument: you can tell a Stoic by his syllogisms, a Platonist by his theory of ideas, a Cynic by his loud mouth and vulgar behaviour, an Epicurean by his greed. There is no serious exposition of creeds, even in *Hermotimus;* nor is there any evidence that the typical features picked upon, especially in *Philosophers for Sale* and *The Dead Come to Life,* were the essential characteristics of the sects in Lucian's own day. The pronounced ethical bent of later Stoicism and the playing down of some of its earlier dogma is not recorded, any more than the typical doctrines of neo-Platonism. In *Hermotimus* Lucian specifically attacks the sects for their lack of eclecticism, although such eclecticism was, to a mild degree, a feature of all philosophical thought in his period. If Lucian betrays no specific knowledge of contemporary philosophy, neither does he betray a coherent attitude towards the creeds as he does portray them. Stoics and Aristotelians, it is true, are always comic butts, whereas Cynics (Menippus and Diogenes) and Epicureans (Damis in *Zeus Rants*) are used as ironists. But then, setting aside the issue of whether these characters really represent their philosophical labels, which in the case of Damis is only partly true, it also has to be noticed (i) that Epicureans and Cynics are themselves sometimes comic butts, like greedy Herman and brawling Alcidamas in *The Banquet,* or the dreadful Theagenes in *Peregrinus* (not to mention the eponymous hero of that work), and (ii) that where a philosopher is used as an ironist, he is fulfilling the same function as Lycinus, Tychiades or any other *porte-parole* to whom no philosophical creed is assigned. It is in that sense a largely literary function, rather than an indication of intellectual adherence. To account for this variety of positions towards the same sects, one can either argue that Lucian changes his philosophical position from work to work like a weathercock in a tornado, which is tantamount to admitting that he has no philosophical position anyway. Or one can attempt to assimilate Lycinus, Tychiades and the rest to a particular sect (Epicurean, Cynic or Sceptic are the usual candidates), while ignoring the fact that they display no consistent features of any given school. It is preferable to accept that the intellectual manner of any character cast as *eirōn* will be controlled by the purely literary requirements of that rôle, whether a philosophical label is attached to it or not.

In all these major respects Lucian's portrait of philosophy is an entirely traditional one; there are, none the less, interesting features which probably do reflect the world around him even if he has not chosen to develop them in those terms. The first is the connexion of philosophy with superstition and magic in *The Lover of Lies*. What more appropriate than that the narrators of tall tales should include a Platonist, and that Arignotus the Pythagorean should appear as the biggest liar of all? More interesting still is the degree to which Lucian's portrait of himself in *Nigrinus*, and of Menippus in *Menippus* and *Icaromenippus*, represents in, respectively, positive and negative images, what one might call the rake's progress of philosophical aspiration in the period. In *Menippus* the hero requires from philosophy one truth, and disillusioned by his failure to obtain it from the traditional sects, has recourse to a magician-cum-oriental prophet for instant revelation. He gets it, but the lesson of the revelation, as spelt out by Tiresias, is to put the present to good use and not to worry about speculation: almost a sketch for *il faut cultiver notre jardin* and identical with the moral of *Hermotimus*. The parallel between Mithrobarzanes and 'the vision of Doctor Thessalos' from a contemporary papyrus has been well-drawn by Festugière. If *Menippus* is read with this in mind, the disparity between the philosophical framework and the ethical clichés which lie at the heart of the dialogue is explained. It is, in a sense, the same disparity as that between the Platonic manner of *The Parasite* and the nullity of thought at its centre. By making the truth revealed through the philosophical quest a simple commonplace that needed no 'relevation', Lucian offers an ironic commentary on the contemporary thirst for metaphysical certainties. Since to read the dialogue in this sense is to eliminate otherwise glaring faults in the literary structure of the work, it is not a case of multiplying explanations for a single element. Tradition supplies the matter of the dialogue, but contemporary reference provides its literary cohesion. Exactly the same can be said about *Icaromenippus*. The flight of a human being up to heaven, though it is fully accountable for as a traditional motif of comedy, takes on, when connected with a philosophical quest, echoes of a neo-Pythagorean doctrine: the soul flies upward to the celestial region, where sun and moon are the isles of the blessed (the same idea may accompany the heavenly voyage in *A True Story*, even if it is borrowed from Antonius Diogenes). As in *Menippus*, the questing spirit is again rewarded by a magical revelation, via the properties of the eagle's wing; but the revelation is an empty one, a lesson in ethics for which one hardly needed a trip to the moon.

Nigrinus is quite different, but it uses an aspect of the same theme; the ideal philosopher as spell-binder and giver of revelations. The exchange which forms the framework for the account of Nigrinus' philosophy is almost entirely concerned with expressing the special condition of one who has received spiritual illumination. From the opening words, 'How grave and uplifted you are since your return', the account develops directly into an evocation of verbal powers that exceed the ordinary. The imagery is celestial or at least mythical: the philosopher's words are called ambrosial and compared in power of effect with the Sirens and the lotus fruit of the *Odyssey*. At the same time there is a thread of psychological and medical analogy; alcoholic intoxication and the infatuation of a lover. In the concluding section of the framework there is an extended description of actual physical response to Nigrinus' words which is more than a little reminiscent of the hysteria aroused by a revivalist preacher (35):

> When he stopped speaking, I suffered the same experience as the Phaea-cians. For a long time I just stared at him, entranced. Then I was seized with a fit of great mental confusion and physical giddiness, and the sweat poured down me. When I tried to speak, I became incoherent, dried up, my voice gave out, my tongue produced the wrong sounds, and eventually I broke down and cried.

This is followed by a long metaphor of Nigrinus as bowman which combines the divine and the medical elements of the initial imagery: the basic archery image (cf. Eros) being embroidered with ancillary images of drugs and their power over the soul, thus returning to the idea of intoxication and heightened states.

This elaborate evocation of the philosopher's power is delivered in so self-consciously rhetorical and theatrical a way (the care with which the types of image are interrelated is a good example), and the first speaker himself is made to lay such open stress on the theatricality of the account (10, 12), that one should be on one's guard against taking it too seriously. But the real problem is that the 'philosophy' of Nigri-nus, as reported to us, not only contains nothing to justify the recipi-ent's ecstasy, but is not philosophy at all. In the course of a lop-sided rhetorical syncrisis of Greece and Rome, Lucian spins out all the satirical commonplaces he uses elsewhere on parvenus, charlatans and hypocrites, proposing as his positive recommendations the simplicity and moderation which he always adopts as the norm against which to measure the conduct of his *alazones*. Certainly the Platonist label attached to Nigrinus means nothing. The fact is that, as in *The Parasite*, *Menippus* and *Icaromenippus*, Lucian has taken a philosophical manner for his framework, but is unable to fill it, and indeed has no intention of filling it, with philosophical matter. In the other dialogues the comic element predominates, making this dislocation more tolerable, and indeed a positive contribution to the satire. In *Nigrinus*, where the effect sought is apparently one of ingenious rhetorical display, the transition is much more uncomfortable. It is a combination that Lucian does not use in any other work, and in this his judgment was probably wise. But it does offer interesting corroboration of his willingness to incorporate a contemporary approach to philosophy, at a very general level, as an essential literary technique in certain dialogues.

In terms of intellectual system, then, one can detect significant traces of contemporary attitudes informing an otherwise wholly traditional picture of religion and philosophy. There is no evidence that Lucian himself subscribes to any particular set of doctrines; nor does he put forward a coherently sceptical or atheistic position. On the other hand, common sense tells one that an ardent believer in any religious or philosophical values would be unlikely, even with the best of literary precedents, to use religious or philosophical motifs, of whatever kind, for purely comic effect. If Lucian had any positive beliefs they must have been very mild ones. This does not mean that his work is not very much a product of its times. A writer is conditioned by his milieu even in the simple act of selecting his material. A critic has said of Molière:

Art, *pace* the aesthetic purists, is not the autonomous structure of their dreams; it does not exist suspended in a void and focused exclusively inwardly upon itself. Being created by man, it is shot through with human elements, and reflects . . . man's inherent propensity for affirmation and negation.[1]

Lucian's case is very similar to that of Molière. Molière did not write *Tartuffe* as an anti-clerical tract; he wrote it as a comedy. He was an actor, not a moralist. But because rigorism in religious observance was both fashionable and at the same time found comic by an important faction at court, who would be prominent in his audience, he adapted his usual gallery of stock types to fit that theme. If Lucian chose certain traditional *topoi*, certain literary models, it was because he expected them to have audience appeal. Now, sceptical humour that is not part of a polemical programme is only possible in an age of religiosity such as Lucian's, because only then is scepticism *per se* a humorous attitude. In that sense Lucian was very much conditioned by the age for which he was writing.

[1] M. Gutwirth, *Molière, ou l'invention comique*, Paris 1966, 158.

As far as other kinds of contemporary reference go, the evidence is rather easier to assess. The main issues are two: is there any reflexion of contemporary social problems in Lucian, and are there significant references to contemporary figures and events? The answer to the first is 'probably not', to the second 'yes, but . . .'. A flat denial of social satire in Lucian will raise some eyebrows. Many critics have pointed to parallels between some of his themes and conditions in various parts of the Empire.[1] But the issue is not one of whether there are elements that could be explained with reference to the author's world; it is one of whether there are any elements that can only be explained by such reference. In writing so self-consciously *l'art pour l'art* the existence of a literary antecedent for an idea or character is sufficient justification for its appearance in a work. Why multiply causes? The first victim of such an application of Occam's razor is the argument that all references to contrast or conflict between rich and poor are a reflexion of a class struggle in second-century society. It is true that there are eleven *Dialogues of the Dead* which use this motif, that the three parts of *Saturnalia* are devoted to it, and that it occurs prominently in *Nigrinus, On Salaried Posts* and *Timon,* to mention but a few. If the satirical method of an author is built on comic contrasts, what hoarier chestnut than the absurdities of the rich as measured against the sober common sense of the poor? *Saturnalia* is a good case in point: in form it is an excuse to exploit three different exercises, a dialogue, the mock laws, and the letters. The dialogue is something of a *Zeus Catechized* in miniature, with the priest fulfilling the function of Cyniscus. Tales about Cronos are recalled, from Homer and Hesiod, and used against him, with Zeus playing the same contrastive rôle to Cronos that the Fates play toward him in *Zeus Catechized.* Into this is inserted other traditional material, such as the 'wish for wealth' motif from *The Ship,* or the inequity of divine justice, as portrayed in *Zeus Rants.* Out of the legends of Cronos, now doubling as the Greek equivalent of Saturn, Lucian takes the world-upside-down tradition of the Roman Saturnalia, but without any of its distinctively Roman features. The laws dictated to the priest by Cronos (the concept of direct revelation guyed again?) are principally devoted to rules governing the giving of presents and banquets, doubtless not the most pressing issues for the urban poor, even if banquets are a constant motif in the picture of the

[1] The view of Lucian as a socially and intellectually committed critic of the world around him is expressed with the maximum of stridency, but not very convincing evidence, in B. Baldwin, *Studies in Lucian,* Toronto 1973.

cliens given by Roman satirists. And the letters, when they are not dishing out the moral commonplaces of diatribe—(30) 'You should remember in your revels that all men must soon die, the rich leaving their riches, the poor their poverty'—are also harping on the theme of banquets, with the rich mocked for their stinginess and the poor for their greed, in the same terms as philosophers are pilloried as money-grubbing and self-indulgent elsewhere in Lucian. This contrast of appearance and reality, demanding that neither rich nor poor are quite what they seem, is not at all out of place if the work is intended on a purely humorous level, for it is a stock element in Lucian's comic technique. As part of a ringing plea for social justice it would be remarkably inappropriate. If *Saturnalia* cannot be shown to have a serious general application to its age, neither can it be said to reflect a biographical incident. The fact that Aulus Gellius recalls (XVIII. 2) celebrating the festival in Athens, with a banquet and little intellectual party-games reminiscent of some details in Lucian's account is scarcely convincing evidence for the suggestion[1] that Gellius and Lucian celebrated the festival together in Athens in 159. Neither the manner, nor much of the matter, nor one single unequivocal reference to contemporary conditions or events can be adduced to show that *Saturnalia* is more than yet another comic pirouette upon traditional material.

Lucian's specifically anti-Roman satire is obviously more difficult to dismiss out of hand. The key texts are *Nigrinus* and *On Salaried Posts;* there are also Roman customs which are given individual treatment elsewhere, such as the client's morning visit to his patron (*The Ship* 22, *Menippus* 12), or the problem of inheritance-seekers (*Dialogues of the Dead* 15–19). The striking similarity between Lucian's material and that of Juvenal is an acknowledged fact. Whether or not Lucian knew and borrowed from the picture of the unpleasant side of Roman life in *Satire* III and of the tribulations suffered by household dependents in *Satire* V is a moot point. If not, there must have been an established tradition on which both authors drew along with Horace, Martial, Petronius and others. What is certain is that this presence of common material of a highly stylized kind is the very opposite of a proof that Lucian was intending to give an eye-witness account of the same life-style as the Roman satirists. Of course some of it, as a well-travelled man, he may have seen. But the argument that, because a man has seen something, he must record it realistically in his writings, is not valid for modern authors, let alone ancient ones. Chateaubriand

[1] J. Schwartz, op. cit., 35–6.

travelled in America, but his *Atala* draws far more on the traditions of exoticism and of pastoral Utopia than on his geographical observations. Whatever the explanation for the coincidence of material, it indicates a literary source for Lucian, one allowing him to expand upon the comic possibilities of the 'vices and shortcomings of the rich' motif in particular by creating a Roman variant on the parvenu type he uses widely in purely Greek contexts, e.g. *The Cock* 10–14, *Timon* 22–3, *The Ship* 22–5. In the case of the *Nigrinus* such material fills the gap left by the need to portray Nigrinus' philosophy with a rhetorical exercise, *psogos* rather than encomium being more conducive to comic effect. In *On Salaried Posts* it allows another set of variants on the type of the philosopher, by crossing it with the clichés of diatribe against wealth. Lust for riches (3), comfort (7) or sexual satisfaction (12) are now not indulged vices, as they are in the other pamphlets, but conditions vainly sought by, or wrongly held against, the wretched aspirant. If the material is in any way real, that is a side effect. It is chosen because it fits into the style of writing that Lucian adopts for his works, and, presumably, because it reflected the tastes and knowledge of some particular audience for whom he was performing. Perhaps a little fun at the expense of the Roman master, portrayed as a national stereotype (cf. South Americans in French farce and comic opera of the late nineteenth century), would always find favour with Greek audiences, even when Rome itself was going through the philhellenic phase of the second century. Perhaps Greek-speaking Roman audiences found such stuff entertaining—the comic who insults his audience to their delight is a common enough theatrical phenomenon. Certainly there is no sign of any more serious desire to paint the vices of the age. It would be surprising if there were, in an author who, setting himself up with the opportunity to view his own country (if one can call Greece such for a hellenized Syrian) through the eyes of an ingénu, to wit Charon, precedes to paint a picture of it consistently six centuries out-of-date.

If there is no apparent attempt to hold a critical mirror to his world, there is, none the less, in *Alexander* and *Peregrinus* (and cf. *The Runaways* 1–2, 7, also dealing with Peregrinus) an undeniable exploitation of contemporary *faits divers* as the central theme of pamphlets. The other pamphlets contain not one shred of evidence to suggest that their central figures—the master of rhetoric, the book-collector and the carping critic—need to be identified with living persons at all. It is indeed possible to draw parallels between the master and various sophists described by Philostratus—Scopelian, Herodes Atticus, Hadrian of Tyre, Pollux—but given the entirely conventional portrait which Lucian gives (see above p. 18ff.) this is clearly evidence for the degree to which Philostratus stylizes his biography rather than for the extent to which Lucian borrows from reality. Are we really to believe, for example, that Scopelian was denounced by a slave for an attempted poisoning (Philostratus 1. 21. 5)? Is not the presence of that accusation in all Lucian's portraits of villains an indication of its rhetorical necessity in any variety of *psogos*, including a superficially biographical work like that of Philostratus? However, there is no possibility of doubting the existence of Peregrinus and Alexander. Peregrinus Proteus was a Cynic philosopher who did indeed burn himself alive at the Olympic games, probably in 165 (the date is given by Eusebius and St Jerome). There are a number of ancillary aspects in Lucian's account that are also historically accurate. The charge that Peregrinus persuaded the Greeks to an armed uprising against the Romans (19) is made at least possible by the fact that a rebellion in the province of Achaea did have to be suppressed during the reign of Antoninus Pius (though there is nothing to connect our hero with it). The Cynic disciple of Peregrinus, Theagenes, is probably a man well known at Rome; his death is recorded by Galen. The account of Peregrinus' attack on Herodes Atticus for bringing piped water to Olympia tallies with Philostratus' statement that Proteus often criticized Herodes (II. 1, 33). Most interesting of all are the famous references to the Christians, about whom Lucian is not uncomplimentary in a patronizing way (the sixteenth-century popes did not see it in quite that light). But it is significant that this account (11–13 and 16) is a little confused, puts stress on unimportant aspects of their life style which were doubtless thought amusing at the time (the choice of their communism may owe something to a certain literary respectability deriving from the similar motif in Plato's *Republic*) and does not develop their potential as comic butts, especially in matters of doctrine and ritual. Possibly the cause was simply that, unlike the Paphlagonians in *Alexander*, they had no literary pedigree as symbols of gullibility. As it is, they provide no more than a little passing local colour. Apart from these few features, there is little ground for believing in any of the other details of the work as *history*. Other sources paint Peregrinus as a serious philosopher, e.g. Aulus Gellius XII. 11 *virum gravem et constantem*: Lucian substitutes a portrait conforming, as we have seen (above p. 18ff.) to the classic villain of every *psogos*. Why he should have chosen to write a highly fictionalized invective of a dead man is a difficult question, which can more easily be answered *à propos* of *Alexander*. But a highly fictionalized invective is certainly what *Peregrinus* is.

Alexander is a much more complicated case.[1] The circumstances of its writing are made clear (apparently) in the text. It was a commissioned work requested by an Epicurean (61, and 1, if Celsus be identified with the Epicurean said by Origen to have lived in the reign of Antoninus Pius). The date of writing was after the death of Alexander and, more important, after the death of Marcus Aurelius (A.D. 180), that is, some fifteen years after the most recent event otherwise datable in the work (the plague, A.D. 165–8). It is an attack on an historical figure and his founding of the cult and oracle of Glycon at Abonuteichus in Paphlagonia; independent evidence for the cult is preserved most clearly in coinage of the city, showing that Glycon worship survived until at least the middle of the third century. Clearly, then, the work has been written to undermine the credibility of a relatively new and flourishing religious centre (if Lucian's arithmetic is anything other than purely fanciful, it would have come into being *c.* 145) and to denigrate the memory of a man who, whether sincere or charlatan, would have had little love for the Epicureans, as the principal opponents of that revival of mysticism of which his activities were a prime example. Though the tales told of Alexander's treatment of Epicureans (38 43–6) may have no substance in reality, they represent an entirely plausible attitude. Numerous references to contemporary events can also be found, particularly between 160 and 168, and a number of leading Romans figure in the narrative, notably Alexander's chief victim, P. Mummius Sisenna Rutilianus, proconsul in 172. Alexander's cult is the absolute type of the new revelatory religion which invaded the empire in Lucian's day. It assimilates its god Glycon to Asclepius by the process of divine reincarnation common in the period, and gives him the kind of titles associated with the oriental deities (king 40, lord 43). It also incorporates a strong neo-Pythagorean strain, has references to the practices and features of the cult of Sabazius, the standard magical paraphernalia—an inspired prophet (12), divine manifestations (13f.), magical medicine (22), autophone oracles (26ff.) and mysteries complete with cult-drama (38–40). The choice of Asclepius reminds us of Aelius Aristides and the hysterical superstition which disfigures his otherwise rather moving account, in *Sacred Teachings*, of his relationship with that god. Aristides is simply

[1] In what follows I am indebted to M. Caster, *Études sur Alexandre* ... (1938).

the extreme example of a phenomenon attested by other writers of the period. Maximus of Tyre also claimed to have had a personal revelation, and Origen, in his *Against Celsus* (III. 24), quotes the claim of Celsus that many Greeks and non-Greeks were cured of illness by such visions. The Pythagorean material is more interesting still, because Lucian has invested so many parts of the account with it. I have noted earlier that neo-Pythagoreanism is one of the few philosophies which Lucian seems to refer to in its truly contemporary aspect. It may not be pure chance either that Lucian is so fond of using Homer in works such as *Zeus Catechized* at a time when Pythagoreans had begun to produce edifying exegeses of the text of Homer for their own religious purposes. But there the identification of echoes is highly speculative: what other material would any rhetorician know so well by heart? In *Alexander*, the evidence is explicit. From the outset Alexander is compared to Pythagoras, apparently on his own say-so, and with hardly convincing protestations of respect toward the master on Lucian's part (cf. the entry of Arignotus in *The Lover of Lies*). He is described as a friend of the Pythagoreans (25); he explains his own divine powers in a Pythagorean way by what was probably, in origin, the symbolic image of himself espousing the moon, a celestial body important in Pythagorean eschatology; he flashes a golden thigh while conducting the mysteries; and he issues an oracle in which, using the Pythagorean distinction between soul and intellect, he lays claim to be in part Pythagoras re-incarnate (40). Some of this material may have been supplied to Lucian by an eye-witness; it is all at least plausible within the context of what is known of other such cults of the day.

So much for historicity. As for the account of Alexander's early history, and the charlatan practices of the oracle, these are pure literature. Alexander, like Peregrinus, is simply associated to the rhetorical type of the villain. Why should we suppose that, say, the episode of the attempted murder of Lucian is real? All villains in Lucian attempt murder; and what greater cliché of popular romance than the hired murderer who falters in his task to dispose of the unwanted hero? Who is to say that Lucian knew and advised Rutilianus? The latter was safely dead, and unlikely to quarrel with a convenient fiction. And if these things are inventions, how much more so are the descriptions of Alexander's motivation, his secret vices and the means by which he carried out his quackeries. Where could Lucian have got his information from on such points? The fact of the matter is that, having obtained the basic information necessary to give the colour of direct reference, Lucian has exploited his commission in the best way he knew how: as a purely literary exercise. Nock, in a rare misjudgment, says of *Alexander*: 'Lucian here speaks with a depth of feeling which is unusual in him.'[1] In fact, Lucian simply achieves a particularly telling literary synthesis of traditional material and local colour.

Alexander, and to some extent *Peregrinus*, do, none the less, represent a considerable excursus into actuality for the writer of *Phalaris*, *Charon* and the *Dialogues of the Gods*. For a possible explanation one must look to the whole question of Lucian's audiences, and what were the circumstances in which his works were performed. This is an extremely hypothetical exercise, since, although we know a little, mainly from Philostratus, about the performance of sophists proper, we have no evidence about figures comparable with Lucian. Two reasonable assumptions can be made from the nature of the writing itself: first, that the works were designed for live performance, and second, that the audience was expected to have a high level of literary knowledge. It seems reasonable to assume that a performer on tour would need a fairly large stock repertoire, which he could eke out with occasional pieces, designed in some way for the particular milieu in which he was going to perform. *The Scythian, Anacharsis*, and *Toxaris* might, for example, all be works prepared for a Macedonian circuit. In this context *Alexander* and *Peregrinus* would be examples of relatively precise commissions for a very particular audience; the encomia of Lucius Verus' mistress in *Essays in Portraiture* and *Essays in Portraiture Defended* would be examples of an equally precise commission for an occasional piece of a very different kind. The bulk of Lucian's work had, however, to be appropriate not for special occasions, but for the general run of audiences from Syria to Gaul. Hence the reliance on the most traditional of traditional sources—Homer, Euripides, Old Comedy—and the most accessible of popular material, the themes of Cynic diatribe.

At this point, certain reservations must be made about the distinction I have hitherto observed between references in Lucian's works which can only be explained in terms of his contemporary world and references which can be adequately explained on a purely traditionalist basis. Let us suppose that much of Lucian's art is a very intellectual form of revue material. The advantages of satirical sketches that rest on traditional types is that they can be appreciated either for their literary skills alone, or, if played in the right context, can be made to have an

[1] op. cit., 15.

apparent immediacy to some local event or figure. A particular audience
readily associates a traditional portrait with a current scandal of their
locality. It seems perfectly plausible, for example, that *The Ignorant
Book-collector* might be admired exclusively for its rhetorical skills as
an example of invective, when delivered to an audience of cognoscenti
in the Pô basin, whereas in some Asia Minor township it would be
received as a very near-the-bone attack on some local celebrity. Lucian
would only have to make a few discreet enquiries before the curtain
went up, as it were, in order to find out what was the talk of the town,
and select a piece from his repertoire that featured the appropriate
vices. The range of human vices is very limited, and Lucian's works
run the gamut of the more popular ones. This idea of selecting a piece
as appropriate to a particular place or occasion is, after all, only an
extension to performance of an idea already accepted as basic to the
composition of rhetoric, that it is audience-oriented.[1] Consider Cicero
on the subject, *Orator* XXI. 70–1:

In an oration, as in life, nothing is harder than to determine what is appropriate. The Greeks call it *prepon*; let us call it *decorum* or 'propriety' . . . the
orator must have an eye to propriety not only in thought but in language.
For the same style and the same thoughts must not be used in portraying
every condition in life, or every rank, position or age, *and in fact a similar
distinction must be made in respect of place, time and audience.* The universal
rule in oratory, as in life, is to consider what is appropriate.

The appropriateness of a topic to its audience can reasonably be taken
to include the likelihood of its appealing to them as an entertainment.
The adjustment of the repertoire to fit the gossip of a particular town
would, in that sense, be the consideration of what is 'appropriate'. It is
even possible that different members of the audience would respond to
different levels of a work. Aristophanes in *Ecclesiazusae* 1154–6 has
the Chorus appeal both to the wisdom of the spectators and to their
vulgar tastes:

I hope the wise will vote for me for my wisdom's sake,
And that those who enjoy laughing will choose me for my humour's sake;
In other words, I am bidding just about everyone to vote for me.

On that principle, the more sophisticated members of Lucian's audience
could respond to the literary skill of the pieces, the less sophisticated to

---

[1] I regard my views on this as a natural extension of points made by D. A.
Russell in his article 'Rhetoric and criticism', *Greece and Rome*, second series
XIV (1967) 130–44.

their scandalous content. In a plainly hybrid genre like the Lucianic dialogue or pamphlet a mixed response would seem perfectly appropriate.

The comparison with revue and the floating of so airy an hypothesis are in no way meant to be derogatory of Lucian's art. They are intended to emphasize that the works should be seen as the products of a performing artist, rather than as a series of literary pieces to be read aloud. Lucian's work, ingenious or comic, seems to take on a unity of content and manner when it is seen in this light. Faults of structure would be less obvious to the ear than to the eye; and the question of contemporary reference would seem less significant than scholarly controversy in recent years has made it.

II
The Later Influence

INTRODUCTION

LUCIAN'S fate at the hands of posterity is a complex one. He is
unmentioned by his contemporaries and apparently unknown to the
immediately succeeding generations. Of literary influence there is
barely a question. Alciphron, whose life probably overlapped chrono-
logically with Lucian's, appears to have borrowed from the *Dialogues
of Courtesans* in his *Letters of Courtesans*. There is also the difficult
question of the novella *The Ass,* which may have been written by
Lucian, and whose precise relationship to Apuleius' *Golden Ass* is impossible to determine. Otherwise, silence, until eventually sparse
references emerge in Christian and late antique authors—Eunapius,
Lactantius, Isidore of Pelusium—leading us on into Byzantium and
the first 'rediscovery' of Lucian's work.[1]

The absence of contemporary, or other informed antique comment
had the effect of completely disguising the true nature of the dialogues.
Aristotle's view of Greek tragedy may have its limitations, but it has
the virtue of stemming from the same intellectual world as the texts
which it purports to define. Lucian's dialogues were much more in
need of a chronicler than was ancient tragedy. There are peculiar
difficulties in appreciating a piece of literature which has every appearance of performing a function other than its real one, especially when
that real function is primarily aesthetic. Lacking any understanding of
the nature of the so-called Second Sophistic, neither the Byzantines nor
the Renaissance Italians were equipped to see Lucian as other than a
moralist who happened to write in a particularly entertaining way.
Furthermore, the moral preoccupations of their own civilizations were

---

[1] M. D. Macleod, in the introduction to vol. 1 of his *O.C.T.* of Lucian, records
the interesting fact that a Syriac paraphrase of *Slander* is preserved in an eighth-
or ninth-century Ms. in the British museum. Since the paraphrase is thought to
be approximately sixth-century, this raises the possibility that Lucian's works
continued to circulate in his home locality long after they had fallen into obscurity
elsewhere.

easily transferred into the interpretation of these texts, with their didactic surfaces. It was a Lucian filtered via such channels who was to reach the Europe of the Northern Renaissance. The bizarre effect of this is that we must turn our backs on the real Lucian, and substitute for him a series of shifting masks, whose common feature is the element of derision (however light) and of moral intent (however negative). Accordingly, with Lucian more than with any other classical author, it is necessary to trace the view of him that each age, each nation, each individual holds, before one can detect the effects of his influence.

This naturally risks becoming a circular process. One defines the major characteristics of Lucian with respect to the work of author X, and then proceeds to find those characteristics in that author's work. There are two ways to guard against this. One is to limit the enquiry to authors who describe their view of Lucian for you, in prefaces, letters etc., and in whose work direct borrowings can be detected. From borrowings, often not very interesting in themselves, one can then move towards an examination of possible parallels in theme and motif, and to literary manner, allowing in each case for the prejudices of the age and the author concerned. The second defence is to look at the picture of Lucian that can be derived from the major translations of him. This is less effective than for some other authors, because of the absence of any substantial vernacular translations until a late date. For a hundred and fifty years the selected Latin translations by Erasmus and Thomas More were the only important version, and though their influence on intellectual circles was enormous, they naturally failed to have the popularizing effect of, say, Amyot's *Plutarch*. The greatest and most lasting of the vernacular translations was to be Wieland's German version, but, coming at the close of the eighteenth century, it marked the end of a tradition, and was without heirs. There were, however, two vernacular translations—the Perrot d'Ablancourt version of the complete works into French, first published in 1654,[1] and the so-called Dryden Lucian, heavily dependent in parts on its French forerunner, and first appearing in 1711[2]—whose influence was very significant. D'Ablancourt's work is really an adaptation, since he freely modifies the work in order to produce a contemporary flavour. His introductory letter shows that this is a question of

---

[1] On D'Ablancourt's translation, see L. Schenk, *Lukian und die französische Literatur im Zeitalter der Aufklärung*, Munich 1931, and R. Zuber, *Traduction et Critique de Balzac à Boileau*, Paris 1968.

[2] On the 'Dryden' *Lucian*, see H. Craig, 'Dryden's Lucian', *Classical Philology* 16 (1921) 141–63.

principle with him. Some of his modifications concern the matter of the works. The improprieties were to be abandoned (homosexual references in particular he thought offensive to French mores—in the age of the Grand Condé!), and the comedy of manners was to be re-expressed in seventeenth-century terms. Even more drastic stylistic manipulation was involved. Over-free expressions were toned down, the jokes were to be given French equivalents, and such basic Lucianic features as quotations from Homer and reference to classical mythology were to be as far as possible omitted or replaced, as being pedantic and over-erudite. Of particular interest is the way in which the irrational aspects of Lucian, for example the parodic fantasy of *A True Story*, were incomprehensible to the rationalist mind of a neo-classical translator. D'Ablancourt clearly expected the work to have a moral dimension. He therefore allowed his nephew Fremont d'Ablancourt to add a two-volume supplement which is entirely allegorical in its fantasy (see below p. 137). D'Ablancourt was fully aware of how drastic the effect of all this was, and cheerfully defended it in his conclusion:

> Therefore I do not always adhere closely to my author's words or to his thoughts: and while remaining faithful to his intentions, I adjust his material to suit the style and manners of today. Each age not only speaks but also thinks in a different way.

The Dryden Lucian is very similar in its attitudes, partly because they are the attitudes behind most neo-classical translation, and partly because Dryden borrowed from D'Ablancourt. The translation itself was carried out by a number of persons, probably in the 1690s, many of them with known deist leanings. In several cases, e.g. Nahum Tate's version of the *Dialogues of the Gods*, the translator has clearly worked with the French in front of him. This is perfectly in accord with Dryden's views on translation as expressed in his 'Preface on translation' prefixed to the *Second Miscellany* (1685) and in the 'Life' of Lucian that was his sole contribution to the project. The translator, according to Dryden, was freely to render the ideas and spirit of the original. He was not obliged to stick close to the text, and, indeed, it was better that he be incompetent in the language of the original than in his own. For the result must be a work of and for the translator's own times. From both the major French and English translations, then, the eighteenth century was to gain a view of Lucian periwigged, rationalist, satirizing humbug and fanaticism with a finely gauged humour, an agnostic with a deep sense of social justice, and above all a gentleman. For this period, at least, we have some idea of the peculiar distortions that the image of Lucian underwent, and which will be reflected in any conscious (or unconscious) imitations.

What follows will in no sense be a history of Lucian's influence on European literature. Such a study would be impossibly compendious, monumentally dull and of dubious value. It is, instead, an attempt to outline the significant features of that influence, showing in what form Lucian came through to Northern Europe[1] and what genres of Renaissance and post-Renaissance literature he contributed to or inspired. The search begins in Byzantium and Italy, partly to show the diversity of interpretation to which the works were open, partly because the northern Renaissance absorbed as by Lucian certain works, notably *Philopatris* and *Virtus dea*, which were in fact imitations created in those earlier eras. Then I shall look at European literature in the period 1500–1800, mainly in England and France but with excursions into Spain, Denmark and Germany, examining the reasons for Lucian's popularity, the nature of his reputation, the forms of his influence which had only limited currency, and the three major genres on whose development his influence was decisive: the satirical dialogue, the fantastic voyage, and the dialogue of the dead.

I. BYZANTIUM

The enthusiasm for Lucian among the Byzantines is a curious phenomenon. Though the virulent comments of Arethas (*c.* 860–*c.* 932) and the equally virulent entry in the *Suda* make it plain that Lucian was known in some circles as a wicked anti-Christian, this reputation seems to have been less damaging to his popularity than it was to be in the Western Europe of the Renaissance. For he was an author not only read by intellectuals such as Photius and John Tzetzes (*c.* 1110–*c.*1180), but considered an appropriate source for educational material, as can be seen from Johannes Georgides' inclusion of Lucian quotations in his *Collection of Maxims* (late 9th c.) and Thomas Magister's use of him in the *Selection of Attic Nouns and Verbs* (*c.* 1300). Creative writers were drawn to him both by the clarity of his style and his rhetorical expertise, and also by his satirical techniques. The earliest datable

---

[1] One of the little ironies of literary history is that almost the last of the European languages into which Lucian was translated was modern Greek, where Constantine Dapontes was the first in the field, *c.* 1770: see V. Cerenzia, 'Dapontes traduttore di Luciano', *Rivista di Studi Bizantini e Neoellenici* NS 12–13 (1975–6) 161–73.

influence on *belles lettres* can be seen in the epigrams of Leon the Philosopher (early 10th c.), but from then until the fall of Byzantium examples of various types of influence are plentiful.

At its simplest this interest in Lucian manifests itself as adaptation. Among the examples of that peculiarly mediaeval exercise, the verse paraphrase of a prose text, there is a version of part of Lucian's *Herodotus* by the poet Manuel Philes (13th c.). Philes has extracted the *ecphrasis* of Aëtion's painting of *The Marriage of Roxana and Alexander* (*Herod.* 5), and turned it into iambics, preserving as much of the phraseology of the original as possible. The picture represents Roxana upon the bridal couch as Alexander is led towards her. A notable feature are the Cupids playing with Alexander's armour, where it lies upon the ground (Botticelli copied the motif in his *Mars and Venus*). Philes extends the ornamental rhetoric of the description by using as his closing four lines the moral with which Lucian interprets the painting at the beginning of 6:

> All you behold is not but art and fable.
> From what is seen, 'tis possible to learn
> That even Alexander at his wedding
> Could not put off his love for warlike things. (Philes 30–3)[1]

The *ecphrasis* was, of course, a frequent subject for Byzantine poetry; one thinks in particular of the many architectural ecphrases of churches. The fondness for verbal recreations of works of art that Lucian shows in the *prolaliai* must have made him a popular subject for transpositions of this kind.

A more creative type of influence, at least to the modern eye, is the *imitation* of a particular dialogue. An example of this is the *Sale of Lives of Litterateurs and Men in Public Life* by Theodore Prodromos (early 12th c.).[2] How close this work is to the Lucianic satire of similar title can be seen from the opening exchanges of Zeus and Hermes:

Zeus   Well, Hermes, we arranged the place and the benches and the rest of the auction-room furniture nicely yesterday, and there won't be any need to prepare it again. Indeed, there won't be much need for a proclamation from you, summoning prospective buyers. For yesterday's announcement was enough for them, in place of a proclamation. Many of them are already gathered here. But there

---

[1] All translations in section two are my own unless otherwise indicated.
[2] The text is only available as transcribed by F. J. G. de la Porte du Theil in *Notes et extraits des mss. de la bibliothèque du roi* 8, 2, Paris 1810, 129–150.

is the point that you ought to run over what lives we have on offer for the buyers. For, those who saw yesterday's announcement have come to buy workers' lives, as is clearly proven by the loincloths, sandals, soot and squalor. But we shall be auctioning literary and political figures.

Hermes And how, Lord of us all, could I make a proclamation to such common fellows, probably manual labourers, given that I'm Hermes? How will they understand the verses? I'm always bidden by you to make my proclamations in verse.

Prodromos, taking up Hermes' promise at the end of *Philosophers for Sale* to continue with a sale of 'common lives', has produced a sequel. He takes out of *Philosophers for Sale* 1 the motifs of arranging the auction-room and of Hermes' summons to the buyers. Into these he inserts the idea of the difficulties that Hermes experienced in finding a suitable tone for his proclamation in *Zeus Rants* 6. He then goes on to the idea of foreign gods with whom Hermes cannot communicate (Bendis, Anubis as in *Zeus Rants* 8, the Colossus of Rhodes as in 11), an extension of the problems between old gods and new that figures large in *Zeus Rants* and is the subject of *The Parliament of the Gods*.

Having established this close relationship with *Philosophers for Sale*, tricked out with motifs from other dialogues, the piece proceeds according to the same pattern as Lucian's. A succession of famous figures—Homer, Hippocrates, Aristophanes, Euripides, Pomponius, Demosthenes—come forward and hold dialogues with their potential purchasers. The tone is bantering. A buyer comments unfavourably on Homer's blindness, and is rebuked by Hermes for criticizing the gods' greatest benefactor—all the best attributes of the gods have been given to them by the poet! Prodromos is playing with the idea behind *Zeus Catechized* and *Zeus Rants*, that the Olympian gods are inventions of the poets. With this he links the notion, ridiculed in *On Sacrifices*, that the gods are dependent on man for their livelihood:

If he had not by good fortune happened to be well-disposed towards us, we should have well and truly thirsted and starved, without so much as a fraction of ambrosia or a half a pint of nectar.

The comic reputation of Homer as charlatan is brought in, together with some fun at the expense of the traditional scholarly controversy over his birthplace and the stock pun on his name (= hostage), both topics used in *A True Story II*. 20, and a great deal of play is made with snatches of the text of the epics, together with some references to the

Homeric hymns. In other words, the procedure is the same as for the philosophers in Lucian, where stock physical traits and snatches of doctrine in a popular form are brought together to burlesque each figure.

Approximately half the piece is devoted to Homer, the other characters being dealt with far more summarily. Both Prodromos and his audience would have known their *Iliad* and *Odyssey* much better than the works of the dramatists, let alone those of prose writers. The characterization becomes virtually one-dimensional. Hippocrates is made to give a comic account of the jargon of medicine; Aristophanes and Euripides converse exclusively via versions of their own lines. A slight variation in the format is allowed in two customers who argue over Euripides. But the first really original touch occurs when Prodromos introduces a new dimension of verbal humour in the character of Pomponius; he shows an inclination to speak in transliterated Latin, which the buyer either mistakes for Greek or fails to understand altogether. This opens the way for a little mild satire on the language of the legal system, as close to contemporary reference as the piece ever gets. At the same time, Pomponius has a literary function derived directly from Lucian. He takes the rôle assigned to the Cynic in *Philosophers for Sale* 9, in that he is made to condemn himself by his analysis of how to achieve success in the law. He indicates the money to be made out of a legal career and then moves on to encourage the cultivation of vices which will assist this:

Just let shamelessness take the lead and nonsense follow close behind; let verbosity be their companion, along with a harsh voice and an overtly bilious condition. You must snarl at the court, pour whole cart-loads of abuse on the opposing litigant, and from time to time leap at the face of his counsel as if about to grab him by the end of his nose. That way you can think yourself the winner, and go away with a high opinion of yourself.

The piece continues with the sale of Demosthenes, ridiculed on the traditional grounds of having been corrupted financially in his political activities while posing as a man of principle. Hermes takes the ironic stance of pretending not to believe the charge. Cowardice in war is also held against him, the old story of his running away from the battle-field being contrasted with various 'heroic' quotations from the *Orations*. And as a final salute to Lucian, Zeus, in proposing to Hermes that it is time to return to Olympus for a spot of supper, introduces the motif of the left-over character—in *Philosophers for Sale* it is Aristippus

(12) whose evident taste for luxury makes him unsaleable. Here it is 'that effeminate perfumed fellow with the fine purple border on his tunic, who is known as the Swan, because of his music, I suppose'. Zeus proposes holding him over until next year, to be auctioned together with the common lives; thus we return to the close of *Philosophers for Sale* once again.

The dialogue is a rare example among Lucian imitations of an art-pastiche. As such it fulfils much the same almost exclusively aesthetic and humorous function as its model. The structure and manner are identical; the same motifs occur, the unsaleable sybarite, the jargon-ridden expert; there are the same attempts to vary stock roles, with Hermes changing from neutral observer to overt ironist, and the *alazōn* who undermines his own position. The main difference between Prodromos and his model is merely that one type, the philosopher, is replaced by a series of types. Yet it is hardly a real series, for the elements of burlesque are much the same in each case. The same type is repeated, with different labels. As for contemporary allusions, in the strictest sense there are none, though some general reference to Byzantine law, and perhaps to medicine, may be found. Prodromos has produced an ingenious jeu d'esprit in which the moral basis necessary for true satire is barely discernible. The fault of the piece is, perhaps, that it apes its model too closely to seem an independent work of art.

Another example of a dialogue calqued on a particular work is *Hermodotus* by Ioannes Katrarios (dates unknown).[1] It takes its form from the pseudo-Lucianic *Affairs of the Heart*. However, it differs in kind from Prodromos' work; first, because its aim is overtly rhetorical rather than satirical, although it includes a possibly didactic element: second, because its theme is not derived all from the same source but incorporates substantial borrowings from other dialogues. In *Affairs of the Heart* Lycinus and Theomnestus, while talking about love, fall to discussing the age-old topic of the superiority of hetero- or homo-sexual passion. The inevitable syncrisis is given a certain variety by turning it into an account, given by Lycinus, of a similar discussion between two friends, adjudicated by himself. Lycinus' judgment, while superficially favouring the heterosexual Charicles, praises the argument of his opponent. *Hermodotus* follows the same structure. Aristocles tells his friend Menedemus about the outstanding physical beauty of a Celt whom he has seen in the city. He recounts how he had talked of the

[1] See F. Schumacher, *De Ioanne Katrario Luciani imitatore*, Bonn 1898.

matter to the sophist Hermodotus, who had expressed surprise that he found physical beauty affecting, and had recounted two speeches on the topic, one of his own and an opposing one of a friend. Aristocles rehearses these to Menedemus, the first in praise of physical beauty, the second rejecting it. Menedemus and Aristocles then give their own judgment, which supports Hermodotus but praises his opponents speech. In both cases the *syncrisis* is the reported speech of two characters not present, and retold by a third party to a largely passive listener; in both, a double set of judgments are given at the end, designed to show off the virtues of both sides of the case. The resemblance between the two dialogues is more than structural, for arguments and phraseology have been borrowed by the Byzantine writer. But as the subject of beauty is only tangential to that of love, he has also called for material upon two other works with subjects more closely related to his own, *Essays in Portraiture* and the spurious *Charidemus*, in both of which beauty is the central theme.

For an example of a really elaborate stitching together of Lucianic material, without, however, a specific dialogue providing the groundplan, we must go to *Philopatris*, an anonymous dialogue, probably of the mid-eleventh century. Here the purpose is genuinely satirical. Triepho comes upon Critias in a state of agitation, and finally gets him to recount how he has heard seditious talk in the street and has been introduced into a circle of conspirators. He was not taken in by them, but it needed the patriotic and religious orthodoxy of Triepho to make him feel himself again. At this point Cleolaos arrives with the welcome news of the emperor's fresh military successes, thus making the prospect of revolution even less plausible. The content of the dialogue is, to say the least, obscure. Its most recent editor[1] has advanced the perfectly coherent hypothesis that it was written in the short reign of Isaac Comnenos (1057–9) and reflects the discord between that emperor and the patriarch Cerularius. A prophecy of the emperor's death in the month of August (22), and a conspiracy involving an inspector of taxes (19) can be traced in historians of the period. But though the conspirators seem to have truck with soothsayers, a charge made against Cerularius (who was suspected of neo-Platonist tendencies), and though monks may be involved in the conspiracy (21, and less certainly 26), the hypothesis is still somewhat fragile.

The evidence for systematic imitation of Lucian in the dialogue is anything but fragile. It is of two types, according to the section of the

[1] Ed. R. Anastasi, Messina 1968.

work in which it falls. Sections 1–18 consist in an elaborate introduction
in which very little is established other than that Critias has undergone
a strange and disturbing experience and that Triepho is an orthodox
Christian who will not let Critias swear by the pagan gods. If, as has
been suggested, the Christian conspirators are guilty of paganism,
there may be a more satisfactory disguised link between the two parts
of the dialogue than is superficially apparent. The conspirators would
be seen as having cast a spell on Critias, who is released from his
trance by the true religion of Triepho. The resemblance to *Nigrinus*
that some have claimed to find is an illusory one. Critias does not
deliberately delay his account to create suspense, nor is he in a
heightened condition. The author of *Philopatris* has simply taken a
standard Lucianic expository formula; in this version of it one character, catching sight of another in a state of agitation, tries to persuade
him to give an explanation. Pallor, puckered brows and anxious pacing
are the key elements of Critias' behaviour: Hermes and Athena comment upon precisely the same aspects in Zeus at the start of *Zeus Rants*.
The subsequent sections are a patchwork of further references. The
tragic exclamations, alases, woes and alacks that Critias pours out are a
less sophisticated version of Zeus' tragic parody in *Zeus Rants*. When
Triepho teases Critias for being, literally, portentous, the list of miraculous occurrences that Critias offers contains several stories recounted
in *Dialogues of the Gods*. Triepho's rejoinder—'I'm afraid that you
may have heard a magic incantation and that the wonder which has
astounded you may affect me, turning me into a pestle or a door'—
refers to the story of the sorcerer's apprentice, related as one of the
'miracles' in *The Lover of Lies* (35). Running through the dialogue
whenever the theme of amazement occurs is the image of a man being
turned to stone like Niobe—obliquely mentioned in 1, used by both
characters in 18 and by Critias at 27. These all draw on the opening
image of *Essays in Portraiture* 1, where Lycinus defines the effect upon
him of the beauty he has seen: 'Struck with amazement, I was all but
turned from man to stone, as the story has it.' So much for the theme
of amazement, which occupies 1–3. From there the author passes to
ridiculing the pagan gods (4–11), by whom Critias inadvertently
swears. Triepho disposes of them after the manner of Damis in *Zeus
Rants* 39–43, giving Zeus as buried in Crete (45), and supplying the rest
from Homer. Just like Damis, Triepho argues that the Homeric account
on which the Olympian tradition rests is an absurd and disreputable
one. Zeus could well say of him what he says of Damis:

The fellow doesn't spare any god, but just lets rip, and fastens upon each in turn, be he guilty or not. (44)

Sections 14–16 transfer the discussion to the relationship between gods and Fate, also used as a weapon by Damis, and the subject of *Zeus Catechized*. Again quotation from Homer is employed wholesale to show the inconsistency and absurdity of traditional views. (The linking passages 12–13 and 17–18 give Triepho's point of view as the convinced Christian, with suitable exposition of dogma and scriptural authority.) So that this entire long introductory section of the dialogue is based on one particular dialogue, *Zeus Rants*, interleaved with motifs and ideas borrowed from others, and made noticeably Lucianic in style by the profusion of verse quotation both open and concealed, including characteristic comic misquotation, paraphrase and pastiche.

The second half of *Philopatris* moves suddenly into a contemporary vein, rather as (we shall see) Byzantine underworld dialogues do. Triepho now changes rôle and becomes the almost passive second speaker of *The Eunuch* or *The Lover of Lies*, while Critias finally launches into a retrospective narrative, like the ironist in those dialogues. The interweaving of conscious reminiscences from Lucian gives way to a hostile account of the conspiracy, in which Critias speaks of the villains, their self-deception and gullibility toward black arts, with the same mixture of sarcasm and invective that Tychiades uses against the credulous philosophers of *The Lover of Lies*. Triepho's response borrows from the words of both Tychiades and Philocles at the end of that dialogue. For Tychiades describes himself as 'going around with a swollen stomach and needing an emetic, like men who have drunk new wine', to which Philocles replies:

I myself have enjoyed the same effect from your account, Tychiades. They say that it's not only those bitten by mad dogs who go mad and are afraid of water, but that if a man who has been bitten bites another, his bite has the same effects as the dog's, and the second man has the same fears.

Triepho, too, speaks (27) of his swollen stomach, and of having been bitten by Critias' words as though by a mad dog. In both cases the remedy is the truth—for Tychiades 'common sense in all things', for Triepho, the truth of Christianity. The news of the emperor's military success merely adds an epilogue to the political element, for the borrowings from *The Lover of Lies* have rounded off the literary structure.

Philopatris is clearly an example of far more independent imitation than the other Byzantine works we have so far looked at. There is no direct model in Lucian for what the author of the work is trying to do, and he has not quite mastered the technical problems involved. There is an uneasy imbalance between the elaborate literary reminiscence of some parts and the obscure references to immediate political reality. This imbalance is equally evident in the one genre of Lucianic work which seems to have developed in an independent Byzantine form, the underworld dialogue.[1] The earlier of the two readily available examples, *Timarion*, can be dated on internal evidence to the first half of the twelfth century. Like *Philopatris*, it falls into an exposition that is closely modelled on Lucian, and a major section that is less immediately derived from him. It is more complex still, however, for the main section itself falls into two very distinct parts. In the first, Timarion gives an account of his journey to Thessalonica for the feast of St Demetrius. This is the occasion for descriptions of hospitality received, of countryside and city, and of the festival itself. There is plenty of opportunity for elaborate formal ecphrases of the highly stylized variety that marks most medieval literature, e.g. the physical beauty of the duke (9) seen as he passes in a procession. In the second part, satire takes over from travelogue. Timarion, taken ill, feels better after a few days, only to be struck down by dysentery and liver trouble. This gives the author opportunity for a little fun at the expense of medical theorists. Then, in the night, two shadowy figures ajudge him medically dead (again a parody) and fetch him forcibly off to Hades. It is a curious underworld, quite unlike the Lucianic one insofar as social equality is not to be found at all. One wonders whether the views of some particular sect occasion the portrait of eternal social injustice in the afterlife. After journeying for a while Timarion comes upon various Byzantine personalities, not all identifiable, in whom the main vice ridiculed is gluttony (17–21). Then he sees the emperor Romanus IV Diogenes (22), which gives the excuse for a brief account of that ruler's tragic misfortunes. At last, Timarion encounters his old teacher, the famous orator Theodore of Smyrna (*flor. c.* 1100), to whom he complains that he has been unfairly ruled dead. Theodore promises to put his case before the underworld court, where the judges are Aeacus, Minos and the iconoclast emperor Theophilos. They progress on to the

[1] For a general description of these works, see H. Tozer, 'Byzantine satire', *Journal of Hellenic Studies* 2 (1881) 233–70. *Timarion* has been recently re-edited by R. Romano Naples 1974. There is also a new edition of *Mazaris*, with translation, notes, introduction and index, by *Seminar Classics* 609, State University of New York at Buffalo (*Arethusa Monograph* V), 1975.

Elysian fields, described with the inevitable ecphrasis of a *locus amoenus*,[1] where the court is to be held.

So far the author has agglomerated a number of Lucianic themes: reluctance to enter Hades, the leisurely survey of its inhabitants, the beauty of the Elysian fields, the necessity of passing through a court of judgment. He seems to have modelled himself in some parts not on underworld dialogues as such, but on similar motifs in other works. The pattern for the essential motif of the piece, the 'man who dies before his time', is given by *The Lover of Lies* 25: Cleodemus tells how he was taken sick, and on the seventh day, when the fever was at its height, a young man in a white cloak appeared to him and led him through a chasm to Hades. But when he came to the underworld court, Pluto rejected him, on the grounds that his thread was not fully spun, and he was led back to the upper world. Some of this new material is actually substituted for traditional motifs—entering Hades without using Charon or his boat, and preferring a messenger after the manner of *The Lover of Lies* instead of the usual Hermes. The extensions to the traditional court theme provide an occasion for particular ingenuity. More satire against doctors is brought in, this time as personified in the figures of Aesculapius, Hippocrates, Erasistratus and Galen, some of whom are on a panel intended to advise the judges in cases where the status of a soul as dead is called into question. The conduct of the trial is a parody of Athenian legal procedure, slightly adapted to fit (one assumes) Byzantine practice. Again much medical evidence is called, extending the parody of contemporary medical theory. Timarion's case is evidently won for him by the eloquence of Theodore, and he is conducted back to the upper world. *En route* he visits the special area assigned to philosophers, where he witnesses a dispute between Diogenes the Cynic and Johannes Italus, a leading philosopher of the late eleventh century. Farther on he briefly sees tyrants undergoing appropriate torments. Prominent among them is, again, a near contemporary, Philaretus, who usurped control over a large part of Armenia in the second half of the eleventh century. At last Timarion returns to the upper world. And the dialogue closes as he and his interlocutor Cydion prepare to go home for a siesta.

It is clear from this account that the Byzantine author has made out of the underworld visit a new type of work which, though modelled on Lucian, is considerably independent of him. The exposition is quite

[1] For a discussion of this trope see E. R. Curtius, *European literature and the Latin Middle Ages*, trans. W. R. Trask, New York 1953.

closely tied to Lucianic models. Cydion greets Timarion with the formula that opens *Lexiphanes*, and tries to persuade him to give a full account of himself with the same insistence on the claims of friendship as Menippus' unnamed companion puts forward in *Menippus* 2. Timarion finally accedes (4) in the same terms as Menippus does (3). Also like Menippus, he finds himself easily falling into the language of Euripides and Homer (though it has to be admitted that Cydion also uses Homeric phrases, without the excuse of having recently left that poet's company, while Timarion's explanation is simply that he wants his narrative to have the right tone, like Hermes' verse proclamation in *Zeus Rants*). Several motifs in the visit to Hades are also Lucianic, notably the Elysian paradise, the trial, and the vision of famous villains undergoing punishment. Into this the author has inserted, in the exchange between Diogenes and Johannes Italus, a miniature 'dialogue of the dead' in reported speech. On a more formal level, it is true that the general presentation of the work, with the superficial dialogue form disguising a direct narrative, the secondary speaker being reduced to an occasional prompt, is widely used by Lucian (e.g. *Menippus* and *The Lover of Lies*). However, in other ways the work is quite different. First, not only the opening but also the journey through Hades itself follow the leisurely pace and descriptive indulgence of the novella: if there is a parallel in Lucian it is the underworld voyage of *A True Story*, rather than those of *Menippus*, *The Downward Journey* or *Dialogues of the Dead*. Secondly, the choice of overtly contemporary material in the satirical passages is quite without parallel in Lucian. In part what has happened is that a new set of types has been substituted for the rich man, the philosopher and the other traditional citizens of Lucian's hell. Instead law and medicine are the objects of fun, as they are in Prodromos' *Sale of Lives*. In part, however, though it is difficult to be certain of quite who some of the characters are, the author has definitely selected figures from his own world. The result is a work which does not seem entirely an exercise in literary art, nor yet a vehicle for a consistent moral message. A leisurely and entertaining narrative has been expounded, with incidental satirical and moral inserts.

That this new type of underworld visit is probably not just an individual quirk of the author of *Timarion* but represents a Byzantine sub-genre is confirmed by comparison of it with *Mazaris' Stay in Hell*. This comes from another troubled period of Byzantine history, for it was composed in the latter half of the reign of Manuel II Palaeologus (1391–1425). The work follows the same conventions as *Timarion*, though the balance of the elements, and hence the literary effect, are rather different. Again, the central character, who recounts his tale in the first person throughout, is carried off by death before his time, in the course of a fever. The exposition, description of the illness and arrival in Hades are dealt with in summary fashion. The elaborate descriptions of the first part of *Timarion* disappear, the portrait of the upper world being transferred into the mouth of a character in Hades itself. This Hades is more recognizably Lucianic than Timarion's. The souls have lost their physical distinguishing marks 'being of one age and without facial features', as in *Dialogues of the Dead*. The bodies of many are 'speckled with bruises and . . . baptized by a multitude of sins', just as sins have scarred the souls of the wicked in *The Downward Journey* (28–9). In other ways, none the less, the Hell of Mazaris retains the overt mirroring of Byzantine inequality that marks *Timarion*, for the first figure met by Mazaris, one Holoboulos, rhetorician, physician and secretary to the emperor, is still an unpurged courtier of the worst type. Almost upon meeting Mazaris, he defines both himself and his world by his advice:

Go back . . . up to life, dear sir; for no-one here has any need of you, poor and obscure as you are, a disregarded fellow not even possessing the two obols for the ferry over, in accordance with the relevant ordinance in force up there.

The poor man unable to pay his fare (Micyllus in *The Downward Journey*, Menippus in *Dialogues of the Dead* 2) becomes the villain in a Hades where riches and status still apply.

The bulk of the work is now given over to an extended satirical portrait of Byzantine society in general and the court in particular. Holoboulos gives a substantial description of the embassy of Manuel II Palaeologus to the West, and analyses, in a mini-dialogue within the narrative, the corruptions of office in the imperial service. Occasional Lucianic motifs are interlarded—the assurances of Mazaris that he will treat Holoboulos' words in confidence (cf. *Menippus* 2), the impossibility of hurting a man already dead (*Dialogues of the Dead* 27), the punishment of a man by denying him the oblivion bestowed by Lethe water (*The Downward Journey* 28–9). During the conversation a certain Padiates is particularly blackly represented; suddenly he springs out in person, brandishing a club, and strikes Holoboulos down. In the resultant furore a number of dead arrive who subsequently engage Mazaris in further conversation about the upper

world. Here again the purpose is evidently the satire of particular
personalities, notably of individual foibles as opposed to general moral
lapses. Eventually Holoboulos leads Mazaris on to a *locus amoenus*
corresponding in detail to the traditional picture of Elysium: (16)
'. . . towering elms and plane trees in profusion grew there, and melo-
dious sparrows perching upon them sang very sweetly and with great
variety.' There is, however, little respite in the satire, for the imperial
choir-master Lampedarius is at hand, and in enquiring about his sons,
delivers a further attack on the greed, sexual indulgence and hypocrisy
of the contemporary world, and specifically of monks. Of the elder
son, for example, he says:

He had his hair cropped and dressed himself in a Jewish turban and cloak.
The cloak covered up all the childishness, ignorance, fatuity and idleness,
even the conceit and all the rest of the intemperance and wantonness in
which he had indulged since childhood. He became one of the long-tunic
brigade, and lives in the monastery of Christ the Benefactor, displaying his
false piety while all the time he is a slave to lust.

Eventually tiring of this barrage, Mazaris expresses the desire to get
away. After a speech that expressly explains how the envy and rivalry
of the lower world is an eternal punishment for the same elements in
all men's lives above, Holoboulos indicates a potential route out, and
the narrative ends abruptly. In a pendant to it, a dream sequence and
three letters, the satire is continued, concentrating on the Despotate of
Morea and the shortcomings of its society.

We have now come a long way from the form of the underworld
dialogue as Lucian exploits it. The personal satire is conducted in a
tone of almost unrelieved invective, although the broader targets—
the incompetence of medicine, the corruption of the law—are treated
more ironically. In its frequent use of quotation from a wide range of
authors, notably Homer and the tragedians, but including Lucian
himself, and in its fondness for puns for their own sake, *Mazaris*
retains a certain reminiscence of Lucianic style. But as with *Philopatris*
and *Timarion*, the imitation is piecemeal. Since, far more than with the
other works, the form is merely an excuse for the content, the effect is
to make the imbalance of literary and historical elements seem excep-
tionally violent. Nothing could be less like the conscious art of the
Lucianic models on which the Byzantine genre is based.

The imitation of Lucian in Byzantium does not seem to have been
limited in type or period, with the proviso that there are no extant

examples datable to before the ninth century. The way in which writers like Prodromos and Katrarios approach the text of Lucian is unparalleled in later literature in the sense that they alone create deliberate pastiches. The explanation for this is partly linguistic. The archaizing fashion of learned literature encouraged close imitation, in which the borrowing of themes becomes inseparable from the borrowing of phrases. The satirical works, however, are written in a slightly more relaxed form of language, though still archaic enough to satisfy the taste of the educated upper-class circles in which they circulated. Here, there is more evidence of creative imitation, the construction of a genre after a Lucianic model, but designed to deal with the *mores* of the contemporary world. There is still substantial pastiching—*Philopatris* and even *Timarion* were able to circulate as genuine works of Lucian, the former unjustifiably being the cause of much of his later unpopularity with the Roman Catholic church. None the less, there is also evidence, as there is in so little 'official' Byzantine literature, of an attempt to create a genuine literary outlet for qualities such as humour, irony, even invective. For this much Lucian is to be thanked.

2. ITALY

From Byzantium, Lucian's works passed first to Italy. The process of transmission was probably coming into effect in the last decades of the fourteenth century, for the first Latin translations seem to date from the opening years of the fifteenth, as do the first scattered references to Lucian in surviving correspondence.[1] Greek scholars had begun to visit Italy, and brought with them the taste for an author firmly established in the Byzantine curriculum. Italian scholars travelling in Greece carried home manuscripts for themselves, or their patrons. What is known of Greek mss. held by Italian scholars and nobles at this period suggests that, as early as the 1420s, texts of the complete works were in Italian hands, plus a proliferation of mss. containing selections or individual works. A large number of Latin translations were to follow, some of them anonymous, some by respectable scholars such as Guarino da Verona (1374–1460) and Poggio Bracciolini

---

[1] For further details see the introduction to my edition of Erasmus' translations from Lucian in *Opera Omnia Desiderii Erasmi Roterodami* I. i, Amsterdam 1969, 363–4. The theory of a 'canon' of versions as set out there is inaccurate in detail but certain works definitely did have greater currency than others.

(1380–1459). The range of works—some thirty odd—that attracted
the attentions of translators was significantly smaller than the range of
texts available in the original; there is a marked preference for the
plainly rhetorical pieces, on the one hand, *The Fly, In Praise of my
Country, Slander* (the latter in no less than four different versions),
and for certain moralistic pieces on the other, *Charon, The Downward
Journey,* and *On Sacrifices* all appearing in more than one version. It is
true that, as early as the second half of the fifteenth century, a large
selection of works was done into Italian, probably by Nicolò da
Lonigo, and was eventually to find its way into print as the standard
vernacular version of the following century (running to four editions:
1523, 1525, 1529, 1536). But here, too, the emphasis of the selection seems to be upon works that could be said to fall into the
same two classes. The sense of concentrating on a narrow range of
Lucianic works is made stronger if one looks at the Latin translations
which actually appeared in print. Again, there is an emphasis on moral
works, *Charon, The Downward Journey* and various *Dialogues of the
Dead* recurring frequently, with *Slander* also popular. On the other
hand, enjoyment of the lighter side is shown by the fondness for *A True
Story* in the version by one Lilius Castellanus. It would be dangerous to
base a hypothesis on late fifteenth-century tastes in Lucian solely on the
number and range of printed versions, when there is so little evidence
about the size of editions or the width of the audience reached. But,
taking manuscript translations and printed editions together, one can
reasonably conclude that certain scholarly circles, or circles with intellectual pretensions, took a close interest in Lucian, that this interest
proliferated, and that something like a 'canon' of texts and translations
arose.

In using the terms 'rhetorical' and 'moralistic' I have already given
some indication of the criteria on which this process of selection was
made. These criteria are clearly important, for to know them is to
have a sound indication of the reputation of Lucian, and hence of the
aspects of his work most likely to promote imitation. The best source
for material on the processes of interpretation and selection is to be
found in prefaces and letters. Not all of it is revealing. The comments
of translators on qualities such as wit, learning and 'philosophy' are
often just the stuff of all Renaissance prefaces. None the less some
points are strongly made. Rinuccio Aretino in the foreword to his
translation of *Philosophers for Sale* is quite specific when, in praising
Lucian's 'verbal elegance' and 'moral seriousness', he adds: 'What

others express seriously in their writings, Lucian puts playfully.'[1]
Guarino's dedicatory letter for *The Fly* is more specific still, commenting on the linguistic virtues of his author—so important in an age when
even the best scholars were tyros in Greek—and praising both the width
of Lucian's knowledge and the forcefulness of his attacks on vice. In
other words, the *general* determining factors are already those which
will attract supporters to Lucian for the next three or four centuries:
one set of virtues appertaining to language and style, another deriving
from the moral qualities of his thought and the gain to that morality
of being couched in a witty or biting fashion. If we look at the *particular* reason why a translator has selected this or that dialogue, the
emphasis on moral relevance appears even stronger. Johannes Aurispa
chooses *Toxaris* as offering a number of useful examples on the important social and ethical issue of friendship. Guarino sends a copy of
Slander to a friend who has suffered the same fate as Apelles. Rinuccio
sees *Dialogues of the Dead* 20 as paralleling his own thoughts on death
and the absurdities of funeral ritual. The 'canon' of works selected for
translation grew up because the topics of certain works fitted the ethical
preoccupations of contemporary humanists, or seemed to reflect the
social conditions of the time.

If, in all these points, fifteenth-century criteria merely prefigure the
stock attitudes of later ages, in one respect they differ substantially.
Little reference is made to the implications for Christianity of the
attitudes toward philosophy and religion which might be detected in
many Lucianic works. It is true that few overtly anti-religious pieces
seem to have attracted translators; *On Sacrifices* and *Zeus Catechized*
get into Latin, *Zeus Rants* and *The Parliament of the Gods* are included
in the vernacular collection. None of these seems to have been read
in other than a purely historical way, as a comic discrediting of pagan
beliefs. The same kind of historical reading was evidently also made of
the dialogues featuring philosophy. It is in any case easy to interpret
many of these as attacks on false exponents of a true art. In the case of
Philosophers for Sale, where the actual doctrines are humorously
presented, the dialogue was simply read in a contrary sense, as a serious
epitome of the view of the major sects. The immediate evidence comes
from a source interesting for other reasons too. Luca d'Antonio Ber-
nardi da San Gimignano, a teacher of grammar active in the second half

---

[1] On Rinuccio's translations see D. P. Lockwood, 'De Rinucio Aretino
Graecarum Litterarum interprete', *Harvard Studies in Classical Philology* 24 (1913)
52–109, particularly 94–102.

of the century, particularly in Florence, used dramatic representations of *Philosophers for Sale* as a teaching aid.[1] For these he wrote a verse prologue which indicates the value of the work about to be seen. The audience are advised that Lucian offers them a review of ancient philosophers, from whom they may choose their own mentors (with the exception of Epicurus, who is specifically discommended as an atheist). Since Luca numbered among his pupils such a figure as Marsilio Ficino, this is probably not an example of an obscure pedagogue getting the wrong end of the stick, but of an influential educator following a current interpretative trend. The wider lesson that this example offers is the simple but disturbing one that humanists of this period, in their effort to find moral instruction in all things classical, may have overlooked the comic element in more works than this.

Fifteenth-century Italy was, then, an age in which Lucian was seen as the expounder of ancient philosophy and the critic of a discredited religion, rather than as the frivolous denigrator of the very principle of religious and philosophical thought. He was, indeed, an author whose works could fittingly be dedicated to a pope, as Lapo da Castiglionchio dedicated his versions of *On Funerals* and *Lucian's Career* to pope Eugenius in the early 1430s. Lacking the label of anti-Christ which was to dog his career in northern Europe, he could pass as a moralist of a Senecan or Horatian variety, the purveyor of good sense in a hypocritical world. To this he had the virtue of adding a clear and amusing style. Here is the essence of Lucian as the Renaissance Italians read him. It is these aspects which they sought to imitate.

The most obvious examples of successful imitation are two works which had the curious fate of passing as translations from Lucian in certain early printed editions. The first is a dialogue by Maffeo Vegio (1407–1458) entitled *De felicitate et miseria,* but circulating as *Palinurus*: the second is *Virtus dea,* whose pedigree was even more complicatedly concealed by its being attributed to Lucian as a translation by Carlo Marsuppini. It is, in fact, one of the *Intercoenales* of Leon Battista Alberti (1404–1472).

Vegio's piece is a dialogue of the dead between Palinurus (the drowned steersman of Aeneas) and Charon. The opening passage, in which Charon commiserates with Palinurus on having lain unburied, and expresses pleasure that he is now entitled to ship him across the Styx, serves largely to place the reader in the right literary context.

[1] This information is derived from N. Caccia, *Luciano nel Quattrocento in Italia. Le rappresentazioni e le figurazioni,* Florence 1907.

Almost immediately the work moves into a didactic tone, in which the similarity of profession between the two characters is used to illustrate the theme of human dissatisfaction with one's lot. Palinurus has deplored Charon's hard life; Charon rejoins that his job is the cause of his 'vigorous and blooming old age' (the phrase is Virgilian). Palinurus accepts Charon's account of his state, but refuses to believe that he himself had no cause to lament the pitiable life he led. The consequent debate allows a further reworking of Virgilian material in description of Palinurus' case. Against this is set a substantial general moral argument about the trials of domestic life, from Charon, in which certain Lucianic themes, notably hypocrisy, are treated in a quite unLucianically abstract way. From domestic matters, the discussion passes to the alleged superiority of the lives of great men, and their hidden disadvantages. The arguments are much those of, say, *The Ship* 26–7, but again the presentation is largely general:

One must consider the hidden places of the mind, one must carefully examine the recesses of inward thought; if you could see them as you do the brow, what a host of ills, what an array of terror and trepidation you would find there. What anguish, care and suspicion, what ulcers, wounds, slaughter, ambushes, swords, would be revealed, what endless varieties of weapons! all preventing their sleep from being peaceful, their meals quiet, their wealth sweet, their power enjoyable, or their pleasures and amusements happy.

It is a style quite unalleviated by the wealth of anecdote and concrete reference which is characteristic of Lucian. The dialogue continues in the same vein, on the themes of war and tyranny, but now examples are offered drawn from Olympian mythology. The later part of the piece, in fact, though as didactic as the central section, is considerably more lively. Vegio takes greater care to maintain the literary fiction of the underworld setting, as when Palinurus asks Charon to row more slowly so that they will not arrive before his account of the drawbacks of power is finished. Similarly, the 'message' is now couched in allegorical terms, with the punishments of Hades and the rewards of Elysium standing as symbols for Christian doctrines. Although the overall effect is certainly not Lucianic in modern terms, the conjunction of themes that are the same as the Cynic doctrines featured in many of Lucian's works with the conventions of the *Dialogues of the Dead,* and with a certain amount of reference to classical myth, offers some points of comparison. It is Lucian moralized, and deprived of much of his specifically literary quality.

Alberti's piece, *Virtus dea,* is much shorter, and cast as a dialogue of the gods between Mercury and the goddess Virtue. None the less, its function seems similar in kind to the Vegio dialogue, even if it is greatly superior in literary terms. Virtue has sent a note to Mercury asking for a meeting. She complains about the treatment she has received at the hands of Fortune. But Mercury warns her that Jupiter and the other gods are unlikely to pay any attention to complaints against Fortune, who is the most powerful deity on Olympus. The dialogue is substantially Lucianic in several major features. The idea of one god complaining of his lot to another is found in *Dialogues of the Gods,* e.g. no. 4, where Hermes protests to his mother Maia. The all-powerful status given to Fortune accords with the portrait of Fate in *Zeus Catechized* and *Zeus Rants.* On a technical level, the opening pattern, with one character coming upon another, occurs in several Lucian dialogues (though not *Dialogues of the Gods*). And the devoting of a large part of the piece to an anecdote is particularly common in the short dialogues, e.g. *Dialogues of the Gods* 16, 21, 24; here, Virtue describes how she and her followers, intellectuals and artists, were insulted and attacked in the Elysian fields by Fortune and her cronies, princes and politicos. Where Alberti's dialogue differs from our view of what is Lucianic, but comes close to Vegio's, is in the overt moral message. Virtue's anecdote is designed to show the relative status of force and intellect in human society, and the lack of respect shown to virtue. The rather gloomy message is summed up in the goddess's last speech, after Mercury has advised her that her best hope is to lie low:

I must lurk in the shadows for ever. Naked and despised, I am cast out.

Maffeo Vegio is one of a number of significant writers of the time, including Pontano and Boiardo, whose work shows spasmodic Lucianic influence. But Alberti is the Lucianist of the age, par excellence. It is to his literary pieces, incidental to his reputation as an architect but important as examples of his range of interests, that one should turn for an aperçu of Lucianic influence on fifteenth-century creative writing. There are three main works of Alberti involved, the *Intercoenales, Musca* and *Momus. Virtus dea* is, as I have said, one of the *Intercoenales.* This is a collection of dialogues interspersed with short fables and narrative pieces, ranging over a multitude of disparate topics, and arranged in eleven books, each with a prefatory piece. The duel function of entertainment and instruction that Alberti proposes in the prefatory letter to bk. 1 accords precisely with the effect attributed to Lucian by his Italian translators. Dedicating his work to a Florentine doctor friend, Alberti makes a comparison between physical and mental healing. The function of his own work, he says, is to relieve disorders of the spirit through laughter. Readers are to find both matter pertinent to their problems and release through mental relaxation.

Lucianic influence on the *Intercoenales* extends over the whole range of potential aspects, in type of satire, in theme, and in form. Alberti uses both fantasy situations and real ones. In realistic dialogues he frequently works through a Lycinus figure, e.g. Libripeta, who mocks the pretensions of his fellow men. In the fantasies, he has examples of gods commenting upon human activity (e.g. *Patientia*) and of gods communicating directly with men (e.g. *Oraculum*). He is particularly fond of introducing personified abstractions, as in *Virtus dea*, a practice which Lucian confines to dialogues featuring both gods and men; in Alberti's pantheon, such goddesses, Virtus, Patientia, Necessitas, Fortuna, are also incorporated into exclusively celestial situations, thus substantially reducing the burlesque element. The main division of his dialogues is, then, into the same two types as Lucian's, but with significant modification of effect in one important area. Thematically, a broad parallel of similar type can be drawn. There is an obvious similarity between the Cynic ethical generalities which Lucian has absorbed into many of his texts, and Alberti's views on such topics as hypocrisy, the trials of power and the vanity of wealth. More significant, perhaps, are parallels of thematic detail. The absurdity of human religious ritual, derided by Lucian in *On Sacrifices*, and, under the aspect of prayer, in *Icaromenippus*, receives a similar mocking treatment in Alberti's *Religio*, with prayer picked as the central example. The vain and absurd arguments of philosophers ridiculed passim in Lucian, are amply demonstrated in *Servus*, where the philosopher's proof that a slave's condition is superior to his master's also partakes of the rhetorical perversity of *The Parasite*.

These general resemblances carry more conviction when seen in the context of the parallels of detail. The common store of motifs offers fruitful evidence of influence. At the broadest level, this consists in the use of categories such as the dialogue of the dead (*Defunctus, Cynicus*), the dream (*Somnium*), and the fantastic voyage (*Somnium*). *Cynicus* is an interesting example of the blending of the borrowed and the original. The situation offered is one that Lucian himself does not exploit. Mercury brings before Phoebus the souls of those shortly to be returned to life in the upper world, in order that he may decide what form they should be transmuted into. Phoebus requires a critical account of their past lives, which is supplied by Cynicus. This intervention of one soul to judge his fellows is a direct borrowing from the role of Cyniscus in *The Downward Journey*. The dead are then presented in groups, by profession: priests, magistrates, philosophers, writers, orators and merchants. In Lucian's *Dialogues of the Dead* such groups are usually represented by individual examples of a type. Alberti none the less presents the types in much the same terms as they are generally pictured in his model. Priests are hypocritical and licentious, like Alexander of Abonuteichus; philosophers are arrogant quibblers and pretentious speculators; writers are liars—he is evidently thinking of historians, after the fashion of *How to Write History*, when he writes:

> They have made up stories about invincible rulers, councils of war, the scaling of mountains and the crossing of seas, and races finally conquered in battle, in cases where there wasn't an enemy to be seen.

Orators are, of course, word-choppers and slanderers (as is recommended in *A Professor of Public Speaking*). And merchants are used to introduce the idea of godless profiteers, the trader who, threatened with danger at sea (or among thieves) makes lavish promises to the gods, but reneges when he reaches safety, as in *Zeus Rants* 15. Thus specific borrowings have in part been reworked, to give them a more general application, and to illustrate a variant on the standard *Dialogues of the Dead* situation, giving rise to a substantially independent work. Motif borrowing also goes on in a much narrower form, with devices such as pictorial allegory. In *Picturae*, which contains the description of paintings on the walls of a room, as in the central section of Lucian's *The Hall*, the paintings are given a specific moral value by the choice of allegorical subjects, after the manner of the supposed Apelles painting in *Slander*. Another minor motif-borrowing of this kind is the self-revealing letter from Asotus to his courtesan in *Vaticinium*, though it lacks the element of preposterous self-deception which makes the letter of Hetoemocles in *The Banquet* so funny. A third motif leads us closer to the category of technique borrowings; a number of people in succession seek the company of a particular character, who rejects them. In *Timon*, the flatterers receive physical violence; in *Oraculum* Apollo deals with his clients verbally, as does the astrologer in *Vaticinium*. The function of motif-borrowing, whether at the level of the very notion of a dialogue of the dead, or in terms of details such as letters and pictures, is probably the purely literary one of allowing Alberti to get as much colour and variety into the text as possible without detracting from the force of its content. If such motifs had worked in the context of similar themes and types of satire in Lucian, why should they not be equally effective when transplanted into the *Intercoenales?*

The last category of influence is one of dialogue technique. On the whole, the celestial dialogues begin, as do the *Dialogues of the Gods*, without scene-setting, but Alberti knows how to use two of Lucian's favourite opening gambits in those situations where, as in all Lucian's realistic dialogues, the form is one of retrospective reportage. In *Servus* the unnamed second speaker comes upon Parmeno laughing to himself, just as Pamphilus comes upon Lycinus in *The Eunuch*. In *Defunctus*, Polytropus overhears Neophron talking and intervenes, just as Menippus is overheard at the opening of *Icaromenippus*. Alberti's borrowings in this field extend to less obvious devices too. Parmeno, in *Servus*, excuses himself initially from telling the whole story, just as the doctor declines in *The Banquet*. Some devices affect the whole narrative manner, rather than one simple segment of it. Parmeno is made to reveal his own character faults in *Servus*, transferring a pamphlet technique (*A Professor of Public Speaking*, but cf. *Philosophers for Sale* 10) to a dialogue situation. Again, the borrowings are part of Alberti's attempt to ensure a proper level of entertainment, the one half of his avowed purpose in writing the works at all.

This brief aperçu of types of influence should be sufficient to indicate the range and depth of Alberti's debt to his model, but it gives no insight into the effect within the context of the individual dialogue. Not all the works offer direct borrowings of the kind observed in *Cynicus;* nor do they all have a satirical manner compounded from Lucianic elements, as does *Servus*. The conversations of abstract deities, e.g. *Patientia*, are only derivable from *Dialogues of the Gods* if we take *Virtus dea* as the middle term. Since the latter represented something indistinguishable by the common reader from the genuine article, then the dialogues resembling it must belong to the same type of imitation. What all the works, fantastic or realistic, do have in common is a plain moral point, reinforced by the allegorical use of the gods in some cases, plainly expressed by a human speaker in others. If there is a central anecdote, as in *Virtus dea*, the moral point will derive from it. If the dialogue reviews a series of characters or situations, the moral point will be extracted from each. It would hardly be fair to speak, as I did in the case of Vegio, of Lucian moralized. Alberti is so much more skilful at associating the meaning of his dialogues with the trappings of their literary expression. But the general picture of the *Intercoenales* does accord with a Lucian interpreted as a didactic writer, whose entertainment was a tool of his moral teaching.

Musca (c. 1443) offers a slightly different approach to Lucianic material on Alberti's part. The prefatory epistle to Cristoforo Landino relates a doubtless apocryphal anecdote in which Alberti describes how, while he was sick of a fever, he received a letter from Guarino, together with the latter's translation of Lucian's *Musca*. He was immediately inspired to compose an answering piece, and the good humour that the exercise aroused in him cured him of his indisposition. True or not, the anecdote shows Alberti as acknowledging a conscious desire to match a particular Lucianic work, whereas the *Intercoenales* are modelled on the Lucianic manner in general. What is more, he takes as his base a purely rhetorical exercise, rather than the more obviously 'moral' works which would seem appropriate to his wider interests. Lastly, he places the emphasis of his piece (and of Lucian's) on the comic element.

The result is not quite what these indicators might suggest. It is extremely interesting, because it shows, perhaps even more clearly than the *Intercoenales* do, where Alberti saw Lucian's virtues as lying. The Lucianic piece is merely an ingenious description of the physical qualities and life style of the fly, in which an essentially trivial subject is raised in status by as many comparisons made to its advantage as the rhetorician can manage. Image, anecdote, philosophical reference and human parallels (the use of 'fly' as nickname) are all called in to give variation; and the piece closes on a proverb with a humorous twist, to underline the speaker's awareness of the frivolity of his task:

> Although I still have much to say, I will stop talking now, lest I should seem, as the proverb has it, to be making an elephant out of a fly.

Alberti completely changes the reader's relationship to his material by giving an exordium that comes to a climax on a moral point. In itself, it is an entirely Lucianic one: the pointlessness of the human obsession with matters beyond the grasp of man's intellect. Just as Menippus in *Icaromenippus* is bewildered by the various claims of the philosophers to understand the scientific complexion of the universe, so Alberti offers us a philosopher who scorns man's incessant talk of 'the circling of the heavens and the movements of the stars and the rest of that sort of thing, which nature herself scarce understands'. The discourse on the fly then becomes, by inversion, the natural opposite—a sure source of instruction from a domestic object entirely within man's observation. The point is accordingly made explicit that, however trivial the creature, man can learn the art of right living from it. And only on *that* note does Alberti pass at last to the rhetorical display proper.

The listing of the qualities of the fly naturally contains much Lucianic material and employs the same devices to amplify the fly's status. Numerous comparisons with other creatures, notably bees, are made, the references to bravery and interest in food are repeated, the musicality of its buzz is mentioned. Image, syncrisis, classical exemplum are again all brought in to advance its status. But there is a much clearer thematic arrangement of the fly's qualities, and this arrangement, whose basic division is between enhancing praise and refuting potential blame, is designed to point the moral comparison. Taking up the last sentence of the exordium, Alberti uses the habits of flies to criticize man in his public conduct (e.g. war) and in his private values. The criticism is not merely implicit:

Would that men themselves might lead lives as gentle, placid and equitable as those of flies! For then more men would not have died at the hands of their fellows than through any other sort of calamity. Trasimene and Cannae would not have been drenched in human gore; rivers would not have been stopped up with bodies, nor so many have lain submerged by fire and the sword and the sad embers of the dead, as the poet has it; nor would Caesar have boasted that he brought more than 400,000 men to their deaths.

The effect is curious. The fly takes on the rôle of the sensible man-in-the-street, a Micyllus figure. The praise itself is not entirely mock-encomium, since the object of the praise, the fly, is neither praised nor blamed. There is a separate target altogether: human imperfection. The tone accordingly sometimes switches, as in the passage quoted above, from the bantering of rhetorical display to a sharpness closer to the direct attack of the Lucianic pamphlets. Almost the only touch of self-conscious humour comes at the end, as Alberti expresses the desire to avoid an epilogue, on the grounds that the subject is not appropriate to extended treatment, a device directly in the manner of Lucian's comically applied proverb. The comedy is otherwise confined to the inherent humour of the contrast between the insignificance of the apparent subject and the dignified treatment to which it is subjected. To write this piece at all, Alberti seems to say, is of itself a criticism of rhetorical triviality. Yet, paradoxically, the piece is an occasion for more serious moralizing than is found in many an overtly serious work.

The resultant work is thus quite independent of its model in effect, although using so many of its elements. It is, at the same time, congruent with the 'morality' of Lucian's work taken as a whole (if one tries to read into Lucian a consequential ethical position). The fly takes on the value of an ingénu society whose values provide a critical yardstick against which to measure man. In that sense, it is a Lucianic work in fifteenth-century Italian terms, although it would not have seemed so in Lucian's day, nor does it so to us.

The most extended and complex of Alberti's works to be influenced by Lucian is *Momus*, an Olympian burlesque in four books.[1] Three different strains of influence co-exist. These can best be understood against a brief outline of the 'plot'. Bk. 1 describes how Momus earns the thorough dislike of the other gods for his wilful (though largely justified) criticism, how he is expelled from heaven, and proceeds to cause havoc on earth. In bk. 2 he is reinstated by Jupiter, and gradually wins a commanding position in that prince's favour. In bk. 3 Jupiter, at Momus' instigation, considers how to recreate creation, and decides to pay special attention to the advice of the philosophers. However, in the course of an elaborate celestial power-struggle, Momus is disgraced, and condemned to be fixed in the sea, rather like Prometheus on his rock. In bk. 4, the most disjointed of the books, the gods, on a visit to earth, suffer a number of uncomfortable adventures, while Charon also visits earth, accompanied by the soul of the dead philosopher Gelastus (= ridiculous). At the close of his adventures, Jupiter finally comes to appreciate the correct conduct of a prince as (to our surprise) Momus had previously set it out in a document unheeded by his master.

Into this episodic structure are inserted certain incidents and anecdotes borrowed directly from Lucian. For example: in the first book, in illustrating Momus' arrogance, Alberti uses the story of a contest between three gods, judged by Momus, which Lucian recounts in *Hermotimus* 20. In bk. 2, votive prayer, an invention of Momus', turns out to be greatly importunate to the gods, for men make many frivolous or downright impious demands that have to be physically blown back from heaven, just as they are in *Icaromenippus* 25. In bk. 3 Jupiter, trying to get an opinion on the philosopher Democritus,

---

[1] I have been helped in my analysis by the edition of G. Martini, *Momus, o del Principe*, Bologna 1942.

consults Apollo, who gives him two absurd and mutually contradictory oracles, just as in *Zeus Rants* 31 Apollo delivers an absurd oracle which is ridiculed by Momus. In addition to this type of specific borrowing (there are many more examples), there is an even greater number of motifs broadly modelled on Lucianic ones. The characters themselves are the most obvious point of contact: on the one hand, the quarrelsome and self-interested gods and their inconsistent leader, on the other the equally turbulent philosophers with their obsession with metaphysics and their lack of moral sense. Episodes are introduced modelled on several aspects of *Zeus Rants* in particular. Momus in bk. 1 plays the rôles of the ironic sceptical philosopher and of the poet who spreads disreputable tales about the gods, eventually causing a decline in the all-important attentions paid to them by man. In bk. 3 Jupiter, in disguise, goes down to earth, only to hear his own existence doubted. Alberti transfers and re-orders elements of these themes, taking events reported by a third party in Lucian and making them part of the action in his own text, using an event to reveal a quite different aspect of character or morality from his model. Some of the borrowings are purely ornamental: the convention of the gods' assembly is used, a mock decree is issued. *Zeus Rants* is not the only piece plundered in this way. In bk. 2 Momus delivers an encomium of vagabonds conceived along the same lines as the praise of sponging in *The Parasite*. In bk. 4 the motif of Charon's arrival on earth is obviously taken from *Charon*, but it is used partly to introduce what are in fact a series of little dialogues of the dead, notably one between Gelastus and Charon on why the philosopher has not been admitted to Hades (a question of money; cf. *Dialogues of the Dead* 2) and another between the tyrant Megalophos and his critic Peniplusius.

All this overtly Lucianic material is then worked into a structure whose meaning, as the prologue makes clear, can only be derived *per ironiam*. The prologue prepares us for that blending of moral instruction and entertainment which is characteristic of both the *Intercoenales* and *Musca*. But it also tells us that the work is a political allegory, in which the conduct of an earthly prince, both as it typically is in Alberti's day and as he would like it to be, is reflected in the figure of the supreme prince, Jupiter, and in his relations with both ordinary mortals and the celestial aristocracy. This is the third and most substantial level of Lucianism. The political ideas themselves are, of course, Alberti's (or at least are unlikely to have been derived from Lucian, unless we suppose him to have read *Zeus Rants* and other

Olympian pieces as themselves allegories along these lines). On the other hand, the underlying morality, with its emphasis on the dangers of the accomplished hypocrite (Momus in bk. 2), the limits of human knowledge (passim), and the fragile position of ordinary man, accord with the general precepts of Lucian's moral world as the fifteenth century seems to have defined it. The narrative form of *Momus* is Alberti's too, though much of it is built up from dialogues bound into a pseudo-narrative. But the requirement to read the burlesque otherwise than at face value must derive from an attempt to see a moral dimension in Lucian's fantasy works as a whole, and from an appreciation of the inversion of values practised in pieces like *The Parasite* and *A Professor of Public Speaking*. I have called the work a political allegory. That is a loose application of the term allegory. Alberti has learnt from Lucian the art of using one world to comment upon another, without the rather simple one-for-one equivalence of values that *allegory* suggests. True, the prologue speaks of the ancients as using the gods as symbols for forces at work in the mind. But the equivalence that Alberti goes on to propose in *Momus* is one in which the characters and actions of the gods are the mirror of the character and actions of the men who surround and influence a prince. In other words, the reader himself is now the ingénu, taken into the absurd world of Alberti's fiction, but encouraged to see in it the realities of his own world ironically concealed under a set of literary types. This is a peculiarly modern attitude to Lucian in its awareness of literary subtleties, yet, paradoxically, it is firmly rooted in the moralistic interpretation which is characteristic of the fifteenth-century approach.

The reception of Lucian in Italy, and his influence on early humanist writing was evidently very different from his career in Byzantium. When not closely pastiching him, the Byzantines took the empty shell of forms and motifs, and filled it with highly specific satire of public figures, events and institutions of the day. The Italians thought they saw, instead, an ethical system of general validity, compatible with Christian beliefs. It was as the perfect example of how to blend humour and instruction that he was imitated. But, as the development of Alberti's works from the *Intercoenales* to *Momus* shows, it was possible to derive a very sophisticated form of didacticism from such imitation, once the complexity of Lucian's literary forms was realized. *Virtus dea* and *De felicitate et miseria* are only Lucianic in historical terms. *Momus* is, arguably at least, quite close to the literary spirit of its model, if farther from it in form. When the humanists of the

Northern Renaissance took over the study of Lucian from their Italian forerunners, it was already a quite complex tradition they were inheriting.

3. NORTHERN EUROPE

By the turn of the fifteenth century, the impetus in the teaching and translation of Greek, Lucian included, was rapidly passing to a new generation of humanist scholars, north of the Alps. Although the presses of Venice, notably the Aldine, continued to produce scholarly editions of Lucian, they were no longer the work of Italian scholars. Similarly, the *editio princeps* of the complete Greek text (Lucian was only the sixteenth Greek author to be printed *in toto*), although it came from the Florentine press of Laurentius de Alopa in 1496, was probably edited by Janus Lascaris, a Greek soon to be taken into the service of France (1503), destined to be the organizer of the royal library at Fontainebleau, and friend and correspondent of Budé and Erasmus. Before 1500, the number of northern scholars who paid any attention to Lucian could be counted on the fingers of one hand: apart from an early German translation from Poggio's version of *The Ass*, Rudolph Agricola had translated *The Cock* (1484) and *Slander* into Latin and Johannes Reuchlin *Dialogues of the Dead* 25 (1495) into German, both the latter works popular with the Italians. With the collection of translations by Erasmus and Thomas More, appearing first in 1506 and in an expanded form in 1512, this situation was entirely changed. By the second decade of the sixteenth century the presses of Paris, Louvain and Basel, the scholars of Germany, France and the Low Countries had firmly taken over from the litterateurs of Florence and Rome. Lucian was printed as far away as Cracow and London. With that special arrogance which northern humanists seem to have reserved for their Italian forerunners, it was held that no previous work on Lucian had really been done. As Petrus Mosellanus put it:

. . . a few others have tried their hand, but as they were not working in the same century, they did not achieve the same success.[1]

Not all the work done on Lucian in the early years of the new century was quite as 'modern' as scholars of the period may have thought it. As late as 1521 Josse Bade in Paris published a translation and learned commentary, by one Johannes Brucherius, of *Dialogues of the Dead*

---

[1] *Luciani . . . dialogi duo Charon et Tyrannus,* Hagenau 1518 aiii.

and *On Funerals*,[1] in which the works are interpreted in an elaborate allegorical sense, accommodating them to traditional Catholic doctrine. Even so respectable a figure as Philip Melanchthon was not above the same approach. In an address given in Tubingen in 1517 'On the liberal arts', he quotes in full a translation of *Dialogues of the Gods* 23 (Venus and Cupid), introducing it as an allegory on the virtues of literature and study. This way of reading Lucian is, in fact, only an extension of the fifteenth-century vision of him as primarily a moralist, a vision which still permeates all the prefaces and notes to Lucian by humanists working in the first two decades of the sixteenth century. Petrus Mosellanus explains the principle very clearly in the dedicatory epistle to his translation of *The Downward Journey*:

> The plain truth, presented directly, is as unpalatable to the human mind as a pill without its sugar coating is to the human stomach. It is a waste of time to try to present moral instruction in a direct form, as it will be so unpalatable that none of it will take effect. You must put it into pretty language, attractive and amusing, just as Christ found it advisable to express his new philosophy through parable and allegory.

Standards of scholarship may have been higher north of the Alps, but the view of Lucian had changed very little.

It is difficult to establish precisely how the shift from this picture of Lucian as a second Cato to one of him as a mocking sceptic took place. In one significant respect the humanists themselves were responsible. For two or three decades all the major work done on Lucian was in the hands of friends and correspondents of Erasmus, most of them inclined to religious reform with or without a capital *r*. They promoted Lucian's suitability as a school text, they pointed out the general moral instruction to be derived from his works. At the same time, however, the implicit application by More and Erasmus of certain texts to controversies involving the traditional academic and theological hierarchies put an emphasis on to Lucian's powers of negative criticism. Ottomar Luscinius used the preface of a 1517 selection of dialogues to contrast the ignorance, folly and feeble humour of contemporary scholastics with the worthy, indeed Christian, laughter aroused by Lucian. Haio Hermann, obliged to leave Louvain after a difference of opinion with the theological faculty at the university, attacked it in revenge in the preface to his edition of three Lucian dialogues (*c.* 1520) as the champion of barbarism, systematically destroying and corrupting what

[1] *Ioannis Brucherii . . . in Luciani Scaphidium et eiusdem de Luctu libellum.*

vestiges of learning the Goths had left. This type of individual polemic associated with Lucian might not of itself have had much effect. More serious was the very public use, by Wilibald Pirckheimer, of three Lucian translations, *The Dead Come to Life, A Professor of Public Speaking* and *The Runaways,* as weapons in the Reuchlin controversy.

Johannes Reuchlin was a Hebrew scholar whose *De rudimentis Hebraeicis* (1506) provided Christian scholars with an adequate grounding in Jewish scholarship which would facilitate the proper study of the Old Testament. When, in 1509, a renegade Jew by the name of Pfefferkorn obtained authorization from the Holy Roman Emperor to confiscate and destroy all Hebrew books in the empire, Reuchlin was prominent in the defence of the important texts, particularly the *Talmud* and *Caballa.* In the course of the consequent imbroglio he, inevitably, fell foul of a reactionary group, in this case the Dominicans of Cologne and the inquisitor Jakob Hoogstraten, who brought charges of heresy against him. The humanists hardly entered this affair until it was referred to Rome by the appeal of Hoogstraten in 1514, but it became clear that it entailed a threat to their own liberties of study if the theologians and conservatives gained the upper hand. Between 1514 and 1516 a number of leading figures such as Eoban Hesse and Ulrich von Hutten joined the attack. Then in 1517 Pirckheimer committed himself by publishing *The Dead Come to Life* with an *epistola apologetica,* both reissued the following year with a dialogue discussing the suppression of the *Talmud.* In 1520, when the case had been allowed to come to a rather indefinite conclusion (the pope made a settlement in favour of the Dominicans but made no attempt to enforce it), he published the two further dialogues, with equally polemical prefaces. In each case the equation between Lucian's *alazones* in the various dialogues and the opposition in the case was firmly established. Pirckheimer could hardly have attacked his opponents in more offensive terms if he had tried.

This kind of application of the Lucian texts, together with the immensely popular works on a Lucianic model issued by Erasmus (see below, pp. 168–91) were in part responsible for the hardening of conservative opinion against the Greek. The acceptance of *Philopatris* as both by Lucian and anti-Christian was another black mark, as were the somewhat casual references to Christians in *Peregrinus.* As the century progressed and the question of religious allegiances became politically as well as theologically vital, it became common among writers of both extreme Catholic and extreme Protestant persuasion to use Lucian as a symbol of lack of respect for metaphysical values of any kind, to the point of atheism, and to detect in his work qualities inimical to any form of revealed religion.[1] Yet at the same time, the view of him as humorist and constructive satirist, very much fostered by Erasmus, persisted. It was really only in the second half of the century that the first tentative and unsuccessful attempts were made to spread the dialogues in vernacular translations, and only then did any systematic opposition to Lucian on the part of the religious authorities become manifest. As late as 1549 the Provincial Synod of Cologne included Lucian in a list of books suitable for teaching purposes, while the Roman Index did not get round to putting a blanket veto on Lucian's works until the astonishingly late date of 1590, although *Philopatris* and *Peregrinus* were condemned from the 1559 Index of Paul IV onward. It seems to have taken the overheated religious atmosphere of the mid-century to drive the extremists into a position where, taking their cue from the tactics of Pirckheimer, they would belabour each other with accusations of 'Lucianism'. The eventual solution to the problem was, as we shall see, only found in the late seventeenth century (when the religious issues were in any case vastly changed): if Lucian would not do as he was, he must be turned by the translator's art into a gentleman.

Just as the initial sixteenth-century interpretation of Lucian differed little in substance from that of the Italian humanists, so his influence continued to exercise itself in much the same modes. Two of them, mock-encomium and theatre, were to prove dead ends. The theatre will bear examination separately, for Lucianic influence there was important while it lasted. The mock-encomium will stand more summary treatment. The direct imitations of Lucian mock-encomia occur in two forms, one purely humorous, the other didactic. Both are reliant on the simple technique of paradox, the praising of the manifestly unpraiseworthy. In the purely humorous class are the vast number of pieces on gout, in imitation of the (probably) pseudo-Lucianic *Tragoedopodagra*. Most of them, like Johannes Carnarius' *De podagrae laudibus oratio* (1553), are in a simple rhetorical form, but others incorporate further standard Lucianic features. Erasmus' *Podagrae et calculi ex comparatione utriusque encomium* uses formal rhetorical comparison of the type used by Lucian in *The Parasite* and *Essays in Portraiture*; Pirckheimer presents his *Apologia seu podagrae*

---

[1] Cf. my article, 'The reputation of Lucian in sixteenth-century France', *French Studies* XXIX (1975) 385–97.

laus as a courtroom scene, that favourite Lucianic setting of *The Double Indictment, The Consonants at Law* et al.; Hans Sachs turned his piece into a dialogue of the gods (1544). There are also paradoxical encomia preserving the theatrical form of the original, e.g. Jacob Ayrer *Ein Fastnachtsspiel aus dem Ritterordem des Podagrischen Fluss* (*c.* 1600). The didactic element so noticeable in the Italian encomia occurs in works taking as their basis *The Fly* or *The Parasite*. A particularly interesting one is Gaspar Heldelin's *Ciconiae encomium* (1534): interesting, that is, because he indicates his source by issuing it together with his own translation of a Lucian dialogue (*Zeus Rants*). How great the proliferation of these little scholarly jokes was can be seen from the early seventeenth-century collections of them, notably Casper Dornarius' *Amphiteatrum sapientiae socraticae joco-seriae* of 1619. The genre did not remain a purely academic one: the examples of Hans Sachs and Jacob Ayrer given above are both from German popular literature, and Rabelais' *Tiers Livre* (1546) already contains a purely comic praise of codpieces. Nor did it flourish in the sixteenth century alone. Eighteenth-century England was particularly prolific in works such as Fielding's *Essay on Nothing*. But from the outset, especially as far as the vernacular languages were concerned, its creative development was controlled not so much by the influence of Lucian, or of the other standard classical examples (Isocrates on Thersites, Synesius on baldness, Ovid's *Nux* etc.) as by the new ironical form given to it by Erasmus in his *Praise of Folly* (1511). From Rabelais' praise of debt in the *Tiers Livre* onward there are very few examples (some of Fielding's journalistic pieces are exceptions) in which there is any case to suppose that the authors of genuinely ironical encomia went directly back to Lucian. Erasmus, of course, cast the exercise in a thoroughly Lucianic mould (see below, pp. 191-7), but in so doing he created a form and function for the genre which was quite different from his original, and which obviated further reference to it.

i. *Lucian and the theatre*

The reason for the end-stopped influence of Lucian on the theatre is very different from the assimilation to a new form that the mock-encomium underwent. There is some evidence that from the fifteenth century onward Lucian dialogues were sometimes performed for pedagogic reasons in schools and colleges. Indeed, one of the major editors of his work, Jakob Moltzer of Strasburg, who assembled and annotated the first bilingual Greek-Latin *Opera omnia* of Lucian, published at

Frankfurt in 1538, got his Latin nickname 'Micyllus' from playing the cobbler in *The Cock*. Scattered attempts were made to adapt Lucianic dialogues into full-scale works, or to model plays closely upon individual dialogues as in Hans Sachs's *Charon and the Departed Guests* (1518). In practice, however, the Lucianic dialogue is anti-theatrical, for reasons which also apply in part to Senecan tragedy. Both genres are armchair theatre, with techniques especially designed to give the reader the illusion of setting, costume and action. Lucian characters identify and describe one-another, evoke the physical circumstances of their meeting, give warning of the approach of other characters 'off-stage', in a fashion that is a replacement of drama, not a recipe for it. In consequence only one work seems to have 'stuck' as a source, and that, interestingly, one in which the material borrowed from Old and Middle Comedy is most blatantly undigested: *Timon*.

The first of the *Timon* imitations is very early indeed. It is the *Claudi duo* of Titus Livius de' Frulovisi, a Latin play written for performance by Venetian schoolboys *c*. 1430.[1] The interest of the work is considerable, for two reasons. First, the author has contaminated his Lucianic material with stock themes and types from Roman comedy. Secondly, he has given his Timon character, and hence the play in general, a coherence lacking in Lucian, where the elements borrowed from comedy and diatribe sit ill together. The Timon-figure, the hero Plusiplenus, is a young man, impoverished by extravagance, who has actually won the respect of upright citizens by his attempt to improve himself. He dramatically differs from his model in not being a misanthrope at all. When he rails against the gods, it is for not fulfilling the requests that he has made; he does not invoke their anger against others. When Jupiter decides, in scene 3, to send riches back to Plusiplenus, it is because he has forsworn the gods of lust and drinking. This moral element is reinforced by the subplot of scenes 1, 4, 7 and 8, in which two unreformed characters, Philaphrodita and Pornovosius (the names speak for themselves) are shown as desperate for money to indulge their lust, and consequently lacking in natural feelings towards those from whom they hope to inherit. Frulovisi takes the ideas in *Timon* 21–3 of sudden wealth going to the undeserving and its destructive effect, plus the idea in 30 that Plutus could easily give his wealth to the

[1] See W. Ludwig, 'Titus Livius de' Frulovisi, ein humanisticher Dramatiken der Renaissance', *Humanistica Lovanensia* XXII (1973) 39–76. For the text of the play, see C. W. Previté-Orton, *Opera hactenus inedita T. Livii de Frulovisiis de Ferraria*, Cambridge 1932, 33–64.

wrong person. Philaphrodita is accidentally visited by Plutus; his mother dies, and he squanders the inherited riches. Evidently the subplot provides an appropriate moral contrast with the new virtues of Plusiplenus. For the rest, the initial action is the same as *Timon*: the dialogue between Jupiter and Mercury, the fetching of Wealth, the despatch of Wealth and Mercury to earth. The final scenes of the play, however, show how far the moralizing can be taken. Frulovisi develops Lucian's idea (31–3) that Poverty comes out of Timon's house accompanied by her children the virtues, and protests at the advent of Wealth. The virtues now become speakers in the dialogue, and instead of leaving with Poverty are persuaded by Mercury to agree to cohabit with Wealth in view of Plusiplenus' changed character. The result of this manipulation of material is to reduce the complex potential of the Timon figure to a one-dimensional moral type, but at the same time to bring out various subordinate elements of Lucian's original in such a way as to strengthen the dramatic unity of the play. As an example of the humanist attempt to revive theatrical forms with a moral purpose it achieves a distinct success.

The sixteenth century was to have its own examples of neo-Latin school drama on Lucianic themes, including the Jesuit Jakob Gretsler's *Timon comoedia imitata ex dialogo Luciani qui Timon inscribitur* (1584). The first vernacular adaptation of *Timon,* in 1494 by Matteo Boiardo (from the Italian translation of Nicolò da Lonigo) is more important,[1] for it represents a hybrid intermediary in the transference from mediaeval to modern staging conventions. Boiardo makes his debt to Lucian plain enough, for he has that author speak a prologue for us in person, in which he announces the unique experience of his becoming Italian for his new audience's benefit—Boiardo's way of claiming novelty in the adaptation of a Greek rather than a Roman source. Some two-thirds of the play faithfully reproduce the main elements of the Lucian plot. Yet the most casual glance reveals that the resultant work is very much an adaptation, into which Boiardo has constantly inserted new detail. In act I, for example, the first three scenes follow Lucian quite closely, but scene iv is a soliloquy for Timon as he is about to go to rest and hoping not to dream of men, who, unlike other animals, are so ill-disposed to their own kind. The whole of the fifth act in particular is an original attempt to give the story a rounded conclusion. Timon

[1] In interpreting Boiardo's play, I have drawn upon several of the papers in *Il Boiardo e la critica contemporanea. Atti del convegno di studi su Matteo Maria Boiardo,* ed. G. Anceschi, Florence 1970.

reburies his gold in the tomb of Timocrates, only to find more gold there. The servants of Timocrates' spendthrift son, now imprisoned, arrive at the tomb on the instructions of a letter left by Timocrates on his death, and meet with Timon. The outcome of which, the epilogue tells us, will be that the son regains his inheritance and the servants share the treasure abandoned by Timon. This conclusion is not designed merely to round the play off. Like Frulovisi's, it conveys a moral, and one very different from the Cynic lesson of the original. Like Frulovisi again, Boiardo has introduced a comparison by which to measure his central figure, in the form, here, of Filocoro, the young spendthrift who, reformed, will benefit from the treasure left him by his father:

> Piu prodigo non sia, ma liberale,
> Spendendo et dispensando cum ragione.

> (Becoming generous in future rather than recklessly lavish
> Spending and distributing his money with wisdom and moderation.)

Meanwhile Timon, himself—we are told by the *argumento*—a spendthrift when young and the victim of harsh paternal judgment, turns his back upon men and retires to reintegrate himself into the world of nature. This strange ending is not so curious when one looks at the new elements inserted into the earlier stages of the text. There are three main points: the insistence on gold as a source of anxiety and corruption, the portrait of a woodland life with the possibility of idyllic escape into nature, and the insistence on moderation as a virtue. Poverty has taught Timon to live *cum ragione*, Filocoro's experiences have taught him the same. The contrast between the final actions of the two, the one turning his back on society, the other reintegrated into it, is less important that the moderation with which both approach their future. This is not to say that the effect of the work is not primarily comic; but it provides a positive morality of the type common in Italian imitations of Lucian, and which makes it very much of its time.

Theatrically Boiardo's piece had, as I have said, its importance as one of the transitional plays between the *representazioni sacre* and *commedia erudita*. The double setting of heaven and earth required by the Lucianic plot was a helpful element in the transition. *Timone* had, however, no immediate Lucianic heirs. The next vernacular play to be overtly influenced by Lucian was not to appear for another whole century. This is the anonymous English *Timon,* a university play of around 1600 (possibly later, if influences of Ben Jonson have been correctly identified in it). It is a very academic piece. The outlines of the main plot are drawn directly from Lucian, particularly the procession of flatterers and the indefinite ending. There are also smaller details—the use of the name Laches from section 58, and verbal borrowings in the speeches of Demeas the orator and Stilpo and Speusippus, two lying philosophers—which do not appear in any earlier post-Lucianic versions of the story. It has been argued that the elaborate subplot draws on other Lucian works. Certainly it uses stock Lucianic characters, e.g. the two philosophers and the lying traveller Pseudocheus, and mocks its *alazones* in comparable ways—Gelasimus the rich but dim man with social pretensions is the victim of deserved gulling. But in its dramatic technique it leans more heavily upon Plautine conventions.

Much more complex is the relationship between Lucian and Shakespeare's *Timon of Athens*.[1] Though the basis of the plot was taken from North's Plutarch, significant details in the play ultimately derive from Lucian. The spendthrift images of Act I come from remarks of Hermes in section 8; the poet of Acts I and V is created from Gnathonides, who offers a dithyrambic ode to Timon in 46; the help offered to Demeas and Philiades in 47 and 49 is the model for the gifts to Lucilius and Ventidius (Act I. i 95–152). Demeas' speeches also offer the fiction of Timon's prowess in battle (50) which may lie behind the genuine exploits referred to by Alcibiades (Act IV. iii 43–5) and which motivates the Senate's offer to Timon of a captaincy against Alcibiades. Quite how these details reached Shakespeare it is difficult to determine. As there was no English translation of *Timon* he is unlikely to have read it, unless we accept the hypothesis that he is distantly remembering Erasmus' Latin translation, which was certainly included in Tudor school curricula. Much of what is common to Lucian and Shakespeare is also in Boiardo, and like Boiardo he has cast the play in a didactic mode, with Timon illustrating the truth of Apemantus' assertion (Act IV. iii): 'The middle of humanity thou never knewest but the extremity of both ends.' Both authors also share non-Lucianic material. Some of Shakespeare's references to woodland life and human helplessness in the face of nature appear in Boiardo; so do the themes of calling on earth to pervert nature to man's destruction and of man as more

---

[1] The literature on the sources of *Timon of Athens* is prolific but rarely helpful. However, G. Bullough, *Narrative and Dramatic Sources of Shakespeare*, vol. VI London 1966, 255–345 is an indispensable aid.

beastly than the beasts. But all this is sixteenth-century commonplace. More interesting is the appearance of the idea of rehiding the treasure in both authors, and the emphasis on gold as a source of anxiety and corruption. It is, however, even more difficult to posit a way by which Shakespeare could have been acquainted with a relatively obscure Italian comedy never printed outside Italy than to suppose a form in which he could have known Lucian. In neither case would the source have provided him with the essentials of the play. *Timon of Athens* is Lucianic only in some second-hand and relatively insignificant way.

There's the rub. Among Lucian's works even *Timon* seems to have been no more than a repertoire of material, rather than an aid to the development of contemporary dramatic art. Once one looks beyond the sixteenth century, this truth becomes even more evident. The only two dramatists to show significant influence of Lucianic material were Ben Jonson and Henry Fielding. Fielding's case is complicated and will be dealt with separately (see below, pp. 201–4), but Jonson is typical of the special nature of Lucian's influence in this particular area. He had some knowledge of the original Greek, for in his library he possessed *Luciani Samosatensis dialogi octo*, one of a batch of school editions published in Paris in 1530.[1] His broader reading would almost certainly have been in translation, probably the popular Erasmus-More selection but extending to several works outside that canon. Jonson's use of Lucianic material runs the whole gamut from verbal reminiscence to full-scale imitation. There are direct references to the author, as when Crites and Amorphus discuss his truthfulness in *Cynthia's Revels* I. i:

Am. . . . It is the same wine that Demosthenes usually drunk, in the composure of all his exquisite and mellifluous orations.

Crit. That's to be argued, Amorphus, if we may credit Lucian, who in his *Encomio Demosthenis* affirms he never drunk but water in any of his compositions.

Am. Lucian is absurd, he knew nothing: I will believe mine own travels before all the Lucians of Europe. He doth feed you with fictions, figments and leasings.

Crit. Indeed, I think, next a traveller, he does pretty well.

Here Crites-Jonson is using Lucian's reputation as a creator of fictions to ironize the pretensions to truthfulness of the traveller Amorphus.

---

[1] See the edition of Jonson by C. H. Herford and P. (and E.) Simpson, vol. 1 Oxford 1925, 266. The notes to this edition record the majority of the supposed Lucianic borrowings and give references to the copious article literature on the subject.

Then, there are possible parallels between various dialogues and some of the masques: *News from the New World Discovered in the Moon* and *Icaromenippus*, *Lovers Made Men* or *The Masque of Lethe* and *Dialogues of the Dead*, *The Hue and Cry after Cupid* and *Dialogues of the Gods* 20 and 23. Similarly the opening encounter between Mercury and Cupid in *Cynthia's Revels* I. i draws on various of the *Dialogues of the Gods*, and includes a little verbal reminiscence. Compare, for example, *Dialogues of the Gods* 11. 1, Apollo to Hephaestus on Hermes:

> Ask Poseidon. He stole his trident. Or ask Ares. He secretly took his sword out of his sheath; not to mention myself, whom he disarmed of bow and arrows.

and Cupid to Mercury:

> O! 'tis your best polity to be ignorant. You did never steal Mars his sword out of his sheath, you! nor Neptune's trident! nor Apollo's bow! no, not you!

More significant is the transference of the end of *Lexiphanes* into the final scene of *The Poetaster*. The play was part of the 'war of the theatres', and should be read *à clef* with Jonson himself hiding behind the portrait of the noble and gifted Horace, while the incompetent Crispinus is Marston, and his side-kick Demetrius, Dekker. In Act V. i Horace performs the rôle of Sopolis, offering to purge Crispinus, the offending poetaster, of his absurd vocabulary. Sopolis had about him a 'medicine mixed for an enraged person so that by drinking it he might vomit (i.e. the bile causing the disorder)'. Horace says:

> Please it, great Caesar, I have pills about me,
> Mixt with the whitest kind of hellebore,
> Would give him a light vomit, that should purge
> His brain and stomach of those tumorous heats . . .

Hellebore, as for a madman, and purging by vomit—the more concrete elaboration of the image none the less betrays its source. The vomiting itself, in the Greek merely described by Sopolis, is now acted out in full, with the doctor's little pieces of advice and commentary distributed among the various characters present. Thus 'Put your fingers down your throat' become Horace's 'Force yourself a little with your finger', and '*Vilipendency* will make a great racket when it comes tumbling out on the wings of the wind' gives rise to

> Hor. Barmy, froth, puffie, inflate, turgidous and ventosity are come up.
> Tib. O terrible windy words.
> Gal. A sign of a windy brain.

Lucian's vomiting scene is followed by a grave speech of Lycinus', recommending sound study of the right models. Stick to classics like Plato and Thucydides; ignore the moderns, notably Lycophron's *Alexandra;* avoid outlandish vocabulary; conduct yourself modestly. Just so Virgil pronounces upon how Crispinus may mend himself:

> 'Tis necessary therefore he observe
> A strict and wholesome diet. Look you take
> Each morning of old Cato's principles
> A good draught next your heart; that walk upon,
> Till it be well digested . . .
> . . . Use to read
> (But not without a tutor) the best Greeks,
> As Orpheus, Musaeus, Pindarus,
> Hesiod, Callimachus and Theocrite,
> High Homer; but beware of Lycophron,
> He is too dark and dangerous a dish.
> You must not hunt for wild outlandish terms,
> To stuff out a peculiar dialect;
> But let your matter run before your words.
> . . . And henceforth learn
> To bear yourself more humbly; not to swell
> Or breathe your insolent and idle spite
> On him whose laughter can your worst affright.

Jonson, in this the third of his *comical satires*, justifies the title of 'Lucian' that Dekker gave him in *Satiromastix*, by adapting to good dramatic and satirical effect a whole episode of a Lucian dialogue. Yet one cannot in this see an important influence on the development of his dramatic writing as such.

Only in one play does Lucianic influence play a determining rôle. That is *Volpone*. The overall plot of the play, with its elaborate account of legacy hunting and the gulling of the aspiring legatees, is modelled upon *Dialogues of the Dead* 19, together with the episode of Eumolpus at Croton from Petronius' *Satiricon*. One aspect of Volpone's character, the man who lives richly for years on the gifts of his would-be heirs, is from *Dialogues of the Dead* 19; another aspect, the man who feigns death while in the best of health, in order to deceive legacy-hunters, comes in *Dialogues of the Dead* 15 and 16. Corbaccio, the *captator* who tries to poison his prey in an effort to speed things up, is out of *Dialogues of the Dead* 17; Mosca, the personal slave who inherits all (at least, he nearly does) occurs in *Dialogues of the Dead* 19.

These are not the only direct borrowings from Lucian. At two points in the text Jonson has taken material from *The Cock:* Mosca's praise of gold in Act V. i echoes Micyllus in Act II, and the doggerel show put on by Nano, Androgyno and Castrone for Volpone's benefit in I. i draws widely on the cock's account of his metamorphoses.[1] Added to which, Mosca's praise of parasites at the beginning of Act III. i, with its 'I muse the mystery was not made a science. It is so liberally profest! . . .' is a mock encomium in the spirit of *The Parasite* (though hardly modelled on it).

The Lucianic and Petronian details have been crossed with an allegory out of Horace, who in *Satires* 2. 5 couples the fable of the fox and the crow with the practice of legacy-hunting. Hence the beast names: Volpone = fox, Corbaccio = crow, Voltore = vulture etc, right down to the very subplot, where Peregrine is the falcon and the prattling parrot Sir Politick Would-be owes his animal rank to his nickname of Pol. But though this fabular structure, and Horace's injunction in the *Ars poetica* (a work later translated by Jonson) to mix the useful with the entertaining, contribute to the moral purport of the play, Lucian evidently had his part to play there too. Jonson has taken two groups of Lucianic *alazones* and set them against one another. Volpone is an Alexander figure, both *eirōn* and *alazōn* by turns as he manipulates the credulity of his victims, only to overplay his hand; Voltore, Corbaccio and Corvino are the archetypal *alazōn*, duped by their own vision of the worth of what they are pursuing. The effect of this matching of villains against one another is to remove from the stage, as from that stage of the world that Menippus so darkly surveys, all positive qualities. It has been observed that 'never before had Jonson painted with so much power humanity denuded of every germ of goodness'. Though he may have had personal reasons for the change in his moral stance, the literary models for his new position could quite well be found in Lucian, especially as Jonson's reading of him would have been influenced by the moralistic interpretation of sixteenth-century scholars, notably Erasmus. Add to this that Jonson's dedicatory epistle to the printed version of the play borrows wholesale from the *Epistola apologetica* to that thoroughly Lucianic work, Erasmus' *Praise of Folly* (see below, pp. 191–7), and the picture becomes more complex still. At one point Folly picks upon *The Cock* for a portion of her argument, illustrating the superiority of animals to men:

[1] I am indebted for this point to H. Levin, 'Jonson's Metempsychosis', *Philological Quarterly* XXII (1943) 231–9.

And so I could never have enough praise for the famous cock who was really Pythagoras. When he had been everything in turn, philosopher, man, woman, king, commoner, fish, horse, frog, even a sponge I believe, he decided that man was the most unfortunate of animals, simply because all the others were content with their natural limitations, while man alone tries to step outside those allotted to him.[1]

This is the very message illustrated by that strange interlude performed for Volpone in Act I. i. It is, in fact, a comment upon the action to come, a comment not understood, of course, by Volpone himself. The thirst for gold that *The Cock* ridicules will bring low not just the inheritance seekers but Volpone too, because *he has not observed his limitations.* Jonson has used Lucian to provide an ironic commentary on the action, disguised as a piece of nonsense in the mouths of Volpone's *fools;* he has painted a black picture of society in accordance with the stock Lucianic portrait of *alazōn* feeding upon *alazōn;* and he has used a number of Lucianic plot-threads to help construct the intrigue.

There is a clear distinction between Lucianic influence on *Volpone* and on the other plays. The scenes in *Cynthia's Revels* and *The Poetaster* are not of themselves very significant, simply because that sort of borrowing is very common in Jonson. As Dryden said of him: 'He invades authors like a monarch, and what would be theft in others is victory in him.' Part of *The Poetaster* dramatizes a Horace satire; the basic situation of *Epicoene* is from Libanius; *The Alchemist* takes off from Plautus' *Mostellaria; Catiline* depends on Sallust and Cicero; the list is endless. Most of the supposed verbal echoes of Lucian are not particularly informative either. Indeed, many of them certainly derive from Erasmus' *Adages,* e.g. the closing line of *The Poetaster,* 'And apes are apes though cloth'd in scarlet'. *Volpone,* however, is modelled on Lucian at several levels, and at the same time presents a change in the tone of Jonson's comedy. This is not coincidental. If we consider that *Cynthia's Revels* (1600), *The Poetaster* (1601) and *Volpone* (1605) form a trio broken only by the tragedy of *Sejanus,* it is obvious that Jonson gradually came to incorporate more and more Lucianic material into his comedies over a narrow period of time, until with *Volpone* he effected a shift in his dramatic manner. The Lucianic material formed a bridge via which he could adjust his concept of comedy to a darker vision of life. In that sense Lucian contributed to the theatre of Jonson

[1] Trans. B. Radice, Penguin Classics, 1971, 115.

as an individual in a way that he did not contribute to the development of any aspect of the theatre in general.

Mock-encomium became an Erasmian genre. Lucianic influence on the theatre flared and sputtered fitfully, its only positive manifestations a handful of Timon plays and the occasional more substantial influence on an individual writer. But in other genres the picture was very different. Satirical dialogue was, for largely political (in the broadest sense) reasons, to become a very important literary form in the sixteenth century, only to fade out along with the social and historical conditions which had bred it. Here Lucian's influence was to be decisive. The 'fantastic tale' was to develop in a particular way over the sixteenth, seventeenth and eighteenth centuries under the influence of Lucian. And the 'dialogue of the dead', practised with enthusiasm by the Byzantines, more sparingly by the Italians and rarely in the sixteenth century, was suddenly to come into its own in the two succeeding centuries, almost exclusively under the stimulus of Lucian. The time has come to look briefly at how and why each of these genres developed as it did.

ii. *Satirical dialogue*

Dialogue was not of itself a new prose form in the sixteenth century. There had been a vast body of mediaeval debate literature, some of it in prose, and the prose dialogue as practised by Cicero had never ceased to be a model. To this highly academic form the Renaissance added the conventions of Platonic dialogue, where a little more local colour and sense of action were permitted. However, the Ciceronian and Platonic forms of dialogue, designed for the reasoned exposition of ideas, were not entirely suited to polemic. In an epoch of violent controversies, the need was for a new form of dialogue through which to dramatize the new conflicts of values. This was the basis of the attraction of Lucian's satirical dialogues as a form. At the same time, the major issues of the day, concerning as they did both the metaphysical and ethical aspects of religion, seemed to find an echo in the very themes and characters of many of Lucian's works. Erasmus was the great popularizer of the genre. His contribution I shall consider separately (see below, pp. 168–91). But there were many ways of imitating Lucian other than the Erasmian one. Let us look at a few representative examples.

In the years following the breach with Rome, satirical dialogue was very important in Germany as a medium for Reformist propaganda. The substantial influence of Lucian in this area was largely the result of the dialogues of Ulrich von Hutten (1488–1523),[1] although not so much because of the popularity of these works in the original Latin, as because Hutten translated four of his most violently anti-Roman works into German, publishing them under the title *Gespräch buchlin* in 1521. Hutten became acquainted with the works of Lucian while a student in Bologna. He had evidently read some of them in Greek— for example, he quotes in the original from *Hermotimus* in *Bulla*. Probably, however, his main knowledge of the dialogues was through the Latin translations of Erasmus. Two of Hutten's pieces betray their source very clearly. The first is *Phalarismus* (1517), a violent personal attack on Ulrich of Württemberg, occasioned by the duke's murder of Hutten's cousin Hans von Hutten. Hutten's response was aggravated by the fact that Hans and his father Ludwig had both been loyal servants of the duke, that the motive for the murder was merely a passing lust for Hans's wife, and that the duke refused to return the victim's body to his family for proper burial. All of these points are raised in the dialogue itself. Phalaris has appeared to the duke in a dream and summoned him to Hades to receive advice on the art of tyranny. Mercury brings him to Charon, and after a troubled crossing of the Styx leads him to Phalaris. In the course of a long account of his crimes, the duke reveals that, if anything, Phalaris could learn a tip or two from him. Hutten has taken two of Lucian's underworld dialogues as his pattern: first, *Menippus* for the idea of a living man permitted to visit the dead, then *The Downward Journey* for the motif of the tyrant brought to Hell and the reaction of Mercury and Charon to him. Megapenthes' haughty notion of his own superiority while on Charon's boat is transferred to Hutten's tyrant and his refusal to take an oar; Cyniscus' 'Tyranny will turn sour on you if you get a taste of my club' becomes Charon's 'If you don't stop making threats I'll break my pole over your head'. Out of *Dialogues of the Dead* too come minor motifs; the idea that a live man weighs down the boat, and that war is a good source of passage-money to Charon. The character of Phalaris in the second part of the dialogue draws on the details given in *Phalaris I*. All this scattered material is worked into an effective satire by the literary structure, which also derives from Lucian. Hutten has preserved

---

[1] I have made some use of O. Gewerstock, *Lucian und Ulrich von Hutten. Zur Geschichte des Dialogs im 16. Jahrhundert*, Berlin 1924, despite its inaccuracies.

the dramatic shape of *The Downward Journey*: Mercury seen approaching, a conversation on the river bank, the crossing itself, Mercury's account of the scenery as they progress on the other side. The theme of the dialogue, the denunciation of the crimes of the duke, is maintained as the sole topic within that structure. But it is presented in two different ways: in the denunciation by Mercury and Charon, and then in the self-condemnation which the tyrant's eulogy of his deeds constitutes. Whereas Cyniscus in *The Downward Journey* accuses Megepenthes of his crimes before Rhadamanthus, the duke, like Phalaris in *Phalaris I*, delivers a mock-encomium of his own ingenuity, his interlocutor only being there to point up the heinous nature of his acts by admiring their superiority to his own. By this process of ironic caricature Hutten completely undermines his opponent without resorting to invective. Using Lucianic themes, motifs and structures he has assembled an entirely contemporary personal satire.

The second piece close to source is very different. *Arminius*, probably written about 1520, is an entirely political dialogue. It forms a sequel to *Dialogues of the Dead* 25, rather as Prodromos' *Sales of Lives* is a sequel to its model. Arminius' own words to Minos make the fact plain:

> When ... you decreed as it were prizes for the best generals, you passed me over as if I had never lived. For Alexander of Macedon, on your judgment, has been pronounced first of the generals in all Elysium and this region of the Blessed, Scipio the Roman is second to him in honour and Hannibal of Carthage third. I am the only one to whom no rank has been allotted; yet I would have been in no doubt of obtaining your vote for first place if I had ever thought of entering into competition with the others.

Arminius brings Tacitus to give evidence on his behalf, with Mercury standing guarantor of his reliability as a witness. Alexander, Scipio and Hannibal agree to a retrial. The bulk of the dialogue, drawing on Tacitus' *Germania*, is then a eulogy of Arminius as the representative of German virtue, contrasting him with the Romans, symbolizing Italian vice. As in Lucian's dialogue, each of the other generals is criticized in turn, until Arminius is declared the winner. It is not a particularly subtle piece, reading like a postscript to the dialogue on which it is modelled. It testifies more to the strength of Hutten's patriotism than to his literary skill.

Phalarismus with its entirely personal subject and *Arminius* with its political one mark the extreme poles of Hutten's Lucianic imitation. In between lie a group of three dialogues, *Febris I* and *II* and *Inspicientes*, which link individual and politics via the satire of religion, more particularly of its earthly representatives. It is a peculiarity of Hutten's satire that though he was so closely associated with the Reformation, he does not write about religion as such. His motives seem to have been nationalistic; the church represents an alien social element hostile to natural German interests. When it became clear that Luther was not going to contribute to the restoration of the empire as Hutten envisaged it, he lost interest in the Protestant movement and concentrated his attention on Franz von Sickingen and the ill-fated rebellion of the Imperial Knights (1522). This reduction of the role of religion to a social theme is evident in the central group of dialogues. In *Febris I* (1518), Fever, about to be expelled by Hutten from his house, asks him to direct her to someone 'given to the pleasures of the flesh, rich and powerful'. He offers her the houses of princes, rich men, merchants and the Fuggers (Augsburg financiers), but his principal suggestions for a new host are Cardinal Cajetan, the papal legate, and monks and priests in general. Fever rejects them all and settles for a 'courtier lately returned from Rome, where he had learned to live at ease in some cardinal's house', the recommendation of his luxury being expressed in a comically exaggerated dialogue of mock-praise. The rôle of Fever here is akin to that of Wealth in *Timon* or Rhetoric in *The Double Indictment* (another lady 'unjustly' turned out of the house). But most of the piece rests simply on the transference to representatives of the church of the vices Lucian attributes to his philosophers—idleness, lust, physical indulgence—each vice being ironically represented as a plus point in the eyes of Fever.

Febris II (1519) continues on the same tone. There is a splendid dramatic opening scene, in which Hutten and his servant attempt to keep Fever out of the house:

Hutten   Heh, boy, can you hear that knocking? Can you hear that noise of the door breaking down? Do you hear it? Do you hear it? Are you going to stand there and let the door be smashed in? Look out of the window, and if it's anyone I wouldn't care to see, tell them I'm not at home.

Fever   Not at home, when I can hear you talking? Open up, and let me in out of this wind and rain.

Servant   It's Fever, master. O Lord! O Salvation! How can we defend ourselves against that plague? Shall I drive her off with stones? With weapons and arms of every kind?

Hutten   Shut the window first, or she'll waft some poisonous breath upon
us, boy. Shut it at once, and shut it tight . . .

This is a form of theatricality that Lucian does occasionally allow
himself, as at the beginning of *The Dead Come to Life*. At the end of
the scene, which is quite long, Hutten returns to an ironic presentation,
with Fever complaining of her treatment at the house of the 'courtier',
where she was soon crowded out by other diseases. The topic moves,
via the courtier's mistress, to the clergy, as Fever expresses her pity
for the trouble that their concubines bring them. This theme, with
lavish illustration, makes up the bulk of the matter that follows, the
tone giving way to one of invective as Hutten denounces the damage
that such clergy have done both to Christianity and to Germany. The
seriousness is broken here and there by Fever's wheedling attempts to
persuade her old host to have her back, and by a little light humour
which Hutten allows at the expense of his own sexual appetites and
general physical indulgence, not an element for which any parallel
could be found in his model. Otherwise the dialogue is a less compact
and hence less satisfactory version of the devices used in *Febris I*.

The third of the dialogues, *Inspicientes* (1520), is more closely
related to Lucian, as its title, drawn from the sub-title to *Charon* (The
Onlookers), suggests. Phaethon and the sun look down upon the earth
to observe the doings of men. Phaethon's first speech suggests the
'vanity of human endeavour' theme which is central to *Charon:*

> It is a long time since we observed the doings of men as we used to do.
> We've kept bringing a mass of cloud between us and them, so that we would
> not see them, some running about, others sailing, others fighting some war
> among themselves, suddenly leading out great armies over trifles, preparing
> to die for the empty glories of a name and a few titles snatched through
> ambition.

The motif of earth observed by the critical eye of a heavenly body is
perhaps borrowed from *Icaromenippus* (where it is the moon); the use
of cloud to hide the deeds of men certainly is (21). The review of the
world and its doings could be taken from either dialogue. But the
substance of Hutton's work is very different from the general moral
lessons of Lucian's. The *onlookers* are seeing the world as it is; they run
through the current military achievements of the Italians, Germans
and Spaniards, i.e. pope versus empire; they comment upon the Diet
of Augsburg (1518), with its visit from the papal legate and the pro-
posals for war against the Turks. At this point the dialogue becomes

merely an excuse for an attack on pope Leo X, who is painted as a crook, using the prospect of a crusade as a way of extorting money from the Germans. The tone is one of sharp sarcasm:

Sun He says he is a shepherd, as Christ once was. The Christians are his sheep, particularly the Germans. So he's sent this chap here to shear his flock and send the wool back to him. Is there anything wrong in that?

The pope and his legate are shown as imposters, on the pattern of Alexander, deluding the innocent and ignorant Germans. This in turn gives an occasion for a long eulogy of German *mores* by the sun, prompted by the questions of Phaethon, a eulogy contrasted with the denunciation of the corruption of the priesthood (including, for once, an attack on a religious practice, confession). And so we return to the Diet of Augsburg and Hutten's favourite Aunt Sally, the papal legate. Cardinal Cajetan is made to abuse the sun for failing to obey his orders to provide sunshine during his stay in the cold north. Lucian in *Timon* makes Timon shout abuse at Jupiter, but not for the purpose of diminishing Timon himself. Hutten reduces Cajetan, by this piece of absurd burlesque, to a strutting manikin, as he threatens the sun with papal powers, eternal damnation, enforced penance and excommunication. When the sun observes that the legate's doings might be better kept in the dark, Cajetan sees the sense of this and orders the sun to keep Germany unilluminated. It is the situation of *Zeus Rants* inverted. Cajetan arrogates to himself the powers of God, but like Jupiter, when the time comes to use his thunderbolt, it seems singularly ineffective.

Of Hutten's other dialogues, *Misaulus sive aula* (1518) and *Fortuna* (1519) show Lucianic affiliations without any close parallels. The former is an invective against the vices of court life having some points in common with *On Salaried Posts,* mostly in details. Life at court is compared to a ship at sea and to being a slave or a prisoner of war; the courtier is subject to the whims of the women in the ruler's family; all hopes of wealth are deceptive; at the end you will be cast off like an old garment after a life of service. In general it is difficult to disentangle any Lucianic influence from that of Juvenal and the whole tradition of anti-court satire (e.g. Aeneas Sylvius' *De curialium miseriis*). *Fortuna* offers certain interesting parallels with at least one Lucian dialogue. After an opening in which Hutten asks the goddess for special treatment, there follows a discursive account of the goddess and her nature, raising the question of the relationship between God and Fate which is central to *Zeus Catechized*. But the philosophical issue is not sustained in what follows. As well as a little humorous satire at the expense of the author's own foibles, the dialogue contains traditional Cynic material on the cares of riches and virtues of poverty, which could be paralleled from *The Cock* or *The Ship* but also from the New Testament. A few images are probably borrowed from other dialogues, e.g. that of the actor who can change from slave to prince in a moment is from *Menippus* 16. *Vadiscus* and the later dialogues *Bulla*, the two *Monitores* and *Praedones*, which are almost entirely denunciatory in tone, do not offer any significant parallels, although the objects of the satire remain the same.

There are, then, affinities between several of Hutten's dialogues and Lucian in both theme and form. They both attack hypocrisy, obscurantism, arrogance and the abuse of worldly power. They both ridicule the difference between theory and practice in those who set themselves up as moralists, and the exploitation of ignorance for personal greed and aggrandizement. They are both hostile to Rome. As to literary devices, it is noticeable that Hutten alone of Lucian's Renaissance imitators is more attracted to the element of invective than to the use of irony. Like Lucian in the pamphlets he relies on a good deal of sarcasm mixed with open denunciation. At the same time he is perfectly capable of employing irony, as in the tyrant's self-condemnation in *Phalarismus* and the reversal of natural values in *Febris I* and *II*. He exploits the humour of caricature, reducing his enemies to the absurd one-dimensional types of the Lucianic comic philosopher. On the other hand, although he uses familiar devices such as the sustained personification of abstracts, the staging of himself as a character (he doubtless thought of Lycinus as Lucian's self-portrait), and a certain amount of apposite quotation, other important Lucianic techniques are missing. There is little fantasy, little anecdote, no parody. In applying his model to serious issues and a polemical purpose, Hutten has produced a rather different, much narrower form of dialogue.

This new form had a limited currency in Germany, but, as I said above, an important one. From 1521 onward, a flood of satirical dialogues more or less modelled on Hutten were issued in the Protestant cause, attacking the abuses of the church in general and the papacy in particular. Very soon, however, there began the gradual alienation of the humanists from the reformist cause, and with it the decline of the relatively intellectual form of polemic which Hutten had helped to foster. It is none the less curious to see how the essentially frivolous and negative works of Lucian contributed to the forging of an important weapon in one of the most serious clashes of values that Europe has ever known.

The principal French example of Lucianic satirical dialogue, and at the same time one of the strangest specimens of the genre, was the *Cymbalum mundi* of Bonaventure des Periers, a group of four dialogues published anonymously in 1537.[1] Des Periers' early years were spent in the company of reformers and humanists; he assisted Olivetan in his translation of the Bible and Dolet in his *Commentaries on the Latin Language;* he was associated with progressive literary circles in Lyon, and then with the equally liberal court of Marguerite de Navarre, to whom he became secretary. Neither this career, nor the poetry and short stories which formed the bulk of his literary output, prepare one for the disillusioned unmasking of the intellectual pretensions of his time which the *Cymbalum* offers. The Catholic response to it was sharp. Both the Parisian Parlement and the Faculty of Theology at the Sorbonne denounced the work; the printer of the first edition was arrested and imprisoned, the book as far as possible suppressed. For the Protestants, Calvin and Henri Estienne both roundly denounced it as atheistic. Nobody knew, or knows, for certain what the full meaning of the work was; everybody agreed that it was Lucianic.

The four dialogues are, at first sight, rather disconnected. In the first, Mercury comes down to Earth, at Jupiter's behest, to have rebound a book, containing 'Chronicles of memorable acts committed by Jupiter before he existed himself. The ordinance of the Fates or the definite disposition of the future. A catalogue of the Immortal Heroes destined to live an eternal life with Jupiter'. At an inn Mercury is recognized by Byrphanes and Curtalius, two unscrupulous characters who rob him of the book, substituting another which, in the third dialogue, turns out to contain reports of Jupiter's youthful love-affairs (a parody of the Old Testament?). In the second dialogue Trigabus describes to Mercury how the philosophers are still fighting to find the fragments of a philosopher's stone which the god had smashed and scattered among the sand of an arena. The two of them go to watch the quarrels between three of these philosophers, Rhetulus, Cubercus and Drarig; the first two names are transparent anagrams for Luther and Bucer, the third probably standing for Erasmus' Christian name, Gérard. Mercury

---

[1] The question of Lucianic influence on Des Periers was examined by C. A. Mayer, 'The Lucianism of Des Periers', *Bibliothèque d'Humanisme et Renaissance* XII (1950) 190–207, but not in such a way as to contribute much to an overall interpretation of the dialogues.

throws further confusion by suggesting that the stone may never have had the powers claimed for it anyway, although the philosophers are much too taken up with their own ideas to pay any attention to him. The third dialogue is much less coherent than the first two: it starts with a long monologue from Mercury, throwing further light on the theft of the book, and listing the errands heaped upon him by the other gods. Then Cupid arrives, and describes the wealth that the robbers are making out of selling information from the book and inscribing new people in it (the Catholic practice of indulgences). The conversation turns to love, and we see a girl turned by Cupid from indifference to her suitor to a desire for his attentions. Finally, Mercury gives a horse the power to talk, and it promptly gets itself into trouble by denouncing its groom. The fourth dialogue returns to a simple theme. Hylactor, a dog with power of speech which derives from having devoured the tongue of the huntsman Actaeon, meets Pamphagus, the other dog who shared that tongue and hence acquired the same power of speech. Pamphagus advises Hylactor of the dangers of betraying his gift to man, but Hylactor is unconvinced.

It is easy enough to suggest borrowings from Lucian at the level of ornamental motifs. The figure of Mercury has all the characteristics attributed to him in *Dialogues of the Gods*: thieving and deceit in no. 11, being harassed by business in no. 4, his general status of messenger-boy to the other gods. The notion of Mercury being sent down to intervene in human affairs occurs in *Timon, The Double Indictment, The Runaways* et al. He is also intimately linked with Charon as the guide of souls to the underworld in *The Downward Journey* 5–6 and *Dialogues of the Dead* 20. Similarly Jupiter is constantly referred to in the mythological terms in which *Dialogues of the Gods* present him: as Mercury's father (no. 4), as lover of Europa, Leda, Alcmene, Danae, Antiope, Semele, Ganymede and the mother of Alexander the Great—nos 4 and 6 cover all but the last, which occurs in *Dialogues of the Dead* 12 and 13. References can be found for some of the tricks of Cupid, the story of Actaeon, the choice of Tiresias and Dodona as oracles, the appearance of talking animals, and even for the coupling of Apelles, Zeuxis and Parrhasius as stock examples of painters (cf. *Essays in Portraiture* 3). Undoubtedly Des Periers could have assembled all this from other sources; in Lucian he would have found it conveniently together.

Identifying motif-borrowing does not, however, help us to determine what the dialogues mean. The significant parallels are ones of thought. The easiest place to start looking for these is in the second dialogue, where the warring philosophers are at once recognizable as Lucianic stock types. The central idea, of the various sects quarrelling over doctrines which substitute speech for action, occurs in *Icaromenippus* 5–10 and *Menippus* 4–6, but it is most substantially expressed in *Hermotimus*. The search for the fragments of the stone is parallel to the search for the right road to the truth; Des Periers' philosophers think they can only find the stone by wearing blue and yellow, or fasting: Lucian's can only reach truth by a westward road, a northbound road, a hard parched one, a pleasant meadow one. The claims for the powers of the stone are like Hermotimus' assertions of the benefits to the man who reaches the city of virtue. Mercury's doubt as to whether Cubercus has found pieces of the true stone, because they do not demonstrate the powers attributed to it, resembles Lycinus' observation that the achievement of the city of virtue does not seem to have had the claimed effect on a certain philosopher. Above all, Rhetulus shares several of the characteristics of the Stoic teacher of Hermotimus: preferring material interest to truth, physically violent against his opponent, and fond of a good dinner in a great house. The conclusions of the two authors are the same. Faced with the endless talking of the philosophers, Trigabus attacks them for the vanity of their search and the quarrelling it engenders. He implies that they would be better employed on some practical task:

> If I were a member of the Council, I would put you all to the plough, find you work in vineyards, or send you to the galleys. Do you think it pleasant to see a bunch of slow-witted fellows waste their lives searching for small stones like little children. If it served some useful purpose, well and good, but they do nothing with their beliefs, dreams and portents.

Lycinus expresses the same point at some length (71–2) and uses the same comparison with children's games (75). In each case the rejection of metaphysical speculation as absurd and useless is the core of the argument. In Trigabus' words: '. . . the man who expects to derive a profit from something non-existent is quite mad and the man who hopes for the impossible is unhappier still.'

The second dialogue is the least allegorical of the four; even without reference to *Hermotimus* and without identifying its anagrams, it is possible to comprehend its major points. The other three dialogues are a great deal less clear. Jupiter and Mercury are plainly the representatives of revealed religion, and imply a perilously close analogy with

God the Father and God the Son. The book which is to be rebound raises the issues of the origin of God himself (cf. *Icaromenippus* 8) and the relationship of God to Fate (Cf. *Zeus Catechized* passim). The question of Jupiter's powers is twice raised *à propos* of the theft of the book. Curtalius, at the end of Dialogue 1, suggests that Jupiter's punishment for the theft may be very randomly distributed; Mercury, at the beginning of Dialogue 3, wonders why Jupiter has not moved to punish those responsible, and how he failed to notice that the act was inscribed in the book of Fate. These ideas are all paralleled in Lucian: e.g. Cyniscus mocks Zeus' inability to direct his thunderbolt to the right target (*Zeus Catechized* 16), Timon denounces Zeus' failure to deal with temple robbers (3–4), Poseidon is told that sacrilege cannot be punished unless the punishment is ordained by Fate (*Zeus Rants* 25). Des Periers is handling very dangerous issues, hinting at the powerlessness of God and openly presenting the inadequacy of the traditional account of him. His treatment of the representatives of orthodoxy, Curtalius and Byrphanes, is no less dangerous and no less Lucianic. They are religious rogues in the Alexander model, exploiting the susceptibilities of their fellow·men in the name of powers that they have improperly usurped.

Dialogues 1, 2 and the opening of 3, once one sees them in the light of their Lucianic parallels, are recognizable as attacks on revealed religion, on its exploitation by Roman Catholicism, and on the vanity of the attempts by reformist theologians to claim for themselves special knowledge of an unattainable and perhaps non-existent truth. How does this sweeping condemnation of contemporary religious dissension relate to the second half of the third dialogue, and the fourth? Running through all four dialogues are images of the thirst for novelty, among gods as well as men. Jupiter wants his book to have a smart new binding; Curtalius demands news from Mercury (1); the philosophers pursue new powers and new knowledge (2); Athene has asked Mercury for the works of Pindar (the 'type' of the innovator in ancient poetry) and of Apelles and Zeuxis, whom Lucian discusses as innovators in *Slander* and *Zeuxis* (3); Hylactor describes men's fascination with 'things absent, new, strange and impossible'. The frivolousness of this insistence on novelty, which is one reason for the dog Pamphagus' desire not to reveal his powers of speech to men, is a frequently found Lucianic theme. Novelty for novelty's sake in religion is attacked in *Icaromenippus* (24) and in *The Parliament of the Gods*, in the arts in *Zeuxis* and other *prolaliai*. In every case men are presented as passing over the fundamentals in preference for the cult of the superficial, a fault allied to the preference for speech over action in Dialogue 2.

The final substantial link between Lucian and the *Cymbalum* is the doctrine of silence in the fourth dialogue. This dialogue is apparently rather different from the others, but the difference is illusory. Mercury has not entirely disappeared; he is present in the references to Anubis, the Egyptian dog-faced form of the god (cf. *Zeus Rants* 9), and Hylactor, the barking dog, is merely an animal symbol for the 'dog' philosopher, the Cynic. The Cynic's vision of the truth can no more usefully be transmitted to men than the Catholic or reformist doctrines. What would be the result?—glory, material advantage, assured success? All these have been rejected by Des Periers in the earlier dialogues. Like Lucian in *Peregrinus* and *The Runaways*, he turns at last on the pure cynic, and exposes him as just as venal and responsive to self-interest as everybody else. Extending the idea of the folly of useless speech in the second dialogue, Des Periers arrives at the logical notion that only silence is justified. This is a message which has its Lucianic parallel too, in *Dialogues of the Dead* 26. When Achilles proposes to bemoan the life he has lost, Antilochus reproaches him:

We can see the uselessness of speech. We've decided to keep silent and put up with it all, lest we become a laughing stock.

Given the fate of the *Cymbalum*, Des Periers might have done well to follow his own message more closely. Ultimately Pamphagus could not resist having his bite at everyone.

It is difficult to say that Des Periers drew his ideas from Lucian. More probably he was inspired as to the general form in which to express ideas he already held by his reading of the dialogues, which was evidently extensive. The literary parallels are almost as strong as the thematic ones—the dramatic form in which the *Cymbalum* dialogues are cast, the blending of burlesque and irony, the opposition between *eirōn* (Trigabus) and *alazōn* (the self-condemning philosophers), the device of the talking animal. The final message, with its negative emphasis, is certainly in key with the negative nature of the world-view that can most easily be derived from a reading of Lucian. It is not hard to see why the work should have been labelled a dangerous Lucianism, and treated with consequent hostility, in a period of rampant dogmatism.

The dialogues of Hutten and Des Periers are, in a sense, only the sort of Lucianism one expects from a French or German satirist writing under the influence of the growth of reform and in the shadow of Erasmus' *Colloquies*. It comes as perhaps more of a shock to learn that one of the most remarkable and sustainedly Lucianic works of the century was written in Spain, around 1552. This is *El Crótalon (The Castanets)*,[1] whose pseudonymous author Christophoro Gnophoso has been uncertainly identified with the shadowy figure of a humanist called Cristóbal de Villalón.[2] In the first half of the century Lucianic influence in Spain had been largely channelled through the imitation of Erasmus, as in such a work as Alfonso de Valdés' extended satirical *Diálogo de Mercurio y Carón* (1528), an attack on formalistic religion and defence of an Erasmian ideal of positive Christianity. The author of *El Crótalon*, also knew his Erasmus. But the framework, much of the detail, and almost all the world-view of his startling work —startling as much in form as in tone—are all taken directly from Lucian, with whose text he was clearly intimately acquainted. The format of the work builds on *The Cock*: a dialogue between the cobbler Micyllus and a cock who is in fact Pythagoras. Lucian's single early-morning conversation, the first six speeches of which are paraphrased to form the opening of *El Crótalon*, becomes the pattern for a series of nineteen 'cantos' (so called 'porque es lenguage de gallo cantar') each ending with dawn and Micilo's return to his day's tasks; the twentieth day sees the death of the cock and Micilo's laments thereon to his friend Demofon. The author acknowledges his source quite fully in the prologue. He mentions his debt to Lucian in style and incident, in his main characters, the device of the dream, and specific borrowings in different cantos from *Alexander, Toxaris, On Funerals, Icaromenippus, Menippus* and *Dialogues of the Dead*. He also says that his work is not a translation 'a la letra ni al sentido', a point which, though true in a broad sense, needs modification, for there are many short passages of direct verbal borrowing.

The use of Lucianic material is rather more elaborate than the author's account suggests. Even the title, reminiscent of Des Periers' *Cymbalum*, has probably been suggested by a passage in Lucian imitated in the twelfth canto (*Icaromenippus* 17). Material from one work may be used at various points in a number of cantos; related

---

[1] I have been helped in my assessment of Lucian's influence on *El Crótalon* by S. E. Howell, 'Lucian in El Crótalon', *Kentucky Foreign Language Quarterly* 2 (1955) 97–103. I have also used, with some caution, J. J. Kincaid, *Cristóbal de Villalón*, New York 1973.

[2] A more authoritative view is that he was an Italian living in Valladolid.

material from different works may be juxtaposed in a single episode. Essentially the cock uses each stage of his Pythagorean metamorphosis for a mixture of anecdote and satire, the additional Lucianic material being imported there, along with borrowings from many other sources. Two whole cantos are adapted from works of Lucian. In the fourth, Alexander of Abonuteichus is transmuted into a contemporary religious impostor, with a similar account of his formative years, powers of deception, ambiguous prophecies and immorality. In the seventeenth, based on *The Banquet*, the wedding has become the ordination of a priest, and the turbulent philosophers are clerics: the same excesses are committed, the names are largely maintained although partly interchanged, and such a characteristic event as the comic letter from Hetoemocles is preserved in full. In other cantos, the author has used the structure of a dialogue rather than precisely reproducing it. Most of canto 12 is based on *Icaromenippus*, with the cock metamorphosed into one Ícaro Menipo, who, despairing of receiving any certain knowledge about the universe from the conflicting views of scientists, sets off to Heaven. In the same canto the idea of viewing the follies of the world from the vantage point of the moon is borrowed, in canto 13 the picture of God receiving selfish prayers, in canto 14 the presentation to God of a petition denouncing the squabbles of philosophers and theologians. In the same way canto 15 and the second part of 16 use the descent into hell motif, as in *Menippus* and *Dialogues of the Dead* 8 and 17, with two of the principal features of *Menippus* preserved, namely a decree that the rich shall be returned to life as donkeys in order that they may serve the poor, and the rejection of philosophical speculation in favour of the common-sense life of the ordinary man.

A further type of borrowing occurs in cantos 11 and 15, where the moral argument of the canto is based upon a Lucianic illustration. In the former, the absurdity of human attitudes to death, as symbolized in funerals, is derived from *On Funerals*, but the central episode of the young man is replaced by a hostile description of the funeral of the Marqués del Vasto in Milan. In the latter, the detailed arguments about the anxieties and suffering of the *cliens* who finds in the end that by going into service he has sacrificed his liberty to no gain, is transferred from *On Salaried Posts* into a fully contemporary account. Details are preserved: some, like the tale of Thesmopolis and his mistress's lap dog, are contracted; others are expanded, for example the rhetorical comparison of the evils of service with the trials of prison and the dangers of life at sea (*On Salaried Posts* 1–2) becomes an extended comparison by the cock of his life as tutor with his sufferings in prison and at sea in an earlier metamorphosis (cantos 9 and 10).

Lastly, there are incidents and anecdotes used, along with material from Boccaccio, Aretino and Ariosto, to illustrate the view of the world that the cock is presenting. The episode in canto 1 where Evangelista (Evangelos in Lucian) fails to win a music contest by relying on extravagant appearance rather than talent, is from *The Ignorant Book-collector* 8–10. The rescue of Albert at sea by his friend Arnao in canto 9 is from the story of Euthydicos and Damon in *Toxaris* (19–20), and the theme of loyalty to an imprisoned friend occurs in the same dialogue (30–3). The tale of a ship swallowed by a whale in canto 18, and of the marvellous land inside the whale's mouth, is derived initially from *A True Story I*. 30–*II*. 1, and two anecdotes developed from *The Dead Come to Life*, the misdemeanours of the trained apes (36) and the story of the donkey who tried to pass for a lion (32), are woven into the same canto.

This is by no means a complete account of the sources and analogues, and it gives no idea of the skilful working in of directly borrowed incidental passages from various dialogues. The opening speech, for example, of canto 17 is closely derived from the beginning of *A True Story*, although the tale that follows is modelled on *The Banquet*. But Lucianic imitation does not stop here. At various points above I have mentioned the transposition of material into a contemporary setting. This is a key part of the use of that material in *El Crótalon*. The author has reinterpreted the world of Lucian's dialogues into the traditional characters and institutions of his own time. The work is densely satirical, insisting on the absurdity of men's aims and ambitions, and, rather more darkly, on the vices and dissensions which disfigure life. Furthermore, it modifies its sources in such a way that the satire does not remain on a general moral level, but presents issues of specific interest to contemporary Spanish thinkers. The Alexander episode of canto 4 is not just a tale of gullibility and hypocrisy. It is an attack on the inadequacy of religious training in Spain, the credulity of the Castilian upper classes, the shameless manipulation of the trappings of revealed religion by the Catholic clergy. Elsewhere, the diverse sects of the philosophers are translated into the nominalists and realists of scholastic philosophy, their terminological finesse being contrasted with the practical Christian morality of the *devotio moderna*. This transposition does not apply only to the negative aspects of *El Crótalon*. Even the Ícaro Menipo episodes and the descent into hell are thoroughly

Christianized; there is no question of scoffing at religion as such, but of correcting its excesses and distortions. The hero rises to heaven not by the burlesque methods of birds' wings, but on the special permission of his guardian angel. The world he looks down upon from the moon, though the text is in part more or less translated, has been modernized to reflect the conditions of Spain and Europe. And the further flight to heaven is accomplished on a note of respect and even awe, rather than with the frivolous irony of Menippus' account. The same transposition of values applies to the torments of hell in canto 16, where the absurd fictions of the pagan poets have become the realities of the Catholic tradition, much closer in tone to Dante than to *Menippus*.

If we take the prologue of *El Crótalon* as at least a partly viable account of the author's world view, then the parallel between the satirical and black side of it and the negative values which can be deduced from Lucian's dialogues is an important one. The author, writing of himself in the third person, says:

... he imagined how, beneath a pleasant and agreeable exterior, he might convey the wickedness to which men of the present day give their time. For at no time better than the present can one see the truth of the words which Moses wrote in *Genesis*: That all mortal flesh follows a way and course of life corrupt and in error.[1]

This pessimistic vision of the world easily accommodates Biblical maxims to the Cynic theme of the vanity of human activity which appears in so much of Lucian's work. The vein of antifeminism also present in *El Crótalon* is not incompatible with the presentation of women by Lucian, nor, for quite different reasons, is the positive, practical side of Christian morality, which overlaps with the practical commonsense preached in *Hermotimus* and exemplified in the character of Micyllus and in Tiresias' advice to Menippus. After all, a doctrine of modest and sensible action is the 'norm' against which Lucian measures the excesses of his *alazones*. The literary structure, too, conforms to Lucianic principles. On the lines of the doctrine expressed in several *prolaliai*, novelty has not been pursued for its own sake; borrowed material has been digested and made the vehicle for something new. Within this structure, the mixture of anecdote and moral statement, grafted on to a dialogue pattern that sometimes reduces Micilo to a mere receptor, and at others allows him his own comment

---

[1] The reference is to Genesis 6.12.

on the world, conforms to the standard pattern of dialogues such as *The Cock* itself. The originality lies in welding so much material into a lively, biting and often paradoxical account of the world of the author, while remaining so close to the form and thought of his model.

In the context of *El Crótalon*, it is also worth mentioning the anonymous *Diálogo que trata de las trasformacyones de Pitágoras* (Dialogue on the metamorphoses of Pythagoras), a work of comparable date and form.[1] It, too, borrows its framework from *The Cock*, though much less deftly. The first nine chapters are a fairly close adaptation of the original. Micilo gets the chance, as he does not in *El Crótalon*, to tell the story of the feast at a rich man's house that he had recently attended, and how his pleasure in this unexpected event was tempered by having to sit next to a particularly tiresome old philosopher. This leads the dialogue on to repeating Lucian's central moral theme: the illusory nature of the happiness of the rich. The cobbler recounts the dream of wealth from which the cock awakened him, and the cock criticizes his concept of the power of gold. At this point, for the first time, the author brings the work into a properly modern context in a speech by Micilo describing the importance of gold in contemporary Spain, and particularly the dangers and suffering of those who pursue the search for it in the New World. The speech ends with Micilo listing the benefits, power, friendship and honour, that accrue to the rich man. The cock in return, deviating in part from Lucian, but replacing the original with equally typical Lucianic material, upholds the thesis that the misery of the rich outstrips the discomforts of the poor, a view which he illustrates by an account of his own life as the tyrant Dionysius of Syracuse. This is extended to include the torments that even the best of rulers undergo, and concludes with a denunciation of the evils of life for those who serve in a palace (an adaptation of the *On Salaried Posts* theme that is quite common in the sixteenth century). Micilo rejoins with an encomium of poverty, which the cock moralizes upon in his turn.

The rest of the work takes up quite separately the notion of metamorphosis, and presents a disconnected string of anecdotes, the first four antifeminist accounts of marriage, the next five borrowing heavily from *The Ass*, the next three an Erasmian attack on the trappings of contemporary religion, a brief account of a happy life as a frog (suggested by *The Cock* 20), and an equally brief account of life as a courtesan (cf. *The Cock* 19). The final chapter then returns somewhat

[1] See Kincaid, op. cit., 51–7.

unexpectedly to the theme of the blessings of poverty. The dialogue is altogether inferior to *El Crótalon* in literary structure, satirical power, and the use made of its sources. The obvious similarities suggest that the one work was influenced by the other, though in which direction is uncertain. However, both authors clearly knew Lucian on their own account, for each work contains borrowed material not present in the other.

Almost a half-century later, in the Spain of Philip II, Lucianic imitation was to look very different. The dialogues of Bartolomé Leonardo de Argensola (1562–1631) are a case in point.[1] Although the author, who held various ecclesiastical preferments, was best known for his poetry—lyrics and didactic verse in the manner of Horace—and for his historical works, he also composed three dialogues in a Lucianic mould, *Demócrito*, *Menipo litigante* and *Dédalo*, the last approximately datable to 1598. He is known to have read Greek, but the fact that his translation of Alberti's *Virtus dea* under the title *Diàlogo de Luciano entre Mercurio y la Virtud* (*Traducción del griego*) was very evidently taken from Nicolò da Lonigo's Italian version of Lucian suggests that this may have been the medium in which he was best acquainted with the dialogues. A comparison between *El Crótalon* and Argensola's works is instructive, in that both assume the validity of Christian belief, and both are concerned to communicate a picture of contemporary Spain. There the resemblance ends. *El Crótalon* was Lucianic to the core. Argensola's use of his model, by contrast, resembles the Byzantine practice of emptying out the dialogues of their essentials and using only the shell.

Demócrito is a general denunciation of the vices of the time, set in the framework of a discussion between the famous physician Hippocrates and a friend, Damageto, on the validity of laughter as a response to human evils. Hippocrates has been converted to Democritus' view of the world, and explains why. The structure is that of a typical Lucian report-dialogue, with Damageto there simply to occasion, and intermittently comment upon, Hippocrates' narrative, which first describes his legendary summons to Abdera to 'cure' Democritus of his supposed insanity, and secondly denounces the vices of court as witnessed on the equally legendary journey to the court of Artaxerxes in Persia. Argensola relies heavily on the spurious letters attributed to Hippocrates as his source, but the vices he attacks are clearly meant to be those of the

---

[1] See O. Green, 'Notes on the Lucianesque dialogues of Bartolomé Leonardo de Argensola', *Hispanic Review* 3 (1935) 275–94.

Spanish court. At the same time, they reflect several stock themes of Lucianic satire: scholars reduced to beggary as in *On Salaried Posts*, hypocritical monks and priests who do not live up to the religion they profess, as religious men and philosophers fail to do passim in Lucian, absurd ostentation and thirst for flattery among those in power, as in all Lucian's portraits of kings. More modern figures are denounced on the same pattern: venal judges, corrupt lawyers, cowardly generals. With such men is contrasted Timocaris, a friend of Democritus who gave up a large inheritance and preferred to live simply on the fruits of his own labour as a farmer; the theme of poverty and toil preferred to the corruption of riches which, again, is common in Lucian, notably in *The Cock*.

Rather more specific is the satire of *Menipo litigante*. The subtitle *Diàlogo de Philopatro* is very strange. *Philopatris* had been on the Index in Spain for many years and is unlikely to have been read by Argensola. There is, in any case, no resemblance between it and the Spanish dialogue, which borrows directly from *Menippus* for its central episode. It is an attack on the legal profession. Menipo explains to Aristas the peculiar advice that he had given Erostratus, that he should disinherit his children. First, he recounts how a lawsuit between himself and his relatives over the inheritance he had received from his father had ended in the lawyers getting their hands on the whole estate (shades of *Bleak House: plus ça change* . . .). Then he tells how, in the course of the case, he descended into the underworld to obtain his greatgrandfather's view on the disputed point in the will which is the source of all the trouble. Argensola here skips through a number of stock themes: the descent, the sufferings of famous mythological figures, the presence of famous philosophers. Menipo's encounter with Plato is particularly coloured by the traditional Lucianic presentation of him (e.g. *A True Story II.* 17):

I was lucky enough to see the divine Plato passing. He was coming from advising Rhadamanthus about some reform or other of that republic, certain precepts which sounded very nice but were impossible to put into practice; but when I told Lucian of Samosata about this journey of mine, I deliberately hid from him the fact that I had seen Plato (for he actually asked me himself if I had) because of the great hatred Lucian always had for the philosophers.

Menipo eventually found his greatgrandfather, who deplored the distortion of his intentions by the lawyers. Using a variant on the Lucianic device of the letter from one world to another, Menipo persuaded

Rhadamanthus to draft an official document setting out the truth of the case for the benefit of the judges. He returned to the upper world, presented it in court, and promptly lost the case. Aristas, hearing this story, is at once persuaded that Erostratus was indeed justified in leaving all his property to the lawyers in the first place. The denunciation of contemporary vice is, as in *Demócrito*, a black one, but tempered by the proper Christian view of the justice of God. When Menipo ventures to protest, in the fashion of Damis in *Zeus Rants*, that man can hardly be expected to take divine power seriously when it allows vice to prosper at the expense of virtue, Rhadamanthus answers 'with great severity' that he should leave these matters to the judgment of omniscient Jupiter, reminding him that 'the truth is ultimately judged before tribunals that owe no man respect'.

The most complex of the three works to interpet is *Dédalo*. The eponymous hero represents Antonio Pérez, the secretary of Philip II involved in the dubious assassination, with or without the king's connivance, of Juan de Escobedo. The dialogue gives Dédalo's account of the intrigue in which he was involved, and then of his escape from the labyrinth; at this point Argensola develops the theme in a more general way, accommodating the story to the general principles of *Icaromenippus*, Dédalo's flight over the earth giving him a critical view of human society. Menippus' absurd flight on one wing borrowed from an eagle, one from a vulture, becomes a divine rescue, with four eagles plucking feathers from their breasts and dropping them down to the imprisoned Dédalo. Some of the details of society criticized in the flight are recognizable borrowings, e.g. the absurdity of waging war for the possession of small areas of land:

Heavens above! What a tiny stretch of land the Cretans are fighting over with the Athenians and the whole of Greece; the country is aflame with the frenzy of war on the mere matter of increasing boundaries and taking over the lands of others!

Heaven, as the goal in which Menippus' flight culminates, is transposed into the seat of Astraea, the Goddess of Justice, who explains her failure to punish men as itself the greatest possible punishment. Instead of justice, earth is in the grip of *amour propre* and *raison d'état*, the worst monsters that Dédalo can envisage.

As with the other dialogues, Argensola balances denunciation of the vices of his time with confidence in the ultimate justice of God. The political theme is really just an illustration of the moral lesson of man's innate evil, such that the skilfully contrived parallel Dédalo-Minos-Pasifae with Pérez-Philip II-the Princess of Eboli adds a satirical frisson to the first part of the work, but is submerged in the general moral lesson of the end.

Argensola's satires, though their relationship to Lucian is clear enough, are only very generally modelled on him. Their world-view is in part compatible with the denunciations of a Menippus: the bulk of the satire consists in invective against the vices of the age, and many of these are also found in Lucian. But Argensola's ultimate lesson is one of Christian optimism. As for the form of the dialogues, they rely on the report convention, with relatively little interest in local colour, and a corresponding increase of emphasis on the didactic elements. This is understandable, given the author's view, as expressed in an essay 'On the proper style of satire', that the grave style of Horace and Ariosto is to be admired. The result is almost a re-accommodation of the Lucianic tradition to an earlier, more discursive form of dialogue, while retaining significant satirical elements. The age of doubt has passed and the weapons of Lucian had to be reintegrated into a more positive form of social and moral comment.

iii. *The imaginary voyage*

The most disparate of the genres to whose development the influence of Lucian contributed is the imaginary voyage. One critic, in attempting to classify the features of the genre, observed that

the various *Philosophic Voyages* are not bound to each other by a community of theme, but rather by their common story-forms, in respect to which certain definite lines of influence and imitation can be distinguished.[1]

The matter is complicated in the case of Lucian by the differences between the 'story forms' of the two texts which employ the imaginary voyage motif, *Icaromenippus* and *A True Story*. The former presents a plainly unreal journey—to the moon by means of wings—and uses the moon itself merely as a vantage point from which to view and satirize human activity on earth. The latter is a parody of travellers' tales, and as such puts forward its fantastic descriptions and events at least partially within the conventions of realistic travelogue. At the same time, it also includes both another moon trip and a journey to the underworld, but uses both as much for their comic value as for any

[1] W. M. Eddy, *Gulliver's Travels: a critical study*, Princeton 1923, 10.

apparent satiric intent. In these two texts, then, the Renaissance reader of Lucian had at his disposal models for both extra- and infra-terrestrial journeys, and a choice between an emphasis on fantasy or satire. Add to this the influence of actual travellers' tales, much in vogue since the discovery of the New World, and of allied forms of imaginative literature such as Plato's *Republic*, and one gets some idea of the numerous combinations of elements which could be used to create an imaginary voyage, and of the variety of purposes to which it could be put.

It is not difficult to establish that Lucian was closely associated in the popular mind with the whole notion of the imaginary voyage.[1] By the early seventeenth century the very concept is never mentioned without some reference to the 'author of the *True History*'. And when a character in Ben Jonson's *News from the New World* speaks of going to the moon, he borrows two of his three examples from *Icaromenippus*:

> There are but three ways of going thither. One is Endymion's way, by rapture in sleep or a dream. The other Menippus' way, by wing, which the poet took. The third old Empedocles' way; who, when he lept into Aetna, having a dry sear body, and light, the smoke took him and whift him up into the moon.

But the difficulty of assessing just what part in the development of the genre the reading of Lucian actually played is made much more com-plicated by the influence exercised by the major writers in the genre on their successors. If one attempts to trace a line from Thomas More's *Utopia* through Rabelais and Cyrano de Bergerac to Swift, and Holberg's *Niels Klim*, the nature of the problem becomes clear. By the end of the seventeenth century it could be said of any teller of travel-ler's tales what Eleria says of her father in Aphra Behn's *Emperor of the Moon* (1687), to wit, that he was infected

> . . . with reading foolish books, Lucian's Dialogues of the lofty traveller who flew up to the moon, and thence to heaven . . . with a thousand other ridiculous volumes too hard to name.

Each of the writers concerned knew his Lucian, each of them chose to write in a Lucianic genre. In each case the resultant work can, even allowing for the distortions of period interpretation, only in a very particular sense be called Lucianic.

In the case of *Utopia*, the issue at stake in asking the question 'Is it

[1] See M. H. Nicolson, *Voyages to the Moon*, New York 1948.

Lucianic, and if so in what sense?' is the basic one of whether to read the work in a serious sense or not.[1] Part of the answer lies in More's own interpretation of Lucian.[2] His fondness for that author can hardly be in question. Aside from the evident influence of *How to Write History* on his historical essay *The History of King Richard III*, there is the testimony of the three dialogues, *Menippus*, *The Lover of Lies* and *The Cynic*, which he translated and published together with Erasmus' group of versions in 1506. It is the prefatory letter to Thomas Ruthall which accompanied these translations that gives the clearest picture of More's reasons for interesting himself in Lucian. The emphasis is on the balance of moral utility and satirical wit, as it is in Erasmus' prefatory letters; and the contemporary application of the lessons to be learnt is stressed *à propos* of *The Lover of Lies* just as Erasmus stresses it in the case of *Toxaris*. But whereas the relationship between Erasmus' activities as translator and his writing of *Praise of Folly* is quite clear, that between More's translations and *Utopia* is less so. If we take the one clue, the balance between moral message and humour, the problem will be more easily solved.

Formally *Utopia* is Lucianic enough, although not because of direct parallels between the events in it and those in either of Lucian's imaginary voyages. The book is framed as an elaborate hoax concocted by More and Peter Giles, and purporting to record the travels of one Raphael Hythlodaeus, a survivor of Amerigo Vespucci's famous expedition to the New World. It falls into two parts, the first containing a satirical dialogue which offers overt criticism of contemporary Europe, the second portraying the land and people of Utopia in such a way as to offer implicit criticism of the real world. Neither the dialogue of bk. 1 nor the travelogue of bk. 2 owes much to Lucian in overall structure. That does not exclude there being considerable borrowings of technique within individual sections. The tale of the Anemolian ambassadors who attempt to dazzle the Utopians with their wealth but are taken for children, fools and slaves is Lucianic anecdotal humour at its mildest, with an echo of the golden fetters of *Hercules*. The sarcasm

[1] A very useful discussion of the issue appears in E. Surtz and J. H. Hexter's edition of *Utopia*, vol. 4 of *Complete Works*, Yale 1965. See also T. S. Dorsch, 'Sir Thomas More and Lucian: an Interpretation of Utopia', *Archiv für das Studium der neueren Sprachen und Literaturen* 203 (1966–7) 345–63.

[2] The evidence is conveniently set out in C. R. Thompson, *St Thomas More: Translations of Lucian*, vol. 3 of *Complete Works*, Yale 1974. Some specific points on Lucianic influence also occur in H. Süssmuth, *Studien zur Utopia des Thomas Morus* Munster 1967.

against lawyers, and the invective against the mercenary Zapoletans
reach the other pole of Lucian's satirical tone. The mock realism
surrounding the circumstances of the narrative is, too, something
More could well have learned from *A True Story*. Quite after the manner of Lucian learnedly speculating over divine footprints is More's
pedantic insistence on the precise length of the bridge which spans a
non-existent river in a non-existent town (prefatory letter to Peter
Giles). Equally after the Lucianic manner is his explanation for this
care in detail:

> Just as I shall take great pains to have nothing incorrect in the book, so,
> if there is doubt about anything, I shall rather tell an objective falsehood
> than an intentional lie—for I would rather be honest than wise.[1]

In the same class of technical influences are the comic proper names:
Hythlodaeus 'distributor of nonsense', the river Anydrus 'waterless',
the country of the Polyleritae 'great drivellers', and many more. In
bk. 2 every single name has a meaning, always apparently inappropriate
to the function of the place or person in the narrative, yet appropriate
in a wider context. Nor are all the shared techniques comic. The progression of the argument by a series of anecdotes, for example, is
fully Lucianic. Thus, to demonstrate that a philosopher's advice is
unlikely to carry weight with a king, Hythlodaeus proposes a series of
specimens of potential counselling, involving anecdotes from his
'travels'.

None of this raises any problem of interpretation. The difficulty lies
in whether we are to take Utopia, with its community of property,
religious tolerance, divorce and euthanasia, at face value as an ideal
system in itself which reflects ironically upon the customs of contemporary Europe, or whether, by an immense Lucianic irony, the
entire structure should be turned inside out, such that Utopia itself
becomes an absurdity, while remaining a critique of the world as More
knew it. In each case the supporting evidence lies largely outside the
text. Those who extrapolate from More's later actions and writings a
picture of a man to whom social rank was significant and religious
toleration anathema hold that his innate social and religious conserva-
tism would not have allowed him to promote so radical an ideal
society. Raphael Hythlodaeus is just what his name suggests, a purveyor of nonsense. The work is then Lucianic after the manner of *A*

---

[1] Trans. Surtz and Hexter, op. cit., 41.

Professor of Public Speaking, by meaning something other than its surface suggests. Those who take the work at face value rely on a comparison with the views and interests of Erasmus in 1515 to compose a picture of an idealist More later to be corrupted by the cares of political office. Curiously enough, it is equally possible to posit a Lucianic basis for this interpretation, for the central tenet of Utopian society is the exclusion of personal wealth. Now, of the three dialogues More translated, two, *Menippus* and *The Cynic,* deal principally with the view that wealth is the root of all social evil. *Menippus* in particular can be seen as an imaginary voyage of sorts (into Hades) in which an egalitarian society is used to show up the inadequacy of conventional materialistic values. On a reading of this sort, *Utopia* becomes a Christian humanist document, in accord with Erasmus' views on social issues (though the section on war remains very puzzling) and partly inspired by the Cynic doctrines of the Lucian dialogues. All that one can say is that either of these interpretations permits of a close relationship between More the translator of Lucian and More the writer of *Utopia,* since in each case a balance between humour and instruction would be maintained.

The imaginary voyages in Rabelais present problems of a different order. Again, it is not difficult to show the author's acquaintance with the text of Lucian. We have already seen his use of the mock-encomium. There are, besides, a substantial number of ideas, motifs, anecdotes and quotations borrowed from the Greek author.[1] Samippus and his dreams of kingship contribute to the projects of Picrochole and his advisers in *Gargantua* 33; the fate of philosophers and kings in *Menippus* is reflected in Epistemon's account of Hell (*Pantagruel* 30); the landscape in the mouth of Pantagruel (*Pantagruel* 32) has features in common with the world inside the whale in *A True Story II*. Often, as with the mock-encomium, it is the comic process, as much as the themes in question, which marks the influence. So the absurd dialogue between Panurge and the sceptical philosopher Trouillogan takes the motif of the dialogue between Pyrrho and a would-be purchaser in *Philosophers for Sale* 27 and uses in a much more burlesque way the same tension between the philosopher's unconstructive laconicism and the growing bewilderment and irritation of his interlocutor. Important

---

[1] The basic evidence is supplied in J. Plattard, *L'oeuvre de Rabelais* (*sources, invention et composition*), Paris 1910. There is also a less than convincing article by C. A. Mayer, 'The genesis of a Rabelaisian character: Menippus and Frère Jean', *French Studies* VI (1952) 219–29.

though these touches are, they would hardly explain what Rabelais' contemporaries found so Lucianic in his writing (insofar as they meant the term to be anything more than a term of abuse). The contribution of Lucian to the prologues, particularly to that of the *Tiers Livre*, is more revealing.[1] This prologue contains two anecdotes borrowed from Lucian: the story of Diogenes at the siege of Corinth from *How to Write History* 3, and that of Ptolemy, the slave and the camel from *A Prometheus in Words* 4. The first story is used, as is the opening anecdote in the *prolalia Bacchus*, to carry the meaning of the piece; the second, as it does in its original context, reinforces the meaning. In each case, the author offers a fable and then passes to its application to his own work, the second anecdote illustrating a point raised by the first. The effect is of the curtain-raising style which Lucian affects in the *prolaliai*. It is designed to establish a particular relationship between the 'audience' and the text which will follow.

If we are to see a connexion between Rabelais' imaginary voyages, first in *Pantagruel*, then in the *Quart Livre* and its continuation, it is one of this type, i.e. the imitation of literary structure and satirical function rather than of motif-borrowing. Rabelais knew the appropriate Lucianic texts well enough: the *Pantagrueline pronostication* (1533) obliquely refers to *Icaromenippus*, and the first chapter of *Pantagruel* does so explicitly. The parallel between Pantagruel's mouth and the whale in *A True Story* I have already mentioned. It is from this latter work that Rabelais may have taken the whole idea of a comic voyage in which absurd marvels would be listed. Some support for this theory can be found in the fact that at the end of the *Tiers Livre*, when deliberating about the journey, Panurge proposes travelling via the 'pays de Lanternoys', the land of lanterns from *A True Story I*. 29, which the travellers will finally reach in the later stages of the *Cinquiesme Livre*. From Lucian's express intention of satirizing travellers' tales he may have derived the scheme of basing the geography of the various trips on the descriptions of actual voyages to the New World, and also the element of literary parody which gives shape to the great search for the Holy Grail-substitute, the *Dive bouteille*. At the same time he could have noted in the Greek author how the wildness of the fantasy is set off by the affectation of realism. The early part of the first voyage in *A True Story* offers stylistic parallels with, for example, the opening of *Quart Livre* 66:

[1] D. Coleman, *Rabelais: a critical study in prose fiction*, Cambridge 1971 36–9.

Can you see that tall rock with two ridges, to port, the one that looks just like Mt. Parnassus in Phocis?

—Certainly, replied Xenomanes. It's the island of Ganabin. Do you want to go ashore there?

—No, said Pantagruel.

—Just as well, said Xenomanes. There's nothing worth seeing there. The people are all thieves and robbers. Still, near the right hand peak there's the finest fountain in the world, and a sizeable forest round about it. You could provision yourself with wood and water there.

The prologue to the *Quart Livre*, with its extended ancillary episode of the council of the gods, points to an entirely different dimension of Lucianic influence, the burlesque satire of human affairs. The principal episodes of the fourth book, as well as their fantastic and parodic aspect, have substantial satirical functions, functions partly evident in the very use of names, Papefigues, Papimanes, Chenaleph (hypocrisy). The *Cinquiesme Livre* then passes almost wholly into invective satire, particularly against theologians, and finally into elaborate moral allegory.

Looked at as a whole, though the admixture of mediaeval and popular elements makes the tone of Rabelais' voyage unLucianic, the objects of satire—pretension, superstition and hypocrisy—and the stock satirical device—caricature—are common to the two authors. Added to which, the familiar Lucianic device of a detached observer free to undermine the absurd through ridicule is inherent in the ingénu situation of the boatload of travellers and the unfamiliar societies through which they pass. Like More, then, Rabelais has transferred into the form of the imaginary voyage dimensions of parody and satire only partially, if at all, present in *A True Story*. He has developed the genre in a Lucianic way, but without producing an imitation as such.

By the time of Cyrano de Bergerac's *Histoire comique des états et empires de la lune et du soleil* (written *c.* 1648–50) the tradition is becoming more difficult to untangle. Cyrano had read his Lucian, but he was also acquainted with *Utopia*, and with the works of Rabelais, who in his turn had already borrowed from *Utopia*. Into the bargain Cyrano had read Francis Godwin's *The Man in the Moon: or a Discourse of a Voyage thither by Domingo Gonzales*, a work done into French in 1648 by J. Baudouin, himself translator of Lucian. Some parallels are clear enough. The idea of a double voyage, first to the moon, then to the sun, is after the manner of *Icaromenippus*, though Cyrano allows his hero to return to earth in between. There are also rare borrowings of details. The inhabitants of the moon are nourished on smells just as in *A True Story I*. 23. Elaborate funerals and weeping over the dead are held in contempt, as they are in *On Funerals* (but also in *Utopia*). The description of paradise on the moon shares features with the picture of the Elysian Fields in *A True Story II*. Then, there are motifs which offer more distant parallels. The phallic trees of *A True Story I*. 22 which produce acorns with men inside them are echoed in the miraculous tree of the sun whose fruit are jewels that metamorphose into men. The inhabitants of both moons indulge in comic species of warfare, though in Cyrano the comedy reflects ironically upon earthly customs. Sexual liberty is a feature of both lunar societies. There are also thematic parallels with *Icaromenippus*. In both works the hero reaches the moon by an absurd method; in both he achieves some religious goal, Menippus meeting Zeus, Cyrano's hero reaching Paradise. And the theme of the relative insignificance of the earth as seen from the moon becomes in Cyrano's version the comic insistence of the *bêtes-hommes* that the earth is the moon and vice-versa.

On a more formal level, there are parallels of literary device. Both the Cyrano voyages contain mock trials of the sort of which Lucian is so fond (e.g. *The Double Indictment*), and there is also a mock decree as in *A True Story I*. 20 and *Menippus* 20. But it is in the similarities of tone between Cyrano's satirical manner and the satire of Lucian in works other than *A True Story* that the sense of influence becomes greatest. Throughout the moon voyage the hero is represented as accepting the scientific and religious attitudes which Cyrano is covertly deriding, using the ironic manner which obtains in the first part of *A Professor of Public Speaking*. At the same time, the text of the Bible is parodied and used to discredit the religious position it purports to uphold, just as Lucian makes fun of Olympian mythology by parodying and satirizing Homer and Hesiod. Cyrano seems to have been influenced by Lucian on the most general plain; firstly in his choice of the imaginary voyage as a form through which to attack contemporary scientific beliefs, as in *Menippus* and *Icaromenippus*, and secondly in the literary approach to the undermining of the various beliefs, institutions and human groups who form the butt of his ridicule. The unanswerable question is simply, how far does all this depend on a close reading of Lucian, and how far on *Utopia* and the *Quart Livre*, that is, on second-hand Lucianism?

With Cyrano the three major stages in the development of the Lucianic tradition are complete. In *Utopia* the influence is confined to satirical manner; in *Pantagruel* and the *Quart Livre* it is extended to burlesque; in Cyrano's two *Histoires* the *Icaromenippus* motifs are added, and the tone of the satire becomes in every sense more 'Cynical'. When Swift came to write *Gulliver's Travels*, he had the advantage of knowing his forerunners in the tradition quite as well as the text of Lucian itself. He also read and enjoyed the works of Tom Brown, the man behind the greater part of the 'Dryden' Lucian and himself a writer of 'Dialogues of the Dead' in the Lucianic manner. *Gulliver*, therefore, cannot be seen in isolated comparison with a classical model; it draws together motifs and satirical techniques derived from intermediary works.[1]

The concrete evidence for Swift's knowledge of Lucian is sparse but convincing: an extended reference to *Dialogues of the Dead* 20 in the *Examiner* no. 21 (Thurs. 14 Dec.–Thurs. 21 Dec. 1710), a marginal note on his copy of Dr Gibbs's *The first fifteen Psalms of David*, in which Swift quotes sardonically from *Timon* (in the original) at the expense of the translation, and a reference in Letter XIII of the *Journal to Stella*, talking of buying her 'three little volumes of Lucian in French', almost certainly in the D'Ablancourt version. Direct borrowings within the text of *Gulliver* are just as sparse, at least in bks 1 and 2. The most interesting parallels at that level are between the key elements of the fictional plot—a visit to a land of pygmies which borders upon a land of giants, entertainment upon an island of magicians, and a long visit to an animal kingdom where the animals live in peace and prosperity under wise government, while savage and degenerate human beings live nearby and are subject to the rule of the animals—and the continuation of *A True Story* done by D'Ablancourt's nephew and published together with the translation. The similarity with the general structure of the adventures in *Gulliver* is clear. Only when we come to Laputa, in bk. 3, does Swift borrow significantly from Lucian himself. Just as the traveller of *A True Story* finds himself whirled into the air and deposited upon 'a great land in the sky, like a shining island', so Gulliver is taken aboard an 'Island in the Air'. The inhabitants of Lucian's moon are engaged in a war with the inhabitants of the sun and are defeated by the enemy king's tactic in cutting off their sunbeams, thus reducing them to total darkness. Whenever the king of Laputa has difficulties with his subjects on earth, one of his ways of subduing them is

[1] Eddy, op. cit., 14–28 contains useful but sometimes inaccurate information on sources and analogues.

by keeping the Island hovering over such a town and the lands about it; whereby he can deprive them of the benefit of the sun and rain, and consequently afflict the inhabitants with dearth and diseases.

At the centre of Laputa is a huge chasm in which are stored the vast range of optical instruments with which the astronomers of the island spend most of their time observing the surrounding universe. While, in a well in the royal precincts on Lucian's moon, a man can look into a looking-glass and see 'every city and every race just as if he were right on top of them'. Finally, both travellers, returning gently to the familiar surface of the earth, express their relief. 'I felt some little satisfaction in finding myself on firm ground,' observes Gulliver. 'When we touched down on the water, we were incredibly pleased and carried away with delight,' says Lucian's traveller.

The borrowing of motifs in bk. 3 is not confined to Laputa. Glubbdubdrib and Gulliver's visit to the spirits of the dead is based on the trip to the isles of the blessed in *A True Story II*. 5f. Swift follows the tradition that the place shall be 'extreamly fruitful', and in his choice of spirits he imitates Lucian on many points. Alexander and Hannibal are there (cf. *A True Story II*. 9). So is Homer, along with the old joke about confronting him with his Alexandrian commentators. As for philosophers, moderns such as Descartes and Gassendi have simply been substituted for ancients such as Aristippus and Epicurus. The tone of the Swiftian account is different in that it is markedly satirical, attacking the political and moral decline of contemporary England through the conventions of the dialogue of the dead. But that is not unLucianic; it merely represents the contemporary view of the purpose of that particular Lucianic form (cf. below pp. 144–63).

If this were the extent of the parallels between Swift and Lucian, one would be excused for finding a high degree of exaggeration in the comment of Booth in Fielding's *Amelia* (bk. 8, ch. 5): 'There is one whom I am convinced he studied above all others . . . Lucian.' Similar echoes from Rabelais and Cyrano are, after all, more frequent in *Gulliver*, and the verbal resemblances more noticeable. But bk. 3 is important because its parallels with Lucian are as much conceptual as based on mere motif-borrowing. In the first place, the extended parody of the Royal Society, its academic preoccupations, and the form of its learned papers, has a function equivalent to that of the parody of the lying historians on which *A True Story* relies. Secondly, the choice of scientists as target creates a significant parallel between the Laputans and the cosmological philosophers who are the satirical butt of *Icaro-*

menippus and *Menippus*. Swift's mathematicians and astronomers have interests that are so entirely abstract that they have come to ignore the evidence of the senses, which leads in turn to their being very bad reasoners. They have turned learning into ignorance, just as Menippus' philosophers arrive nowhere, because they have detached themselves from any sort of empiricism by their airy metaphysics and speculative scientific systems.

If we put Laputa back into the context of the other three books of *Gulliver*, we can see that this more fundamental parallel with Lucian is part of an overall vision which is itself essentially Lucianic. The satiric basis of the first two voyages, to Lilliput and Brobdingnag, relies on the notion of relative size. Man, in the form of Gulliver, is placed violently out of proportion to his environment, in order to focus our critical attention upon aspects of him that are normally taken for granted. This is, of course, a stock technique of a number of Lucianic dialogues, notably *Charon* and *Icaromenippus*. The king of Brobdingnag expresses the idea in precise terms:

> ... he observed, how contemptible a thing was human grandeur, which could be mimicked by such diminutive insects as I. And yet, said he, I dare engage those creatures have their titles and distinctions of honour; they contrive little nests and burrows that they call houses and cities; they make a figure in dress and equipage; they love, they fight, they dispute, they cheat, they betray.

Just so does Menippus see the world as a vast ant-hill (*Icaromenippus* 20), and describes 'men committing adultery, murdering, conspiring, plundering, perjuring, fearing, and being betrayed by those closest to them'. The difference does not lie in the moral stance, nor in the form of the image that expresses it, but in the response of the character in whose mouth the criticism is placed. Menippus laughs; the king of Brobdingnag condemns:

> I cannot but conclude the bulk of your natives to be the most pernicious race of little odious vermin that nature ever suffered to crawl upon the surface of the earth.

The parallel between the king of Brobdingnag and Menippus can be extended to include a general parallel between the Brobdingnagians and Lucian's *eirōn*s in so far as they do not only reject human pretensions and criticize human conduct, but despise theoretical speculation. 'As to ideas, entities, abstraction and transcendentals (says Gulliver) I could never drive the least conception into their heads.' And again, whereas in Lucian the positive implications of this are barely developed, Swift makes a much more serious moral statement by having the people of Brobdingnag use their intellectual faculties on a practical level to improve human conditions.

Despite the differences, the first three voyages of *Gulliver* can reasonably be seen as falling into Lucianic modes of thought, though deepened and made much more complex by the modern political and scientific circumstances from which they derive. Much the same can be said of the purely literary devices that Swift uses. The affectation of precision and the use of parody are obvious examples, but more important, perhaps, is the blend of invective and irony with which the criticism of mankind is delivered. This is particularly evident in the second voyage. At one level Swift works through invective, as in the example of the king of Brobdingnag's comments on 'little odious vermin' just cited. But to vary the effect, and deepen the satire on man's egoism, in ch. 7 Gulliver is made unwittingly to play the role of self-denouncer, like the 'professor' of public speaking in the dialogue of that name and the Cynic philosopher of *Philosophers for Sale*. Gulliver's enthusiastic account of the glories of his own civilization damns it, while his criticism of Brobdingnag points its virtues. As in most Lucianic inversions, the correct standard of values is quite plain. When one has heard the King deplore Gulliver's account of gunpowder and Gulliver reprove the King's refusal to be privy to the secret of its making, there is little likelihood of mistaking Swift's position vis-à-vis Gulliver's further criticism of the absence of the science of politics from Brobdingnag and the excessive simplicity of its legal system. What one is describing here is Lucianic. It is, of course, impossible to say that Swift consciously derived it from Lucian himself. The balancing of invective and the ingénu who condemns his own position is already to be found in Cyrano. Yet what Fielding and others saw as Lucianic in *Gulliver* (and other Swiftian works) becomes clear: a little direct borrowing, certain attitudes of mind, the art of manipulating a particular range of satirical devices. Add to this Swift's awareness of all the 'modern' Lucianic works in the same genre, and it is easy to see his satire as wholly Lucianic in the sense in which the eighteenth century would have used that term.

The development of the 'fantastic voyage' as a Lucianic genre was not quite complete with Swift. The final word must go to a near-contemporary work by the Danish litterateur Ludvig Holberg, *Niels*

Klim's Subterranean Journey, originally published in Latin in 1741. For all Holberg's substantial knowledge of the Classics as revealed in his epistolary essays and *Moral Reflections*, one would be tempted to see *Niels Klim* as deriving exclusively from post-Lucianic sources, notably Swift, were it not for Holberg's acknowledgment in his *Memoirs* of his general debt to the Greek author, an acknowledgment couched indeed simply as a rebuttal of too close an identification between Lucian's brand of satire and Holberg's own:

> It has been generally believed that, as I have imitated Lucian in my writings, I have imbibed a good deal of Lucian's spirit, and that I am equally indifferent with regard to religious subjects. In this respect I have shared the fate of all who have the courage to oppose credulity; but though I applaud and imitate that philosopher when he makes war upon superstition, I detest and abhor him when he attacks true piety.[1]

This passage of the *Memoirs* was written some time before 1728, and actually refers to works written before *Niels Klim*. The numerous references to, and quotations from, Lucian in the *Epistler*, short essays on diverse topics cast in the Senecan mould of letters, show that the same interest in Lucian and the same attitude towards his work appertained in Holberg's last writings (1748–53). *Niels Klim*, written on the author's own admission some years before its publication, sits squarely between these points in time. Even in theory there would be no reason to suppose it less Lucianic than his other works.

Where, then, can we look for its Lucianic features? In the prefatory essay to his *Moral Reflections* (1744) Holberg said of *Niels Klim*, together with his Latin epigrams, that they were 'full of moral paradoxes, as in them I have undertaken to refute common misapprehensions so as to distinguish the reality of virtue and vice from their appearance'. Earlier in the same piece, when talking of imaginary voyages as such, he observes:

> Some of the 'travellers' tales' are of the same ilk as Lucian's, which are merely a piece of fun. The fictitious voyages written in our time by the famous English doctor Swift are a mixture of entertainment and instruction, though so constructed that the first always predominates. In *Klim's Subterranean Journey* both aspects are also present, but more particularly the latter.

[1] L. Holberg, *Memoirs: an eighteenth-century Danish contribution to international understanding*, trans. and ed. S. E. Fraser, Leiden 1970, 151. (Other quotations from Holberg are in my own translation.)

Taking these statements together, it would seem likely that Holberg's work, though it might owe something to the humorous aspect of *A True Story*, *Icaromenippus* and perhaps the underworld voyage of *Menippus*, will be Lucianic, if at all, on the independent plain of satirical method, an influence which would at the same time have to be disentangled from that of Swift.

In practice there are more parallels of material between Lucian and Holberg than one would have supposed. Some are of a general kind and merely supplement other known sources. Klim arrives in the subterranean world—a whole new miniature universe complete with solar system—by descending into a cave, like Menippus entering Hades, and leaves via a cleft into the same cave. Other parallels are points of substantial detail. In exploring the various provinces of the planet Nazar, on to which he eventually descends, Klim meets, in the words of the *Memoirs*, 'with a number of surprising adventures, calculated to astonish and delight the reader. Many wonderful creatures, such as nobody ever imagined before, are suffered to be the inhabitants of this new world; trees, for instance, are introduced endowed with the gift of speech, and musical instruments are here capable of philosophy or finance.' The reference to talking trees is an allusion to the citizens of Potu, the description of whose principality fills the whole of chs 2–8. The idea for these tree people Holberg takes from the vine-women of *A True Story I*. 8. Lucian's plants are female from the loins up, with branches growing out of their fingertips, and leaves, tendrils and grape clusters for hair. They cry out in pain when the voyagers try to pick their fruit. Their human characteristics extend to speech. They are also capable of sexual union with the sailors (with the typically Lucianic outcome that those attempting it are held fast by their erection, which grows in and takes root). The element of absurdity and bawdiness is present in Holberg's version, though in a more muted form. Klim, fleeing from a bull, climbs a tree, only to find it is the wife of an important Potuan citizen, and that he is put under arrest for attempted rape. The physical characteristics of the trees are closely modelled on the Greek text. The trees communicate: '. . . they uttered murmuring sounds, properly articulated indeed but which sounded strange to my ears.' They have branches that function like arms, with buds for fingers. They have heads 'not unlike human ones' placed at the top of their trunks. What in Lucian merely provides a lewd comic incident has been worked up by Holberg into a central motif, but the source is still clear.

As well as parallels of motif, there are thematic similarities. In the course of describing the customs of the arboreal people, Holberg uses such familar notions as the rejection of elaborate funeral rites (ch. 3) as in *On Funerals*, and the scorning of sacrifices and similar cult excesses (ch. 5) as in *On Sacrifices*. The most extended treatment of a Lucianic theme is the attack on philosophers in ch. 9. Klim has left Potu to explore other regions of the planet. He arrives in Mascattia, land of the philosophers. At the very opening of the episode, we meet a familiar idea. Enquiring as to the reason for the abominable state of the road, Klim is told that the inhabitants cannot find the time to deal with these little practical matters, for they are too busy with things celestial. The satire of pointless speculation is extended by another familiar trait, quarrelsomeness and readiness to resort to physical violence. Klim reacts angrily against an absent-minded philosopher who urinates against him. Before long enraged reinforcements arrive and a full-scale battle gets underway, in which no pleading on Klim's part can obtain mercy from his 'philosophical' attackers:

I learnt that no anger is stronger than the philosophical variety, and that the commentators on morality are a long way from practising it.

The gap between the theory and practice of philosophy is, as in numerous Lucian dialogues, perfectly illustrated.

Though these thematic parallels are interesting, they are hardly conclusive. The same attitudes to death and funerals occur in both More and Cyrano. The picture of Mascattia is as close to Swift's Laputa as to the world of *The Eunuch* or *The Banquet*. The same problem poses itself when we try to trace analogies of style. Holberg makes Klim an unaware commentator, convinced of the superior virtues of European manners, just as Gulliver is in Brobdingnag. It becomes unrealistic to sort out the influence of different levels of the tradition on elements such as Klim's encomium of the dubious virtues of the legal system to the unimpressed Potuan prince. A particularly elaborate example of the technique is Klim's 'critical' rejection of the social structure of Cocklecu, where men perform women's tasks and have much of their sexual rôle. He describes with amazement and disgust a society in which the inadequacy of the relationship between the sexes in eighteenth-century Europe is pointed up by the simple exchange of characteristics. Finally, the irony of unconscious self-condemnation slips over into invective, keeping the reader aware of true values, just as Lucian does in *A Professor of Public Speaking:*

O thrice, nay four times blessed is our Europe, above all France and Great Britain, where the submissive sex corresponds to its name, where women blindly yield to man's rule and whim, so that they seem more like machines or puppets than substances endowed with free will.

Not even the Cynic of *Philosophers for Sale* condemns himself more clearly. But again the manner is totally Swiftian.

Holberg, in fact, represents the point at which the various strands of the imaginary voyage tradition that owe something to Lucian have become totally fused. In his preference for pure fantasy over the semi-realism of *Gulliver*, he returns to Lucian. In his clear moral stand and his use of sustained, sometimes complex, irony, he is recognizably following Cyrano and Swift. And he has something uniquely his own to add, too, in the choice of a single voyage structure with a cumulative moral point. Klim is not only the observer of worlds whose characteristics are a comment upon reality; he also becomes a man of vast power in this new domain, until the natural faults of ordinary men assert themselves, and he is expelled from the fantastic universe, and back into reality. Holberg's satire demonstrates that, although perhaps the fantastic voyage could have evolved as a genre without reference to Lucian, there is a clear Lucianic branch of it which develops in the sixteenth, seventeenth and early eighteenth centuries, each author drawing both upon the manner and the matter of the Greek and upon his own predecessors' absorption of it.

iv. *Dialogues of the dead*

The last of the major Lucianic genres to establish itself was the dialogue of the dead.[1] Although popular in Byzantium and to a lesser extent in Italy, the sixteenth-century examples are relatively rare. In the early decades of the seventeenth century, they were rarer still; but the situation was suddenly reversed in both France and England in the second half of the century, the outpouring of dialogues growing to epidemic proportions in the period 1680–1780, only to fall away again after that. In Germany, where the development of the genre was very much influenced initially by its manifestations in France, the graph

---

[1] General information on this topic is to be found in B. Boyce, 'News from Hell: satiric communications with the Nether World in English writing of the seventeenth and eighteenth centuries', *PMLA* 58 (1943) 402–37, and J. Egilsrud, *Le 'Dialogue des morts' dans les littératures française, allemande et anglaise 1644–1789*, Paris 1934. L. Schenck, *Lukian und die französische Literatur* . . . (1931) also carries relevant material.

starts its curve a little later, *c.* 1690, and tails off at the beginning of the nineteenth century.

It is difficult to account convincingly for the short, rapid but very successful career of this very limited literary form. Attempts to demonstrate that the predominance of the rationalist spirit in France or the instability of political life in England in the late seventeenth century were phenomena parallel to the age in which Lucian himself wrote are undermined by the inaccuracy of the view of second-century life and letters on which they are based. It is rather easier to account for the decline of the genre. Its form was quite unsuited to the metaphysical and emotional interests which became dominant in European literature in the period 1780–1820. Its disappearance as a vehicle of journalistic satire, though more problematic, doubtless stems from the mere question of fashion to which that sort of ephemera is subject.

If the tenor of the times is not a safe cause to attribute to so much new activity in Elysium, the appearance of popular translations of Lucian's work as a whole does account for some of the stimulus. The D'Ablancourt translation (1654) and its offshoot in England the so-called Dryden Lucian (published 1711) both predate the bulk of really literary imitations in their respective countries, and the modernization of Lucian which they attempt certainly facilitates the updating of the dialogue of the dead conventions to include the manners and even the characters of more recent times. As the genre gained in popularity, the connexion with Lucian himself became slighter, even in writers purporting to be imitating the original. Fontenelle acknowledged his debt to the D'Ablancourt translation, itself very much an interpretation to fit the tastes of the age. Voltaire knew his Fontenelle as well as his Lucian, and likewise Lord Lyttelton his Fénelon. For the majority of anonymous Grub-street writers, both the form and the Lucianic label were only convenient accessories to give literary status to types of satire that were already in vogue. In consequence, dialogues of the dead came to conceal a range of sub-genres quite diverse in content, manner and purpose.

In the first sub-genre the form was used as a vehicle for satire on particular people and controversial topics of the day. In France, Boileau's *Les Héros du roman* (written *c.* 1665) made fun of the *précieux* novel; in England William King's *Dialogues of the Dead* (1699) ridiculed the manners and theories of the classical scholar, Richard Bentley, *à propos* of the controversy over the so-called epistles of Phalaris. Fontenelle used some of his dialogues (1683–4) as preliminary shots in the skirmish of the *Querelle des anciens et modernes,* as did Tom Brown in his *Letters from the Dead to the Living* (1702). Brown's collection, whose success finally persuaded his publisher Briscoe to issue the Dryden Lucian (ready *c.* 1693 but postponed for financial reasons), is in fact a microcosm of the type of themes current in both England and France; they include satire on religious extremists, on individuals (Bentley again), and on fashionable pursuits such as astrology, together with portraits of the London of the day.

Quite different in kind are the dialogues whose principal intention is the discussion of abstract ideas. Fénelon's *Dialogues des morts* (1712) were part of his educational programme, designed to inculcate a moderately progressive morality in the heir to the throne, with whose instruction he had been charged. This line of development led two ways. From it derives the respectable, rather platitudinous moralizing represented by Lord Lyttelton's dialogues (1760). But it also has something in common, in purpose if not in style, with the various political dialogues which appeared in the period 1700–60, mostly published abroad, and, for reasons of discretion, anonymous. Typical examples here would be the dialogues included by Emmerich de Vattel in his *Poliergie* (1757) on such themes as justice and sovereignty. In Germany Fassmann's immensely popular periodical *Gespräche in dem Reiche der Todten* contrived to combine instruction with the ephemeral. A similar monthly magazine had been issued by Thomasius in 1683, with the intention of giving the reader instruction in history and politics on a largely anecdotal level. Fassmann's journal, which ran from 1718 to 1739, adhered to the same formula, adding to it a mixture of moral platitude and scandalous detail. The success of this publication encouraged the proliferation of others like it, and also of the extension of the use of the form to purely occasional interests— obituary eulogies and accounts of sensational events—which had nothing to do with the educational purpose of the tradition they derived from.

Thirdly, and perhaps most important, there were the dialogues of the rationalist tradition, launched by Fontenelle. *Libertin* circles had shown some interest in Lucian even on a serious plane; François de la Mothe le Vayer's *Jugements sur les anciens et principaux historiens grecs et latins* (1646) contains material modelled on Lucian's *How to Write History.* But Fontenelle was the first writer of like persuasion to use the dialogue of the dead for a sustained critical purpose, cutting down to size contemporary pretensions about politics, religion and various forms of intellectual activity. His major successors here were Voltaire and, in Germany, Wieland, although minor imitations were numerous, for example, J-F. Demachy's *Nouveaux dialogues des morts* (1755). At the same time, Fontenelle's dialogues belong very firmly to a style of salon literature that was quite as flourishing in the eighteenth century as in his own day. It is to this aspect of his work that belong C-E. Pesselier's *Nouveaux dialogues des morts* (1753) and the whole psychological analysis aspect of Demachy's work. This trend reached its peak in the dialogues of Vauvenargues (*c.* 1745–7). Not published until long after the writer's death, these show how the form has become an animated psychological maxim. The sense of underworld environment is reduced to one reference to 'Ombre illustre' in no. 15, all element of satire is absent, and the characters—mostly figures from seventeenth-century France—embody the tensions between reason and emotion which one would expect from the author of the *Réflexions et maximes*.

This brief account gives some idea of the range which the genre attained, but not of the variations of form to which it was subject. Many of these are of no interest for our purposes because, like that of Fassmann's anecdotal compendia, their form in no way derives directly from Lucian. Equally, the minor literary figures tended to take their form directly from Fontenelle, rather than develop it individually. Let us look in turn at each of the major writers who were certainly directly acquainted with Lucian, if only via translation, and compose, from a view of their work, a picture of the variety of guises under which dialogues of the dead were presented.

The closest work in form and spirit is Boileau's *Les Héros du roman. Dialogue à la manière de Lucien*. Pluto has heard that gallantry, and the absurdities of language associated with it, has affected all the in-habitants of the underworld, even the heroes in Elysium. He is telling Minos of how he has sent for the most famous of the heroes, when Rhadamanthus arrives with news of an uprising against Pluto's admin-istration. Steps are taken, but the arrival of the heroes becomes a matter of greater urgency. However, Diogenes the Cynic appears, casting doubt upon the usefulness of the expected warriors. The bulk of the dialogue then consists in the advent of a succession of famous figures, largely classical in origin but figuring in contemporary works too: Cyrus, Tomyris queen of the Massagetae, Horatius Cocles, Clélie, Lucrèce, Brutus, Sappho, Astarte, Ostorius. With them are two mediaeval characters, Joan of Arc and Pharamond king of the Franks. Each proves to have degenerated into nothing more than a gallant lover. Eventually Pluto's mounting fury and despair are assuaged by Mercury, who brings news not only that the arrival of Jupiter's artillery has put an end to the uprising, but that the so-called heroes are impostors. He introduces the shade of a newly deceased Frenchman (in an earlier version the satirical novelist Scarron) who identifies the sighing lovers as his neighbours: 'Ce sont tous la plupart des bourgeois de mon quartier. Bonjour, monsieur Brutus. Bonjour, madame Lucrèce.' Pluto orders them off to a fitting fate, and the dialogue closes with the off-stage approach of the real heroes and Pluto's retiring to sleep off the fatigue brought upon him by the sentimental excesses of the usurpers.

The piece is plainly Lucianic in its setting and situation. In ways that can easily be paralleled from some of the *Dialogues of the Dead*, Boileau pays attention to the dramatic illusion gained from the manipulation of exit and entrance and the suggestion of decor. Even the sense of physical progression through a world is there:

(Pluto)   ... But first of all, Minos, let you and me go through into this salon which, as I told you, I have had prepared ... and where I have instructed that our seats should be placed, with a hand-rail to divide us off from the rest of the gathering. Let us go in. Ah, splendid. Everything has been arranged just as I wanted it. Follow us, Diogenes ...

Pluto, Minos, Rhadamanthus all exercise appropriate rôles. Diogenes is given the function of ironic observer which he shares with Menippus and Cyniscus in the *Dialogues of the Dead*. Boileau also throws in borrowed motifs as extras: for example, the reference to a notorious miser, newly deceased, who considers a second death rather than part with his obol for Charon, although it concerns a historical person, also offers a variation on the theme of the obol-less traveller in *Dialogues of the Dead* 2 and *The Downward Journey* 19. But the overall effect is not so much that of a Lucianic dialogue of the dead as a piece in his more burlesque manner. The underworld deities are given the chatty diction and uncertain temper of Lucian's Olympians. The review technique of seeing each character in turn is on the pattern of the succession of philosophers in *Philosophers for Sale;* as there, each character reveals his own absurdity, typical doctrines being replaced by typical actions and accoutrements. Indeed, Boileau emphasizes the fact of self-revelation by having Pluto ridicule Diogenes' account of each hero, only to be confounded by the reality that follows. Above all, great use is made of literary satire. Quotation, misquotation and cento all abound, as they do in *Zeus Rants*, with the centos toppling over into parody as Joan of Arc expresses her loyalty to Pluto in a series of awful lines jigsawed together from Chapelain's *La Pucelle*. Each character is precisely modelled, down to the style of speech, on his or her equivalent in a popular novelist or playwright, La Calprenède, Mlle de Scudéry, Quinault, the abbé de Pure etc. And at the same time as the characters betray their creators, Diogenes makes direct or indirect fun of both character and creator in his commentaries to Pluto. The major difference between what Boileau is doing and the literary games of Lucianic burlesque is only one of intention. The former is expressing his disapproval of the sentimental excesses of a certain contemporary literature, mainly the novel: as he defined it himself in the *Discours* written to accompany the first official edition (1710):

. . . as the satirical spirit was beginning to get a hold over me, I could not rest until I had composed a dialogue after the manner of Lucian ridiculing these novels. In it I attacked not only their triviality, but also the affectation of their language, their vague and frivolous conversations, the liberal admixture of flattering portraits of people who were either of very average good looks or sometimes exceedingly ugly, and all that endless verbiage about love.

Lucian, on the other hand, even in the evident parody of *How to Write History*, has a less clearly defined didactic purpose, if didactic at all. He seeks purely to amuse and to dazzle. In most of his work what counts is the skill with which literary borrowings, usually from a much earlier period, are reworked. This difference noted, the effect of Boileau's burlesque is surprisingly similar to that of his model.

At the opposite end of the spectrum of imitation, Fénelon's dialogues owe their resemblance to Lucian far more to a shared store of moral clichés than to form or literary manner. The very title, *Dialogues des morts composés pour l'éducation de Mgr. le Duc de Bourgogne*, and the good bishop's position as preceptor to the heir to the throne, give a clue to the difference in intention behind the composition of the material. Fénelon's educational works stress the need to approach the moral via the entertaining. The adoption of the Lucianic genre, severely shorn of most of its frivolous (and characteristic) features is his concession to entertainment. The nearest to a direct imitation is the dialogue *Alexandre et Diogène*, which reproduces a situation used by Lucian in *Dialogues of the Dead* 13. The opening is more or less the same:

(Fénelon)	(Lucian)
D. Isn't it Alexander I see here among the dead?	D. What's this, Alexander? Have you died too, like all the rest of us?
A. You are not mistaken, Diogenes.	A. You can see I have, Diogenes.
D. What! Can gods die?	It's not strange for me to have
A. Gods cannot, but men of mere mortal flesh do.	died, given that I was human.

Lucian goes on to make play with the picturesque argument about whether Philip or the god Ammon had been Alexander's father. This is eliminated in Fénelon in order to put greater stress on the general point about human mortality. Otherwise the sentiment is the same. The other major ideas in Fénelon's piece also are mentioned in one or the other of the first two *Dialogues of the Dead* that feature Alexander. The tradition that Alexander consciously manipulated the oracle that he was son of Ammon so as to increase his power is drawn from the opening of *Dialogues of the Dead* 12; the importance of flattery to Alexander is part of Diogenes' mockery of him in *Dialogues of the Dead* 13. Yet neither dialogue is so consistently turned to a single moral message, the pernicious power of flattery upon princes. And the rôle given to Diogenes by Fénelon is notably more muted in its language, less ironic in tone, than the Greek model.

Aside from this piece the dialogues are at their closest to their model in the three Romulus dialogues. In *Romulus et Rémus* the general theme is the transience of power. Remus greets his brother with the admonition:

Well, here you are, my brother, in the same condition as I; it was not worth the trouble of having me killed. The few years you held the throne alone are over, leaving no trace behind. You would have had a smoother time of it if you had lived in peace and shared the cares of government with me.

The concept of the equality of men before death is fundamental to the Lucianic Hades, and so too is that of the vanity of kingship, though the nuance here, that greatness attained through crime cannot be the basis for lasting honour, is one not found in the Greek writer. The same dialogue also contains an example of the motif-borrowing that Fénelon occasionally permits himself. Remus concludes: 'How it is you have come down here? You were said to be immortal.' To which his brother cynically returns that the Romans were stupid enough to think so. It is, again, the theme of Alexander's divinity gainsaid by his death, with which Lucian begins *Dialogues of the Dead* 13. The presentation of the interchange through two characters with equal narrative status is an unusual one in Lucian, though the dialogue between Philip and Alexander would be an example. Even there, Philip merely ridicules his son, whereas Remus denounces Romulus. Philip shows Alexander the triviality of his actions, and the unsound basis of his reputation, in order to undermine his pride. Remus reproaches his brother with well-balanced maxims, of which the two most important are: 'To be more just and virtuous would have been compensation enough for the loss of power' and 'Before one can become a great man, one must be a gentleman'. Fénelon's manner is accordingly less reductive.

In *Romulus et Tatius*, the notion of two villains questioning one another about their downfalls follows the pattern used in some of Lucian's legacy-hunting dialogues. Tatius' ridicule of Romulus' military and political achievements is like Philip's ridicule of Alexander's. And the idea that crime in pursuit of power or pleasure breeds further crime occurs in *Charon* and *The Downward Journey*. Once we turn to *Romulus et Numa Pompilius*, however, we get a clearer picture of how far the dialogue form of Fénelon avoids a satirical manner. Here there is a degree of straightforward conversation between the participants quite foreign to Lucian. There is no Philip, let alone a Diogenes, to undermine the pretensions of the villain. The vanity of Romulus' career is simply revealed implicitly by the contrast with Numa's peaceful and wise reign. When a borrowed motif, such as that of illusory divinity (again), is developed at some length—'I had heard you had joined the gods . . . how then do you come to be here?'— it is less exploited for its reductive value than as a peg for more maxims —'Men like to be deceived; flattery is a balm for great woes'. We have left the world of Lucian for that of Plutarch.

The dialogues of Fénelon do not all lack charm. The conversations between Parrhasius and Poussin, and Leonardo da Vinci and Poussin, are pleasantly instructive on the art of painting. Nor do they lack for variety. Some of them are not dialogues of the dead, in the technical sense of dialogues conducted in the underworld, at all. *Charles Quint et un jeune moine de Saint-Just* is simply a conversation piece on true religious inspiration; *Harpagon et Dorante* is a literary jeu d'esprit on the subject of avarice. In general, Fénelon does not consistently exploit the trappings of the Lucianic Hades, or the dramatic conventions of the more theatrical dialogues, or the reductive satirical method of the static ones. Perhaps the key to this ambiguous relationship, in which he has borrowed as little as he decently can without totally losing contact with his model, is to be found in the dialogue *Hérodote et Lucien*. Herodotus reproaches Lucian with his mockery of religion and philosophy. Lucian defends himself on the grounds that the contemporary religion was unworthy of respect. Herodotus further accuses him of mockery for mockery's sake. To Lucian's defence that he attacked vice, the abuse of power and excessive devotion to material pleasure, he rejoins:

It is true that you have spoken well of virtue, but you did it in order to attack the vices of the whole human race: it was a taste for satire you revealed, rather than a firm philosophy. Even virtue you praised without any desire to get back to the basic religious and philosophical principles which are its true foundation.

The dialogue shows a close enough acquaintance with the text of Lucian, read as a moralist manqué. Fénelon clearly approves of much of the matter, but has reservations about much of the manner. His own dialogues accordingly follow Lucian's at a consciously maintained distance. In them, the element of entertainment, though essential, had to be secondary to the element of positive instruction. They were to be not merely illustrations of moral maxims, but illustrations, for the benefit of the future ruler, of the shortcomings of the great men of the past. The format of the dialogue allows him to stage these great men without reference to the prejudices and questions of interest which weighed heavily with them when alive, and also to attribute to them a liberty of self-revelation incompatible with their historical existence. The result is, on a simplified level, an anatomy of power and its corruption, in which the irreverence of the satirist could have had very little place.

If Boileau and Fénelon represent opposing poles of the new tradition of dialogues of the dead, Fontenelle is at its centre. Whereas the other two found few followers, Fontenelle's work was the fountainhead of a great stream of imitations, in England and Germany just as much as in France. In Fontenelle's case our comparison with his model is much facilitated by the very explicit statements of the 'Epître à Lucien' that served as his preface. There he states that he has deliberately suppressed the underworld paraphernalia: 'I have done away with Pluto, Charon, Cerberus and all the worn-out trappings of Hades.' He regrets the areas of moral maxim into which he feels he cannot justifiably follow the master:

How vexed I am that you have exhausted so many fine topics: equality in death, the regret the dead feel for life, the mask of courage which philosophers adopt in dying, the absurd misfortune of youngsters outlived by the very old men whose heirs they expected to be and whose favour they courted! But after all, since the literary format was your invention, it was reasonable enough that you should reserve its finest possibilities for yourself.

Then he turns to what is positive in his own imitation. He has, he says, at least tried to imitate Lucian's aim in writing dialogues:

All your dialogues contain a moral, and I have given all the dead in my dialogues a moral to propound; otherwise there would have been no point in setting them to speak—live characters would have done perfectly well to express trivia.

In practice the moral purpose of Fontenelle's dialogues is often as difficult to find as that of many of Lucian's. There is, however, a clear intellectual purpose, which is to undermine accepted standards of knowledge, religion, and to a lesser extent social order. Such a purpose it would be possible, too, to base upon a certain way of reading Lucian. For example, the dialogue between Aristotle and Anacreon attacks the scientific pretensions of philosophy in exactly the same terms as they are ridiculed in *Icaromenippus*, coming to the conclusion that the only significant form of philosophy is ethics, and that ethics are better practised than preached. It is the common-sense 'message' of the presentation of philosophy in works such as *Menippus*, *Icaromenippus* and *Hermotimus*. The dialogue between Homer and Aesop similarly presents ancient religion as a series of poetic fictions, as Lucian does in *Zeus Catechized* and *Zeus Rants*, in such a way as to attack revealed religion per se. Fontenelle's use of Aesop as interlocutor is designed merely to set up the final *bon mot*:

Men like the gods to be as crazy as themselves, but they do not like animals to be as clever.

Man accepts, and prefers, the gods in his own image. But a fable that raises animals to human status remains merely a fable. It is an extension of the attack on man's selective credulity as portrayed in *On Sacrifices*, or (read in a serious sense) in the *Dialogues of the Gods*.

Parallels of general morality entrain parallels of particular motifs. Anacreon's definition of the hypocrisy of philosophers introduces the themes of venality and quarrelsomeness which are basic to the philosopher-type portrayed in *The Dead Come to Life*, *The Banquet*, *The*

Eunuch et al. Similarly, the introduction of figures whom Lucian uses, such as Alexander and Aristotle, permits the borrowing of traditional reproaches against them—that Alexander owed his glory to the actions of his soldiers, that Aristotle was a prey to ambition and greed. Sometimes the motif is introduced in a way incidental to the context, as with the absurdity of burial monuments (*Dialogues of the Dead* 29) to which Phryne refers in her dialogue with Alexander: '. . . all outstanding people, whatever their trade, have an obsession with monuments and inscriptions.' The Lucianic influence is less obvious when it comes to the element of *galanterie* which entirely takes over certain dialogues—'Sappho et Laure' for example, or 'Callirhée et Pauline'— or substantially controls the direction of others such as 'Hélène et Fulvie', where the idea that great events are bred by chance out of small details (shades of Scribe and Second Empire costume drama!) is illustrated in terms of beautiful and ugly wives and their control over their husbands. In fact, even the *galanterie* is not entirely without connexion with Fontenelle's model, if we remember that he almost certainly read him in D'Ablancourt's translation, whose salient characteristic was precisely its rendering of the classical world into the manners and even the ideas of the seventeenth-century French upper classes.

This much said, there is still a whole world of difference between the literary structure of the Fontenelle dialogues and those of Lucian. In the first place, there is the insistence on paradox as a tool of moral instruction. As the 'Avertissement' to the third edition puts it:

. . . the charm of a dialogue (if it has any) lies entirely in the bizarreness of this combination; it is a way of stimulating one's awareness of relationships which one might otherwise not have perceived and which always lead to a moral point.

So, we are offered the proposition that Phryne's activities as courtesan were more significant than Alexander the Great's because she caused the walls of Thebes to be rebuilt, whereas he merely had them knocked down: the proposition that there is more philosophy in the songs of Anacreon than in the *Ethics* of Aristotle: the proposition that one should die in a frivolous mood like Hadrian, rather than with gravity like Cato. Equally un-Lucianic is the insistence on the *bon mot* not just as a satirical weapon but also as a final thrust encapsulating, like the last line of a Parnassian sonnet, the full meaning of what has gone before. So Brutus concludes his conversation with Faustina on the well-turned paradox: 'Libertarian feelings gain strength from an admixture of spite.' The attack on the supremacy of reason, which occurs more often than any other single theme (with the possible exception of the rebuttal of the superiority of the ancient over the modern) is particularly likely to appear in epigrammatic form. 'Prejudice and reason are two sides of the same coin. What the one lacks, the other supplies,' says Raphael di Urbino to Strato; '. . . if there is any form of happiness for which reason is responsible, it is like the kind of "good" health which is entirely dependent on medicine—never strong or stable,' Mary Stuart observes to Rizzio.

The most important of the stylistic differences is that the balance oɪ dialogue between the two speakers is frequently even. Not only does Fontenelle ignore the type of dramatic presentation used in *Dialogues of the Dead* 20, and the progressive structure of *Dialogues of the Dead* 10, not only does he always limit his dialogues to two speakers (eight of the *Dialogues of the Dead* have three or more speakers), but he rarely uses one character exclusively to undermine the attitudes of the other, as Menippus and Diogenes are used by Lucian. Even in a dialogue such as *Dialogues of the Dead* 23, where the two speakers, Ajax and Agamemnon, carry the same potential weight, Lucian does not characterize Agamemnon at all, but uses him as a mouthpiece for probing the story of Ajax. Fontenelle prefers to set up a balance between the values represented by the two characters, either polarizing them, as with Milo and Smindirides, or drawing a paradoxical parallel, as with Alexander and Phryne. The comparison can be conducted throughout the interchange, as in the last-named example, or, as with Hadrian and Margaret of Austria, by constructing the piece in two sections, each dominated by one character. The nearest example to this in Lucian would be the contest for recognition as greatest general, in *Dialogues of the Dead* 25; but there the framework is that of a formal competition, with Minos as judge, and each speaker has the opportunity to denigrate his rivals. Fontenelle hardly resorts to reductive satire at all, for wherever the values of one character are implicitly or explicitly undermined, they are replaced by the values of the other.

Clearly Fontenelle creates a form of dialogue of the dead very different in kind from that of his model, yet regards it, as the *Epître* shows, as being essentially Lucianic. This prepares us for the dialogues of Voltaire, which seem to have even less to do with their model, but are still the fruits of a writer who acknowledges a debt to Lucian.

Though it cannot be claimed that dialogues of the dead play any substantial role in Voltaire's work, the one extant example, together with
the handful of pieces cast in that related form of ingénu satire in which
the dead visit and comment upon the living, does throw some light on
the eighteenth-century view of Lucian in general and his underworld
dialogues in particular. Voltaire's contemporaries thought the genre
appropriate enough to him to pass off as his Jean-Baptiste Suard's
Dialogue entre Periclès, un Grec moderne et un Russe (1763), in which
Pericles converses with the shades of two new arrivals in Hades. The
ostensible theme is the fate of nations at the hands of Time. Pericles is
astounded by a modern Greek, who is a slave and ignorant of the past
culture of his land. He is equally astounded by a Russian, descendant of
barbarian Scythians but a man of culture, who is as well-versed in the
classical past as the Greek is ignorant of it. The subject has its own inherent ironies, but it is developed for its philosophical implications,
and with more than a little attention to eulogizing Russia, a trait that
made the attribution to Voltaire all the more plausible, given that his
current patroness was Catherine the Great. However, Voltaire's own
underworld dialogue, *Conversation de Lucien, Erasme et Rabelais dans
les Champs Elysées,* is a more substantial affair. He uses Lucian to
interrogate Erasmus and Rabelais on the evils of their time. The core
of the work consists in a series of unflattering witticisms at the expense
of religious fanaticism, monks, cardinals and the pope. All of the satire
is equally applicable to religion in Voltaire's own day, and fits into the
general tone of his anti-Catholic satire in the 'Ecrasez l'infame' phase
(it was published in 1765). Yet in the course of the dialogue Voltaire
paints an unexpectedly modern picture of Lucian himself, for as well
as being termed 'mocker of all things', he is presented as a tilter at
windmills for the pure pleasure of tilting. Erasmus, observing a difference between the two of them, says:

There was an enormous difference between the absurdity of people in your
day and in mine. You were only dealing with gods who were 'sent up' in the
theatre, and with philosophers whose standing was even lower than that of
the gods; whereas I was surrounded by fanatics.

Lucian himself is made to emphasize the point later when he questions
how his companions had the courage to mock their master, when he
himself had been careful not to attack the Roman emperors, i.e. anyone
who mattered. Clearly it is not the moral applicability of the content to its
own world that was the essential of a Lucian dialogue in Voltaire's eyes.

The key to what Voltaire did see as Lucianic characteristics, and to the way in which he must have seen his own satire as Lucianic, can be found in one of the ingénu pieces, *Dialogue entre Marc-Aurèle et un recollet* (1751), and in a letter to Frederick the Great of Prussia, which accompanied the gift of the dialogue. Marcus Aurelius, returned to Rome, meets an ignorant and arrogant friar. Their conversation serves as an occasion for the friar to reveal the shortcomings of Catholicism, and for the emperor first to elicit this self-condemnatory account of the modern world, then to express his own (deist) philosophy. Little in this would draw us to a comparison with Lucian had not Voltaire written of it:

I have pleasure in sending Your Majesty this dialogue, *Marcus Aurelius*. I have tried to write it in the style of Lucian. Lucian is a straightforward chap, he gives his readers food for thought, and there is always a temptation to add a dialogue or two to his. He is not interested in wit. The trouble with Fontenelle is that he is not interested in anything else.

Voltaire, like Fontenelle, suppresses the machinery of the underworld, and does not particularly interest himself with the traditional themes of equality before death and the like. For him, Lucian is an entertainer, but one who makes his readers think. The comment on wit is harder to interpret, for in *Marc-Aurèle*, as in the *Conversation*, the barbed witticism is not absent. But the comparison with Fontenelle which follows, and which Voltaire extends into an interesting critique of his *Dialogues*, suggests that Lucian is not interested in the paradoxical wit, in the cleverness that Fontenelle adores. The Voltairean dialogues are, as I said, not of great importance in themselves but they do show how far the eighteenth century went in paring down the form of the dialogue of the dead that Fontenelle had used, while still claiming to be writing within a significantly Lucianic mode. Contrast, irony and the attack on unreason seems to be the full tally of the legacy here. But if Voltaire does not use the form for any of his major works, the reason does not lie in any inherent limitations of the genre as he envisaged it. It is simply, as he makes Erasmus say at the close of the *Conversation*, that:

The great pleasure in it is to show one's friends where they have taken the wrong path, but the dead never ask anyone the way.

The three *Gespräche im Elysium* of Christoph Martin Wieland (1780) provide an interesting contrast with the French dialogues at which we have been looking. It was hardly surprising that Wieland should venture into the genre, since he was probably the writer the most profoundly influenced by Lucian in the whole history of European literature.[1] Setting aside the remarkable translation of the complete works which was completed comparatively late in his life (1788–9) there is ample evidence for his interest in Lucian, an interest reflected in most of the works that postdate his 'conversion' in the mid-1750s to the critical spirit of the Enlightenment. Parallels with Lucianic motifs and techniques have been suggested for the novels *Sylvio* (1763) and *Agathon* (1764–5). There are certainly clear textual affinities to be found in the *Comische Erzählungen* of 1765, a volume of four verse tales containing 'Das Urteil des Paris', 'Endymion', 'Juno und Ganymed', 'Aurora und Cephalus'. The dedication to Das Urteil emphasizes the relationship, with its little pen-portrait of Lucian. The tale itself borrows closely from *The Judgment of the Goddesses*, 'Endymion' relates to *Dialogues of the Gods* 19, and the whole set, with their burlesque, intended to caricature society manners of the day in an amusing way without providing a substantial satire of its vices, relies on techniques of humour modelled on Lucian's Olympian pieces in general. In *Musarion* (1768), Wieland moved closer to the potentially serious side of Lucian, with a satire of the pretensions of philosophy, be it at its most rational or its most mystical. This greater seriousness of satire was later to reflect itself in the thirteen *Göttergespräche* (1790), which range over subjects from religion to the French Revolution. It also modulates into the positive affirmations about human nature represented first by the three *Gespräche im Elysium*, and later by the philosophical 'novel' *Peregrinus Proteus* (1791), a work not only stimulated by Lucian's *Peregrinus* but also cast entirely in the form of an extended dialogue with Lucian himself as one of the two speakers.

The three *Gespräche in Elysium* are unified in their view of life, but disparate in their style. The first uses the theme of the new arrival in Hades and of the old hand who interprets the environment of Elysium and its contrast with the world above. Wieland takes from *Dialogues of the Dead* 20 the motif of men shedding their physical characteristics (beauty, money) and, more important, their abstract vices (lust, pride), and makes the loss itself more dramatic and more symbolic. The newcomer, Diocles, cannot recognize Elysium in the world of twilight where he finds himself. He is also worried by a strange sensation of

[1] For a study of the wider influence of Lucian on Wieland, see J. Steinberger *Lucians Einfluss auf Wieland*, Göttingen 1902.

change which he is undergoing, of losing physically something that seems to fall from him like scales, or roll off in a cloud. He catches sight of another shade who proves to have been none other than Lucian himself in the upper world, and who explains to him that new arrivals have as yet insufficiently purified souls to perceive their environment properly. Diocles has undergone a rebirth, and his senses must adjust. Such drama as the ensuing conversation possesses derives from Diocles' growing fear of disintegration as each piece of knowledge that Lucian offers causes him to lose more of his scales, the delusions imposed upon him by man's self-conceit. For the first time a philosophical position is being proposed that could easily be derived from reading the *Dialogues of the Dead* in a serious sense. Early in the dialogue Diocles is made to espouse the same view of life in a phrase that could stand for the whole Cynic morality on which the *Dialogues of the Dead* are based:

If this is so, what a puppet show and shadow play of delusion and deception the thing that I called my life was!

For Wieland's Lucian, the worst of man's deceptions is in fact to suppose oneself other than a common man, since all men are but that. Worldly greatness is nothing. By contrast, Elysium is a place of perfect equality and calm, from which pleasure and pain, both the fruits of human illusion, are absent. In Elysium the souls have achieved perfect self-knowledge and perfect communion with each other:

In a word, there is nothing but complete frankness between us here, and that is the very reason why we are so happy.

The remainder of the dialogue is used simply for Lucian ruthlessly to reveal Diocles' remaining illusions about his political and personal motives in life. Only here is there anything approaching a sharp tone in the exchanges. The piece then closes on Lucian quietly advising Diocles to go on to a grotto where he may bathe away the remainder of his earthly taints.

In the first dialogue, then, Wieland has adapted both the general morality of the *Dialogues of the Dead* and a particular motif borrowed from *Dialogues of the Dead* 20. He has, however, forged these into a much more coherent metaphysical exposition than his model. What is more, he has imported, at least initially, a very lyrical tone quite alien from Lucian, as Diocles responds to his new environment:

Where are the pure crystalline streams? Where are the ever-green, flower-laden meadows that poets and sages promised me? Where is the sun that shines eternally, day and night?—There's nothing but twilight and more twilight!—and a calm so still, so very still, that I could hear the swaying of a lily rocking to and fro upon its stem. This literally is a 'land of shades'.

The centre of the piece has become a philosophical exposition from which both anecdote and humour are absent. Even the final reductive exchange is not satirical in form, but a dramatic clash of values. Wieland's reading of Lucian seems to have placed in the foreground elements normally thought ancillary. By developing these elements as the dialogue progresses, he has moved away from the spirit of his model even as his contemporaries might have seen it.

In the second dialogue, which is a continuation of the first, this move away becomes still more apparent. Yet curiously the ostensible subject of much of the piece is a Lucianic work, *Essays in Portraiture*, which Wieland was translating at the time. Diocles returns from his bathe and questions Lucian further on the contrast between the world and Elysium. The emphasis changes towards a discussion of how the shades can coexist without illusions, and from there, to the subject of Lucian's own enthusiasms, first for Diogenes, then for Panthea (the mistress of Lucius Verus and subject of the eulogy in *Essays in Portraiture*). The rest of the work, which includes the appearance of Panthea herself for a brief while, allows a deepening of the discussion of the nature of beauty, in which the distinction is made eventually between the true appreciation of beauty and the distortion imposed upon man by his carnal lust. The tone is so alien from the Greek model, that Wieland at one point makes Lucian admit that what he is saying will sound strange coming from him: '. . . imagine that it is Pythagoras or Plato speaking to you through me.' The whole dialogue is a philosophical interchange, without satire, humour or drama of any kind, in which the doctrines of perfect truth and true humanity are exemplified via the case of beauty and the corruption of man's instinct for beauty by his earthly desires. Lucian's *Essays in Portraiture* is used as the parallel example of how great writers have an instinctive perception of the ideal, an instinct which only artistic genius possesses, and which they express not in doctrine but in the act of creation.

If the second dialogue is not in any meaningful sense Lucianic, the third—which exemplifies the point about lust and beauty from the second—certainly is. Wieland here has *Dialogues of the Dead* 30, on the ephemerality of human beauty as exemplified by Nireus, in mind. Out of this motif he makes a much subtler point. Again a newcomer is introduced, this time another legendary beauty, Phaon, Sappho's male lover. The motif of vices that must be shed is several times referred to: 'The fellow is clearly a recent arrival, and has a lot to strip off.' Nireus, in a mysterious way which gradually becomes clear to the reader but not to Phaon, has 'kept' his beauty: Phaon has not. His consequent obsession with a sense of having lost his identity leads him to tell his own story, including his part in the death of Sappho. Everything in Phaon's behaviour reveals him as still the victim of the delusions which we saw Diocles losing in the first dialogue. Nireus' beauty clearly derives from his spiritual regeneration, Phaon's ugliness from the faults for which he has yet to atone. When Nireus finally leaves him in disgust, the same idea is expressed by the introduction of Sappho, who still sees Phaon as beautiful because she herself is not yet fully purified. But she has begun to see wisdom: 'What we called life up there was a puerile state of affairs.' She is explicit in a way the courteous Nireus was not. In a dramatic moment she highlights the paradox of the two types of beauty when, in concluding her catalogue of Phaon's charms she says: 'In a word, Phaon, you're so beautiful it makes me feel sick.' She goes on to explain that her punishment is to be courted every day of the week by a different young man as beautiful and silly as Phaon. Her condition would be worse than a place in Tartarus, were it not for the attentions of wiser, older men—Nestor, Simonides, Solon, and her beloved Anacreon (cf. Fontenelle's paradox). As, revolted in her turn by Phaon's spiritual ugliness, she turns to leave him, Anacreon comes to announce that her period of atonement is over. She drinks her draught of Lethe water, and is finally released from the blandishments of the upper world. Only Phaon remains, uncomprehending still.

Here, for the first time, Wieland is using the full dramatic possibilities of the form. Though he permits himself the luxury of stage-directions and asides, he generally adheres to the Lucianic convention of allowing a character to inform us about his own past and the physical presence of others. If we find Phaon ugly, it is because Nireus tells us so; if Nireus and Sappho are beautiful, it is their reflection in Phaon's words which conveys the fact. The landscape of Elysium is also brought into use, so that, for example, Sappho is seen by Phaon and described as she approaches from a bower. This close relation to the literary manner of certain Lucian dialogues extends beyond narrative manner to satirical technique. Wieland exploits the irony of the *alazōn* who is quite unconscious of the absurdity of his pretentions.

Yet the effect is only satirical in an incidental way. It is almost tragic irony that Phaon takes the beauty of Nireus for a solely physical manifestation, since we, as reader of the previous dialogue, recognize it as the spiritual form of beauty, purified of the carnal trappings of mere physical beauty. Phaon *is* absurd, but, unlike Lucian's *alazones*, he is not primarily absurd.

These three Wieland dialogues stem from the same rationalist tradition as Fontenelle and Fénelon. Although he reveals a much closer knowledge of Lucian, the precise admixture of thematic borrowing and structural imitation varies enormously between the dialogues. At the same time, they are unique in their period as forming a unified philosophical entity in which is displayed, first symbolically (*Dial.* 1), then didactically (*Dial.* 2) and finally dramatically, a particular view of what is ethically wrong with mankind. The self-consciously paradoxical wit of Fontenelle, the prosaic moralism of Fénelon and the purely negative attack of Voltaire, are replaced by a positive definition of *humanity*, in which an emotional, almost personal element appears, unparalleled in any other imitator of Lucian.

The main forms of Lucian imitation in the dialogues of the dead are typified by Fénelon and Fontenelle. Boileau's literary piece, though nearer to his original in tone, is a sport, restricted to salon recitation for many years, and only printed when the fashion for the genre was well established. And Wieland, coming at the very end of the genre's development, stands alone both in his knowledge of Lucian and in the use to which he put his imitation. Each of the major authors has his own contribution to make to the genre, though each gives it a primarily didactic function. The unanswerable question is, as I said earlier: why should the genre have gained favour at this point in time? Perhaps Fontenelle's *Epître* gives a clue to a solution that would apply not just to himself but to the period. He says:

. . . One advantage is that you can suppose that the dead are people whose experience and leisure allow them periods of deep reflexion. You have to believe that, to their credit, they think a little more than people usually do while they are alive. They can give more rational consideration to the things of the world than we do, because they look upon them with greater indifference and tranquillity, and they like to reason upon such things, because they retain a little interest in them.

Shorn of its dramatic interest and local colour, as it is in all but *Les Héros du roman* and the third of Wieland's *Gespräche*, the dialogue of the dead becomes a way of combining the debate element natural to all rational enquiry, with a temporal perspective that encourages a belief in the unity and continuity of human nature. Sometimes, as in those dialogues that are part of Fontenelle's contribution to the *Querelle des anciens et des modernes,* or Suard's *Dialogue entre Périclès, un Grec moderne et un Russe,* which expresses a simplified example of the eighteenth-century view of history, the temporal perspective is essential to the theme of the work. At other times, it merely aids that sense of dealing in eternal truths which is essential to the moralist. The theory advanced by one critic that all the major writers using the dialogue of the dead form suffered from excessively developed rational capacities and atrophied imaginations merely reveals a fundamental incomprehension of, and dislike for, the major trends in eighteenth-century literature. There is no question of deficiency of imagination. The dialogues take their place in that great mass of literature of their time devoted to the same ethical and social issues. Wieland even takes them to the brink of the primacy of emotions that dominates much of nineteenth-century literature. But the form will not extend to the expression of the exclusively emotional, any more than of the exclusively personal. Hence its demise along with that of the age of absolutes in which it had flourished.

III

Erasmus and Fielding

INTRODUCTION

In the second section of this book I have shown that Lucian's contribution to the evolution of various genres in European literature from the ninth century to the end of the eighteenth was a decisive one. This would have been a sufficient legacy in itself. There is, however, a deeper and perhaps more interesting way of considering literary influence. One can attempt to trace it in those outstanding cases where an individual writer digests the work of another and absorbs what he has digested into an essential function of his own literary creation. Before such a process can be traced, there needs to be very substantial evidence for that individual's knowledge of his model, for his attitudes toward that model, for his efforts to incorporate identifiable borrowings from that model. Then one can move beyond the stage of sources and analogues to consider the parallels which mark, in the finished mature work of a great artist, the affinities with the writings that initially so profoundly impressed him. The works of Lucian exercised an influence of this sort on several major European figures. To give some idea of how diverse that influence could be, I have elected to look at two very different authors, writing in different genres, languages, countries and centuries, but in each of whom Lucian bred certain unconscious habits of mind which governed the selection of a form, a theme and a style even from the material and traditions of their contemporary worlds. The first is the most famous of all the Renaissance humanists, Desiderius Erasmus; the second is one of England's most prolific and talented eighteenth-century playwrights, journalists and novelists, Henry Fielding.

I. ERASMUS

No creative writer has left more evidence for his knowledge of Lucian and for the way in which he interpreted him than has Erasmus.[1] The

---

[1] For further details see the introduction to my edition of *Luciani dialogi* in *Opera Omnia . . . Erasmi* I. i (Amsterdam 1969). A brief list of other works touching on the subject is given on p. 377 of that volume.

wealth of quotations in the *Adages* alone would be sufficient testimony to his familiarity with the text. But it is to the volume of translations that we can best turn. Erasmus' interest in Lucian appears to have grown out of his use of him as a 'reader' when first learning Greek. Among his earliest efforts at translation was a version of *Gout,* abandoned when he found that he could not cope with the epithets in the choruses. This false start was soon followed by a substantial collection of translations, the first edition of which appeared in 1506, with an augmented edition in 1514, to be followed by a series of reprintings all showing minor alterations apparently contributed by Erasmus himself, right up to 1533, only three years before his death.

The various dedicatory epistles which accompanied the translations, coupled with remarks in *De ratione studii* and *De conscribendis epistulis,* give a clear picture of what Erasmus saw as Lucian's principal merits, and of why he chose certain dialogues to translate rather than others. In the first place, he thought Lucian an appropriate author for someone just beginning the study of Greek, on grounds of linguistic clarity and elegance. and also in terms of entertainment value. On the other hand, as far as schoolboys were concerned, he thought selection necessary to eliminate, not so much the improper, as the merely frivolous: in *De conscribendis epistulis* he picks on *Dialogues of the Gods* 12 and 13 as examples of amusing material which unfortunately lack moral relevance to everyday life. This brings us to the second and more important element in Lucian's attractiveness for Erasmus—his value as a source of ethical instruction. The prefaces insist on the 'fruitfulness' of certain works, notably *Toxaris* and *Alexander; The Cock* is said to be *succo praesentaneo salubrem et efficacem,* and a fine example of how to blend the useful and the entertaining, in accordance with Horace's precept. Indeed, so convinced is Erasmus of the moral worth of what Lucian writes that, confronted with the (to put it mildly) ambiguous message of *Astrology,* he proposed that it must have a moral content, simply on the grounds that Lucian was its author.

Some of this didactic value clearly lies in Lucian's stand on broad ethical issues, e.g. the critique of wealth in *Timon* and *The Cock*. The attraction goes, however, rather deeper than general moral usefulness. Erasmus saw direct contemporary application for what Lucian was saying. This is true at the level of individual institutions; in the preface to *On Salaried Posts* he observes that the parallels are much wider. The vices against which Lucian's satire was directed, and the characters who personified those vices, seemed the very mirror of all that Erasmus most detested in his own times. Erasmus' great concern was with the moral decadence of Christianity, especially within the priesthood itself. This decadence he associated with charlatanism, and with disputatiousness and violence among intellectuals. It is to these same elements in Lucian's world that he points: superstition, hypocrisy, pride and quarrelsomeness. And he explicitly parallels the character in which they are most often personified, the philosopher, with the theologians and clergy of his own day. *A propos* of *The Cock* he says of Lucian:

> He does not touch upon anything in passing without disposing of it with some shaft of wit. He is especially hostile to philosophers, among them Pythagoreans and Platonists in particular, because of their magical tricks, and similarly the Stoics, on account of their intolerable arrogance. And quite right too. For what is more detestable, more intolerable, than depravity wearing the mask of virtue? That is why he has been given the name of *blasphēmos*, that is, slanderer—but by those, that is, whose sore spots he had touched. With equal freedom he also scoffs at the gods in all his works, and takes them apart. That is how he gained the title atheist; but it is a name which even does him honour, having been given to him by the impious and superstitious.

The question of hypocrisy and superstition he develops in respect of *Alexander,* which he sees as

> unparalleled in usefulness for detecting and irrefutably exposing the impostures of certain persons who in our time, too, are in the habit of imposing upon the common people by magic and miracles, fake religion or pretended pardons, and other tricks of that kind.

Similarly he sees religious dissension reflected in *The Banquet:*

> . . . we see the philosophical and theological schools quarrelling among themselves much more childishly and fighting no less savagely. And the battle between professors of religion is just as bloody as the one at the dinner party which Lucian has invented or reported.

The parallelism extends also to the positive aspects of Lucian's thought. Erasmus praises the picture of 'untrammelled poverty, light-hearted and contented with its own lot'. More important, he proposes the account of friendship in *Toxaris* as a picture of what the relationship between Christians, and between Christians and Christ, ought to be, but alas no longer is. For the subject of friendship, as Lucian propounds it, should be important in an age when 'it has so far fallen into disuse among Christians that not merely its traces but its very name have vanished'.

On a smaller scale, and with less precision, Erasmus also gives some indication of the literary qualities which attracted him to Lucian. He notes two kinds of humour, light and dark:

All the dark humour which men attribute to Momus and all the light they ascribe to Mercury may be found in plenty united in the one Lucian. (preface to *Alexander*)

He emphasizes the dramatic presentation, the way in which the message derives from the action as much as from any commentary by the participants:

He paints men's manners, passions and desires, and sets them forth not to read but plainly visible to the eye. (preface to *The Cock*)

And he particularly draws attention to characterization, praising Lucian's skill at preserving the individuality of the numerous characters in *The Banquet* and picking on the importance of characterization by language in *Toxaris*:

For how totally Greek is the flavour of the dialogue of the Greek, Mnesippus! amiable, witty, jolly. Whereas, how utterly Scythian is the perfume of the Scythian's speech! simple, artless, rough, industrious, serious, powerful.

What reflection of all this can be found in Erasmus' own work? For Lucianic influence one need look no farther than the *Colloquies*, of which Luther wrote: 'On my deathbed I shall forbid my son to read Erasmus' *Colloquies* . . . He is much worse than Lucian, mocking all things under the guise of holiness.'[1] Some of the *Colloquies* betray the original purpose of the collection as a Latin reader for schoolboys; many others are perfectly serious discussions or compendia of learned information after the manner of Athenaeus or of Plutarch's various symposia. But there are a hard core which are primarily satirical, and whose themes and techniques do indeed reflect Erasmus' reading of Lucian.[2]

Primary evidence of this lies in the few direct allusions to Lucian, the verbal borrowings and reminiscences. One of the early *formulae*

---

[1] Quoted by P. Smith, *Erasmus: a study of his life, ideals and place in history*, New York 1962 (2nd ed.), 300.

[2] I have found useful M. Heep, 'Die Colloquia Familiaria des Erasmus und Lucian', *Hermaea* XVIII (1927), and, on a more general level, G. Thompson, *Under Pretext of Praise: satiric mode in Erasmus' fiction*, Toronto 1973.

from which the colloquies developed cites *A True Story* as the classic example of the far-fetched tale, *The Godly Feast* refers to the description of the Isles of the Blest in the same work, *Knucklebones* quotes from *Affairs of the Heart* on dice-play. More interestingly, *The Lover of Glory*, where the path to true glory is outlined, refers at its climax to *Harmonides*, the bulk of which is an anecdote on the same theme. When Erasmus writes

On this I have no better advice than that which the flautist gave his fellow flautist; see that you acquire a good reputation in the eyes of those who have already silenced envy by their own renown; find yourself a way into the friendship of people whose recommendation will readily bring you popularity.[1]

he is paraphrasing the advice of Timotheus to Harmonides:

This is an immediate and very simple way to glory. If you choose the cream of Greece, a few of those who are at the top admired without reservation, and of unimpeachable judgment, and if, as I say, you give a display of your flute music to them, and they praise you, you can think yourself famous in the eyes of all Greece in as short a while as this. (*Harmonides* 2)

Similarly, the opening exchange of *Military Affairs* in which Hanno makes fun of Thrasymachus for leaving 'as though wing-footed' and returning limping, is a playful inversion of the image of Wealth in *Timon*:

Wealth ... whenever I am sent off by Zeus to visit someone I am slow and lame in both legs—I don't know why—so that I have difficulty reaching my goal, and the man has often grown old waiting for me. But whenever I have to go away, you'll see that I sprout wings and am much swifter than dreams.

Some of the reminiscences are more *à la manière de* . . . than this but still stem from a given motif. The account of why God is too busy to attend a woman in labour because of the terrible state of the world follows the general line of Zeus' lament (*The Double Indictment* 2–3) over the parlous conditions which have prevented him from attending to outstanding lawsuits. In the same way, the idea of presenting one of the theological victims as a fish in *Synodus grammaticorum* is modelled

[1] In general, passages from the *Colloquies* are quoted in the translation of C. R. Thompson, Chicago 1965. In this instance the translation is my own, as Thompson's version is unsatisfactory.

on the presentation of the philosophers as fish in *The Dead Come to Life:*

Bert.   What does an anticomarita fish look like?

Canth. It has black scales all over except for a white belly.

Bert.   I think you'll make the fish into a Cynic in a long cloak. What does it taste like?

Canth. Nothing's more disagreeable. Why, it's a plague. It breeds in stinking pools and sometimes in privies, it's sluggish and muddy. The mere taste of it causes a thick phlegm you can hardly rid yourself of by vomiting.[1]

The matching of the fish's appearance to the dress of the monk for whom he stands follows the general idea of the Aristotelian fish with the gold stripes or the spiny Stoic fish: the outside offers a confirmatory symbol of an essential aspect of the person attacked. And the reference to Cynics, coupled with the emphasis on the inedible, brings to mind Diogenes' comment on the Cynic fish: 'He is inedible, hideous, tough and worthless.'

The most elaborate example of this type of motif-borrowing occurs in *The Dedicated Liar and the Man of Honour*. This colloquy contains a description of the art of lying (cf. the opening of *The Lover of Lies*) based on the idea of Simon's explanation of the art of scrounging in *The Parasite*. Pseudocheus, like Simon, defends the status of his profession as an 'art', rejects any notion that he should feel ashamed of what he does, adduces classical authority (Ulysses), and quotes examples of successful practice. However, Erasmus uses none of the mock-Socratic manner which characterizes *The Parasite*. Indeed, a long section of the colloquy borrows the same technique from *The Sham Sophist* that Erasmus exploits so successfully in *The Imposture* (see below, p. 173), though here the appositeness is dubious and the humour heavy handed. Pseudocheus simply tricks Philetymus with a series of so-called lies, in order to show his expert command of the art. Moreover the tone of the colloquy is, in fact, very much affected by the evident personal reference which dominates the anecdotes of the last section. Lucian's villains are rarely quite so explicit about their roguery.

On a more substantial level it is possible to detect the appearance of important Lucianic themes as the central ideas of two colloquies. The first is *Cyclops*. The major character, Polyphemus (nickname for a

---

[1] C. R. Thompson, op. cit., 398.

former clerk to Erasmus), is described in one of Erasmus' letters as habitually carrying with him 'a beautiful decorated volume of the Gospels, though nothing could be more soiled than his own life'. Erasmus adapts the theme of *The Ignorant Book-collector* to this real-life incident, stressing the man's ignorance of the content of his book but his pride in its beautiful appearance. It is a theme which he evidently likes, for he uses it to comic effect in *A Meeting of the Philological Society* where the abbot of St Bavo is described as forming a collection of expensive and beautiful books with no regard for the triviality of their content (betrayed to the reader by their titles). As in Lucian's pamphlet, the emphasis in *Cyclops* goes on to the difference between the contents of the book and the character of its bearer. As Cannius puts it:

> But it would be well if, as you've decorated the Gospels with various ornaments, the Gospels in turn adorned you. You've decorated them with colours; I wish they might embellish you with good morals.[1]

For the exposing of this gap between text and reality, Erasmus introduces a rather different format from Lucian's direct attack, though it is still a Lucianic presentation. Invective is supplemented by self-betrayal. Like many of Lucian's philosophers, Polyphemus' grasp of the doctrine he professes proves faulty. This can be revealed in passing:

Cann. What if someone hit you hard?
Poly. I'd break his neck for that.
Cann. But your book teaches you to repay insults with a soft answer; and 'Whosoever shall smite thee on thy right cheek, turn to him the other also'.
Poly. I've read that, but it slipped my mind.[2]

But there is also a set-piece of self-unmasking, after the manner of the Cynic in *Philosophers for Sale:*

Poly. Usually I confess to God, but to you I admit I'm not yet a perfect follower of the gospel, just an ordinary fellow. My kind have four gospels. Four things above all we gospellers seeks: full bellies; plenty of work for the organs below the belly; a livelihood from somewhere or other; finally, freedom to do as we like. If we get these, we shout in our cups, '*Io, triumphe; Io! Paean!* The gospel flourishes! Christ reigns!'[3]

[1] ibid., 417.   [2] ibid., 419.   [3] ibid., 421.

Polyphemus' vices are in fact more those of the philosophers of *The Banquet* than the ignorant book-collector's: violence, drunkenness and lasciviousness, in that order. Meanwhile his interlocutor Cannius combines two separate rôles, delivering invective and commenting ironically on Polyphemus' assertion of his own moral worth. The texture of the satire is made more complex by the fact that Polyphemus is allowed to deliver attacks on other traditional objects of Erasmian satire, e.g. 'A haughty spirit often lurks under an ash-coloured cowl', as though Lucian's philosophers were, in condemning themselves, also to be permitted to make justified criticisms of his rhetoricians.

The other colloquy which uses general thematic imitation is *The Ignoble Knight*, in which instruction is given in how to substitute the appearance of a quality, nobility, for its substance. The principle is the same as that in *A Professor of Public Speaking*, which also gives a lesson in how to obtain the maximum of return for the minimum of effort, by the same sort of counterfeiting. In both cases the importance of outward appearance is stressed. Nestor advises Harpalus to dress fashionably, adopt a noble name, surround himself with accomplices who will treat him with great respect in public, talk only of appropriately noble topics and persons. So the rhetorician advises elegant clothes (15), describes the social up-grading of his own name (24), recommends the carefully arranged adulation of friends (21), and a superficial command of the right sort of language (16). The directions given in both works on how to conduct one's private life are in a like relationship to one another. The rhetorician prescribes:

> In your private life make up your mind to do absolutely anything: play dice, get drunk, fornicate, debauch married women—or at least boast you do, even if you don't, tell everyone about it and show them *billets doux* supposedly written by women. For you should try to be a fine fellow and take trouble to give the impression that women are crazy about you. (23)

Nestor observes:

> Unless you're a good dicer, a famous card-player, an infamous whoremonger, a reckless spendthrift, a wastrel and heavily in debt, decorated with the French pox besides, hardly anyone will believe you're a knight.[1]

And both works mention the potential financial advantages of cultivating one's attractiveness to women. Lastly, constant reference is made in both to the need for boldness. *A Professor of Public Speaking*

---

[1] ibid., 428–9.

15 and 22 recommend effrontery and shamelessness, while Nestor punctuates his advice with such phrases as '. . . Stop at nothing. Put on a bold front', and 'Here's where you must remember to put on a bold face. Above all bear in mind that insolence has never passed more readily for wisdom than it does today'. Naturally, some of the emphases in the two works are slightly different. Much more is said about slander and abuse by Lucian, much more about robbery and quarrelsomeness by Erasmus. But in general the definitions of villainy are remarkably alike.

A further two colloquies could be described as sustained imitations of particular works. These are *Charon* and *The Imposture*. The latter is a light-hearted piece of linguistic ingenuity, modelled on the pseudo-Lucianic *The Sham Sophist*. In that dialogue, a sophist who prides himself on his ability to avoid grammatical blunders, and to detect them in others, fails to notice an interminable series of deliberate errors concealed in the words of his interlocutor. The dialogue follows this pattern:

Lucian . . . I say you can't catch me, because there are things what you know and things what you don't.
Sophist Just say something.
Lucian But I've just made another howler, though you didn't notice it.
Sophist How so, when you don't say anything?
Lucian I am saying things, and making howlers, but you don't keep up with me as I do it. I hopes you can follow me this time.
Sophist I'm surprised to hear you say I won't be able to recognize a howler.
Lucian How could you recognize one when in your ignorance you've missed three already?[1]

In *The Imposture*, Erasmus takes another Lucianic device, the character who cannot help breaking into verse (e.g. Zeus in *Zeus Rants*, Menippus in *Menippus*) and substitutes this motif for the idea of grammatical solecism. Livinus addresses Philip in apparently conversational tones, but in metrical units. For example:

Phil. I suppose I'm dealing with a magician, for I don't perceive any deception.
Liv. Watch again/, be on guard,/ you've been fooled/ by me more than once;/ now I mean/ further tricks/ to play.
Phil. I'm ready; begin.

---

[1] Trans. M. D. Macleod, Loeb vol. VIII, 7–9.

Liv. What you've asked of me/ I've per/formed al/ready.
Phil. What's been done, or what performed? I don't see any trick.[1]

Erasmus' dialogue has three great advantages over its model. First, it is quite short. Secondly, it has a clear didactic purpose demonstrating a wide series of metres, eventually identified by Livinus. Thirdly, he has the neat idea of allowing Philip to turn the tables by slipping into un-detected verses of his own, giving the piece an extra humorous dimension and a more pointed end.

Charon is a more substantial imitation, though of a general kind. Erasmus clearly has in mind *Dialogues of the Dead* 14 and 20, *The Downward Journey*, and Lucian's own *Charon*. The situation, in which Charon, on the way to the upper world to fetch himself a new boat, meets the avenging angel Alastor bringing down news of fresh wars and dissensions, belongs to the underworld variant of ingénu satire; but Erasmus has avoided the dramatic presentation which marks *The Downward Journey* and *Dialogues of the Dead* 20, and chosen the reportage presentation of *Menippus*.

The suggestion of action is limited to the opening and closing phrases:

Charon Why the hustle and bustle, Alastor?
Alast.   Well met, Charon! I was speeding to you.

and

Alast.   Hurry back, so the crowd won't overwhelm you.
Charon Oh, you'll meet over two hundred thousand on the bank already, besides those swimming in the swamp. But I'll hurry as much as I can. Tell 'em I'll be there right away.[2]

For the rest, Charon retells the account of human affairs given to him by Ossa, and Alastor supplements it from his first-hand experience. The advantage of this slightly ambiguous format is that it allows Erasmus to use motifs borrowed from both dramatic and descriptive works. The initial donné of the work, Charon buying a new boat which is to be paid for by the obols which come in greatest profusion during wars, is adapted in broad outline from *Dialogues of the Dead* 14, where Hermes brings Charon a new anchor and other fittings for his boat, only to learn that the boatman is a little embarrassed for ready cash:

[1] C. R. Thompson, op. cit., 413.
[2] ibid., 390 and 394.

It's impossible [to pay you] just at the moment, Hermes; but if a plague or a war sends me crowds of victims down, I shall be able to make a profit by cheating on the fares in the mêlée.

Then, running through the colloquy, are the motifs of the sinking of Charon's boat, the stripping of extraneous qualities from the shades of the dead, and the paradox of the 'heavy' shade:

Alast.   But you haul shades, not bodies. Now, how light are shades?
Charon They may be water skippers, but enough water skippers could sink a boat. Then too, you know, the boat is insubstantial.[1]

The first of these, Charon's shipwreck, and the shades left 'swimming with the frogs', is an expansion of the threat at the beginning of *Dialogues of the Dead* 20 that the boat may easily founder, and of the attempt of Micyllus to swim the Styx rather than be left behind (*The Downward Journey* 18–19). The second two also draw on *Dialogues of the Dead* 20. Lucian makes physical trappings and character faults equivalent examples of weight—stripping a tyrant, athlete, general or philosopher in the same way of both concrete (diadem, mantle, armour, trophy) and abstract (pride, effeminacy, contentiousness, vanity). Erasmus extends this into a distinction between weightless souls, who died from consumption or fever, and those 'plucked on the sudden from heavy bodies [which] bring a good deal of corporeal substance along with them', a class for which war is particularly responsible. The heaviness, like Lucian's, falls into concrete (bulls and benefices) and abstract (debauchery, gluttony), and the paradox of the heavy shade is resolved by blaming the weight on dreams:

Alast.   But they don't bring these along with them. The souls come to you naked.
Charon True, but newcomers bring along dreams of such things.
Alast.   So dreams are heavy?
Charon They weigh down my boat. Weigh down, did I say? they've already sunk it![2]

Around this structure of references to the underworld tradition, which both repeats Lucian's parody of earlier traditions and further parodies them by insistence on the comic possibilities of the logically absurd elements in the tradition, Erasmus constructs an attack, very different in tone, on war, particularly the complex contemporary wars

[1] ibid., 392.
[2] ibid., 393.

involving England, France, Holy Roman Empire and papacy. This war theme also provides a direct link with *The Downward Journey* and *Dialogues of the Dead* 20. The crowd of nameless dead who arrive in the former (6) and the general in the latter are swelled into the multitudes expected by Charon:

> Whenever there's a war on, so many come to me wounded and cut up that I'd be surprised if any had been left on earth.

Another feature of war, its omnipresence, is stressed in Lucian's *Charon* too. Into this substantive theme is then woven a more particular attack, on monks, which has no immediate parallel in any of the models, but which introduces an important Erasmian variant on the Lucianic hypocrite figure. Defined by their cloak and beard, as it were, these 'creatures in black and white cloaks and ash-grey tunics' are portrayed as purveyors of falsified religion, hungry not merely for power but, like Lucian's philosophers, also for a good dinner—'it must be partridges, capons and pheasants if you wish to be an acceptable host'—and for money:

> Alast. They make more profit from the dying than from the living. There are wills, masses for kinsmen, bulls, and many other sources of revenue not to be despised.[1]

The ingredients of Erasmus' dialogue, then, owe much to Lucian. The effect is in many ways very different. The Lucianic theme and manner, helped out by the satirical references to underworld *pittoresque*—the description of the Furies now bald from having let all their snakes loose on the world, the Elysian groves chopped down to provide wood for burning the shades of heretics—are clearly the vehicle for an attack on a particular society at a particular moment in history. References to contemporary war, plague, religious strife, are made more particular by the addition of the ironic attack on Erasmus himself for his attempts to promote peace. Nothing could be less like the timeless reference of *Dialogues of the Dead* or the archaic world surveyed in *Charon*. But of course, in Erasmus' eyes, the inclusion of this sort of material falls within the bounds of what he considers Lucianic satire to be. He is merely bringing to life the parallel made explicit in the prefaces to his translations between Lucian's world and his own.

So far we have been talking in terms of one-for-one parallelisms. Once one moves to a broader level of comparison, as with the monks

[1] ibid., 392.

in *Charon* and the stock type of the philosopher, the Lucianic tone of the strictly satirical colloquies becomes strikingly obvious. Three of Erasmus' main targets, war, hypocrisy and superstition, are standard themes in Lucian. Of these he develops war the least. None the less, it is a constant feature of human life as presented in the 'overviews', *Charon* (27) and *Icaromenippus* (18). Criticism of soldiers and generals occurs in various underworld dialogues, notably *Dialogues of the Dead* 20. 7, *Dialogues of the Dead* 25 passim. To this can be added the theme of the vanity of the lives of kings, again notably in *Charon*, the two themes coming together in the wish of Samippus and its criticism by Lycinus in *The Ship*. Erasmus concentrates on two separate aspects. One of these is the destructiveness and pointlessness of war itself; the other is the debasement of those who wage it. The two are essentially connected, for as he put it in *Querela pacis* (1517), 'If you want to see what a wicked thing war is, just consider the men who wage it'. *Military Affairs, The Soldier and the Carthusian, Cyclops, The Ignoble Knight, Things and Names*, all include ridicule against the pretensions and vices of soldiers; *Charon* and *A Fish Diet* attack the greed and folly of kings. The model for the soldiers is, of course, the *miles gloriosus* of Roman comedy, but Erasmus may also have in mind the bragging, violent, and by implication dissolute, soldiers who form the subject of *Dialogues of the Courtesans* 13 and 15. Hypocrisy and superstition bulk much larger in Lucian's work. All the dialogues on philosophers, plus *Alexander*, fall under the first heading, *On Sacrifices* and *Zeus Rants* under the second, while *Peregrinus* and, in particular, *The Lover of Lies*, combine the two. Erasmus' stock portraits of the monk and theologian have all the characteristics of Lucian's philosophers. First, stylization of appearance: the beard and cloak become, inevitably, the cowl. The use of this motif in *Charon* I have already commented upon (above, p. 176). In *The Seraphic Funeral* the adoption of Franciscan garb is ironically assumed to effect an instant change in a man's life. And the moral is openly pointed in *The Old Men's Chat* where Pampirus, having tried every imaginable sort of monastic order, with all the consequent changes of clothing, comes to the conclusion that 'there's a lot of difference between wearing a cross on a cloak or tunic and wearing it in the heart'. As the butcher puts it rather more strongly in *A Fish Diet*, where the point is discussed at length and with several illustratory anecdotes:

If a priest lets his hair grow long or wears a layman's garb, he is thrown into jail and punished severely; if he boozes in a brothel, if he whores, if he dices, if he corrupts other men's wives, if he never touches a Bible, he is none the less a pillar of the Church. I don't excuse a change of costume, but I deprecate a preposterous judgment.[1]

Secondly, as the passage from *A Fish Diet* indicates, the monks share various vices with the philosophers. The butcher mentions drinking and sexual indulgence. Gourmandizing is another common failing. The Augustinian and Carmelite friars are 'bought off' in *The Funeral* by the promise that as much food will be sent to them at their house as is given to those remaining at the dying man's bedside (cf. Hetoemocles in *The Banquet*). Various combinations of the same charges are levelled in other colloquies. The Minorite brother of *The Sermon* is 'a huge fellow with red cheeks, big paunch, a fighter's frame; you'd have called him an athlete. And, unless I miss my guess, he'd drunk more than a pint at lunch'. In *The Girl with no Interest in Marriage*, Eubulus charges the prior with excessive devotion to wine, and describes 'gross monks who are always puffy from overeating'. Moreover he accuses them of the corruption of nuns, just as the priest in *Exorcism* is caught out for having had relations with a girl three times in one night. Another vice common to both philosophers and ecclesiastics is that of the pursuit of financial gain. This can have the air of legality, as with the fat incomes of some priests and priors (*A Fish Diet, Charon*), the selling of indulgences and relics (*A Pilgrimage for Religion's Sake*), or the jockeying for a share in an inheritance (*The Funeral*). Or it can be achieved by totally dishonest means, as in *Alchemy*, where the priest poses as a successful alchemist in order to cheat a foolish old man out of his money. Finally, in addition to these types of moral turpitude, Erasmus denounces a series of equally un-Christian attributes which again are shared by the philosophers: quarrelsomeness, coupled with verbal abusiveness and readiness to resort to physical violence, after the manner of *The Banquet*. The dissension of the sects at the wedding is matched by the strife between the parish priest and the various orders of monks at the death-bed in *The Funeral*. Over the matter of the dying man's confession, 'a bloody battle between the priest and the monks very nearly broke out', with insults exchanged about the claims to learning and morality of the various contenders. Ignorance is in itself a separate subject for attack, as in *The Abbot and the Learned Lady*, where the abbot prefers drinking and low entertainments to reading, which, he claims, drives people mad. The combination of

[1] ibid., 343.

ignorance and quarrelsomeness receives its fullest treatment in the portrait of the wretched Merdardus of *The Sermon,* whose Latin is inadequate to the task of understanding the Magnificat properly, but who crudely abuses Erasmus for his mistakes (after the fashion of Lucian's supposed enemy in *The Mistaken Critic*).

There is no question, of course, of Erasmus *deriving* these attacks from his reading of Lucian. Doubtless the abuses he denounces had a firm basis in reality. In some cases identifiable persons and events are involved. The translation prefaces give one cause to think that what he saw in Lucian was a literary model, in some sense a literary authority, for representing the same material in satirical form. Such matters had already been the subject of fifteenth-century invective against the monks, but without the stylization of character that is markedly shared by Erasmus' monks and Lucian's philosophers. One can, furthermore, draw up a 'type' for the Erasmian villain, be he monk or soldier, which contains most of the characteristics of the Lucianic villain, from the deceptiveness of appearances to the indifference to human life (the Dominicans burying two young men alive in *The Seraphic Funeral*). It is this marshalling of charges, real or traditional, into the formal patterns of a literary type that constitutes an important part of Erasmus' debt to Lucian.

A similar relationship exists between the treatments of superstition in the two authors. Erasmus presents superstition in two distinct areas, secular and religious. In the first, he attacks the pseudo-sciences, astrology, palmistry, alchemy. The most substantial treatment is accorded to the latter, with Misoponus' description of how to fake an experiment, which provides the central anecdote in *Beggar Talk,* and with the full-length account of an alchemist's deceit in *Alchemy.* Here we are very much in the realm of the fake miracles of *Alexander.* In the religious sphere, the literal faking of miracles is described in *The Seraphic Funeral* (as in *Alexander*) by a hostile witness. Four Dominicans are accused of chicanery:

By faked apparitions and bogus miracles they tried to persuade people that the Virgin Mary had been tainted with original sin; that St Francis had not had the true marks of Christ's wounds; that Catherine of Siena had had them more genuinely, but that the most perfect stigmata were promised to a converted layman whom they had secretly bribed to play this rôle; and for the purpose of this imposture they took liberties with the Host and later used even clubs and poisons.[1]

[1] ibid., 509.

However, Erasmus is much more exercised by the everyday manifestations of superstition which are encouraged by the clergy to their own
financial advantage. The excesses of Mariolatry, saint-worship in
general, belief in demons, the cult of relics, the making of vows, the
sale of indulgences, are all exposed to the sort of ridicule which
Lucian pours on the traditional religious beliefs, funeral customs,
oracles and magical practices of paganism. Three major colloquies,
Exorcism, The Shipwreck and *A Pilgrimage for Religion's Sake*, are
devoted entirely to these topics. They do in fact bring together the
topics of hypocrisy and superstition, since in each priests or monks are
shown as either victims of superstition themselves, or hypocritical
exploiters of it in others.

In addition to the obvious general parallels, all these three colloquies contain substantial echoes of the treatment of similar motifs by
Lucian. *Exorcism* describes a trick actually played by Thomas More
and a relative. A priest is tricked into exorcising a fake demon. This
main character has all the qualities of the philosophers of *The Lover of
Lies:* he is gullible, stupid, lascivious and greedy, his credulity extends
to all the magic arts of his day, yet at the same time he prides himself
on his wisdom. 'He looked upon himself as uncommonly wise, especially in divinity.' In two respects there are apparent direct reminiscences of Lucian. Exorcism is the subject of one of the tall tales in *The
Lover of Lies*, and the pretended representation of demons as a practical
joke is also mentioned in that work. The phoney apparition is prepared
for by the equally phoney 'portent' that Polus affects to see, a huge
dragon with fiery horns in the sky, and which he persuades his companions, by sheer insistence, that they too can see, such that within
three days report of the appearance of such a portent had spread
throughout England. Just so does the speaker in *Peregrinus* maliciously
foster, for his own amusement, stories of the portents that greeted
Peregrinus' death on the pyre, such that he is soon hearing the same
stories, with embellishment, from people who swear that they were
eyewitnesses. On top of this, the supposed letter from heaven in which
the tormented soul announces his deliverance is after the example of
such sky-born correspondence in *Saturnalia*. The only point for
speculation, and it is an unanswerable one, is whether, as one critic
has suggested, the Lucianic elements were incorporated into *reality* by
More, when playing the joke (it was he who translated *The Lover of
Lies,* among the group of Lucian dialogues which he contributed to
the 1506 edition of Erasmus' translations). It seems just as plausible

that Erasmus has written up the event in a more Lucianic style, recognizing the spirit that had informed its conception.

The Shipwreck describes a storm and shipwreck (the subject of an anecdote in *Toxaris* 19–21 too), with the emphasis on men's response to imminent death, and particularly their religious response to it. The choice of recipients for prayers, and the rash vows made, are the main objects of satire, starting with the lavish titles of the Virgin as (improbably) protectress of sailors, shown to be an extension of the pagan assignment of that rôle to Venus (cf. *Affairs of the Heart* 11). The general tone is, as in *On Sacrifices,* one of sarcastic comment, mocking the assumption that divine action can be purchased (cf. *On Sacrifices* 2) and that different saints or deities have limited geographical spheres of action (cf. 10). One particular incident, the man who vows a monstrous wax taper to the effigy of St Christopher in the tallest church in Paris, is after the pattern of a similar vow by a sailor in *Zeus Rants* 15. In Lucian the man inevitably fails to come up with the lavish offering promised in the moment of stress: in Erasmus, the comedy is heightened by the man's express intention, even as he makes it, of not fulfilling the vow. The extra humour comes from elaborating on the literal concept of oral prayer by assuming that the saints cannot hear what is said sotto-voce:

> Then the other, lowering his voice—so Christopher couldn't hear him, of course!—said, 'Shut up, you fool. Do you suppose I'm serious? If once I touch land, I won't give him even a tallow candle.'[1]

Though not specifically Lucianic, this play with literalness is in the style of *Zeus Rants* 9, where Zeus complains that he cannot hear the prayers of the faithful because of the hubbub caused by quarrelling philosophers.

A Pilgrimage for Religion's Sake is even closer in spirit, and contains a larger number of borrowed motifs. Ogygius, returned from a triple pilgrimage to St James of Compostella, Our Lady of Walsingham and St Thomas à Becket at Canterbury, recounts what he has seen. This allows Erasmus plenty of room to ridicule two main targets, saint-worship and the cult of relics. The message of the whole colloquy can very well be summed up in the openings words of *On Sacrifices* (one of the works translated by Erasmus):

> I do not suppose there is anyone who is so downcast and depressed as not

[1] ibid., 142.

to laugh, when he sees the absurdity of what is done, at what foolish people do in sacrifices, religious festivals and processions, and at what they pray for, their vows and religious beliefs. And sooner than laugh, one will, I think, ask oneself whether they should be called devout and not, on the contrary, the enemies of true religion and possessed of evil spirits, for having assumed that the divine is so mean and lowly that it needs men, is pleased by flattery, and is angered by neglect.

Passages from this same treatise offer a clear parallel for specific aspects of the colloquy: mockery aimed at worshipping effigies as though they had divine power (11), at making dedicatory offerings (12), at presenting the gods as dependent on man for their livelihood (9), and at assuming the power of the gods to be limited geographically (10). Other works also offer parallels. The idea of locals making a living out of telling lies to tourists occurs in *The Lover of Lies* 4, and references to tombs of gods, particular that of Zeus in Crete, as tourist attractions are frequent (e.g. *The Lover of Lies* 3, *Zeus Rants* 45, *Timon* 6). The miracles described, the richness of the Church and the immorality of monks have, as we have already seen, many parallels in Lucian, not least in *Alexander*. But there are also direct echoes. Take the passage where the activities of the reformers are described as having brought about a downturn in pilgrimages, with disastrous results for the condition of the saints:

Men. Tell me, how is the excellent James?
Ogyg. Much colder than usual.
Men. Why? Old age?
Ogyg. Joker! You know saints don't grow old. But this new-fangled notion that pervades the whole world results in his being greeted more seldom than usual. And if people do come, they merely greet him; they make no offering at all, or only a very slight one, declaring it would be better to contribute that money to the poor.
Men. A wicked notion!
Ogyg. And thus so great an apostle, accustomed to shine from head to foot in gold and jewels, now stands a wooden figure with hardly a tallow candle to his name.[1]

The panic stirred up in *Zeus Rants* by the atheist pronouncements of Damis rests on just the same point. Zeus puts it to the assembled immortals (18) that since not only all their honour but also their income derive from men, then, if men are persuaded that the gods do not

---

[1] ibid., 288.

exist, there will be no sacrifices or presents, and they will 'sit starving in heaven, deprived of all the feasts, festival games, sacrifices, vigils and processions' that they used to enjoy. In *Timon* (84), as in *A Pilgrimage for Religion's Sake*, this state of affairs is not threatened, but already present. It is an extension to this theme which offers the most thorough-going example of Lucianism in the colloquy, the letter of the Virgin to a Lutheran. As I said *à propos* of *Exorcism*, the idea of the heaven-sent epistle can be paralleled in *Saturnalia*. Its content falls into two sections. The first contains Mary's complaint at the nature of the prayers offered to her. Like the prayers that Zeus listens to in *Icaromenippus* 25, they are all highly unsuitable demands for personal advancement, or worse. In Lucian the idea is expressed in very general terms:

There was this sort of thing: 'Zeus, may I be granted the throne!', 'Zeus, may my onions and garlic flourish!', 'Gods! let my father die quickly!' And someone would say 'Let me inherit my wife's fortune!', 'Let my plot against my brother go unsuspected!', 'May I be granted to win my lawsuit!', 'Let me win the gold medal at the Olympics!'

The only classes of wisher specifically mentioned are sailors, farmers and launderers, who merely make wishes characterizing their professions. Erasmus does that in his use of countryfolk and sailors. But he also uses the theme of the inappropriate wish to satirize a broad range of types. As well as the outrageous prayers—the merchant entrusting his mistress's chastity to the Virgin, or the soldier praying for rich booty—we find an unmarried girl asking for a rich and handsome bridegroom, a priest for a rich benefice, and so on.

The second part of the letter is similar in tone to the preceding passage of *Icaromenippus* (24), where Zeus complains about the decline in his worship. The burden of the complaint is that the traditional gods are being neglected in favour of new deities, whereas Mary represents her plight as part of the general decline in saint-worship. The effect is none the less the same. Just as Zeus protests that '. . . they think that they have done me sufficient honour, getting on in years as I am, if they sacrifice to me every fifth year at Olympia', so Mary sadly observes that honorific titles, rich treasure and annual income are all deserting her steadily. The reference to loss of cloths and jewels is itself reminiscent of the contrast between the rich metals of the new interlopers into Olympus and the mere bronze and marble of the old deities whom they displace, in *Zeus Rants* 7–12, and, more strongly, of the instant impoverishment wrought by temple robbers in *Zeus Cate-chized* 8. The passage closes with Mary's threat to carry off the infant Christ from the churches unless a change of policy occurs. As well as reflecting the playful assumption passim in Lucian that the gods are as they are traditionally portrayed—Christ still a child in the arms of his mother is like, say, Apollo still beardless though father of Asclepius (*Zeus Rants* 26; cf. *On Sacrifices* 11)—this passage also introduces the motifs of a god powerless to deal with offenders, as Zeus is unable to use the thunderbolt to good effect (*Zeus Rants* 25, *Zeus Catechized* 16, *Timon* 4) and of the belligerent appearance of other saints and gods (e.g. *On Sacrifices* 3). So that the letter is beautifully constructed out of a series of updated Lucianic motifs within the framework of a form— the divine letter—which is also Lucianic in pedigree, though mediaeval in real reference. The borrowed motifs are not necessarily conscious reworkings of given passages; they show how Erasmus wrote up a contemporary abuse in the manner in which he had found it described in one or two places in Lucian.

The borrowings and parallelisms of theme and motif are, though interesting in themselves, ultimately significant as marking the extent to which Erasmus' whole approach to the art of satire was influenced by his reading of Lucian. In discussing content I have, inevitably, already dealt in passing with characterization and the burlesque reduction of characters to a type. Let us go further and look at questions of form. First a caveat. When comparing the style of the colloquies with Lucian's dialogues, one must bear in mind certain obvious limitations on the significance of parallels. Many characteristic devices of Lucian's prose style—the use of anecdote, quotation and maxim for example— have such widespread currency in other classical authors, and consequently in the rhetorically-derived style of most sixteenth-century prose, that similarities are of dubious significance. There are, however, techniques inherent in the pseudo-dramatic form of Lucianic dialogue which are probably more significant if found in a writer of Erasmus' period than in a later writer, since mediaeval dialogues made little use of such techniques and contemporary drama was too little developed to have stimulated their re-invention. If we compare the colloquies with Lucian in respect of dramatic conventions, there certainly are important similarities, especially given the fact that Erasmus, to judge by his other works, had no particular interest in, or skill at, inventing details of purely literary finesse.

Lucian's dramatic technique is very carefully worked out to ensure that in recitation the audience possesses the necessary facts to identify character, scene and action, as relevant, and receives such information about events prior to the dialogue as will throw light on the conversation itself.[1] Erasmus is not writing for oral delivery, but he is interested in preserving a general dramatic quality. Consequently he borrows selectively from Lucian, and the elements he borrows are not always the most obvious ones.

As far as the bulk of the dialogue goes, the preservation of distinctness of character and the communication of changes of scene are a much simpler problem for Erasmus than for Lucian. It is unusual for a new character to appear half way through a colloquy, and where one does, as with the inn-keeper in *The Well-to-do Beggars* or the two carriers in *The Old Men's Chat*, the subject matter, and in the latter case the linguistic register, are left to indicate the change to the reader. There is none of the sighting of characters off-stage which Lucian relies upon. Similarly Erasmus avoids entrances and exits, and leaves the content to indicate a change of scene. So that the evolution of *The Old Men's Chat* from the pastor's house to the inn is much less carefully prepared than the crossing of the Styx and the arrival at the court of Rhadamanthus in *Cataplus*. This is not to say that Erasmus never prepares his transitions. Glycion's proposal to hire a wagon, in *The Old Men's Chat*, and his announcement that he has made the arrangements and the party can now climb aboard, follow a similar pattern to the discussion of Charon's boat and the boarding of it in *Cataplus*. But this sort of transition is relatively unimportant in a text intended for the eye.

Expositions, however, are an area in which Lucian's influence is very strong. Both authors have to face the problems of establishing scene, action and character. Again, Erasmus adopts a simpler approach by largely limiting himself to two characters (with the exception of the various *Feasts*, which rarely reflect Lucianic devices of any sort), and by presenting scenes whose setting is not material to the 'action', as Lucian also does in a substantial number of cases, e.g. *The Eunuch*, *The Banquet*, *Hermotimus*. Where Lucian does give indications of scene, he prefers to do it minimally and by implication, as does Erasmus in *The Old Men's Chat*, *The Repentant Girl* or *The Girl with no Interest in Marriage*, e.g.:

Eubulus I'm glad dinner's finally over, so that we may enjoy this walk.[2]

[1] See A. Bellinger, 'Lucian's dramatic technique', *Yale Classical Studies* 1 (1928) 3–40.   [2] C. R. Thompson, op. cit., 103.

Interestingly, Erasmus' *Charon*, the one example of a genre in which Lucian regularly gives clear, if indirect, indications of place—the Underworld dialogues—is a rare example of a colloquy in which one wishes Erasmus had been rather more precise about setting. Charon is somewhere between Styx and upper world, but this is all one can glean.

As for the identification of characters, there we find a number of divergencies between the two authors. Almost without exception, a named character in a Lucian dialogue will actually be addressed or referred to by that name in the course of the dialogue. Very often in Erasmus the characters' names nowhere occur in the text. Lucian's names often carry an implied personality with them, being those of gods, heroes, stock figures of comedy, or names descriptive in themselves—Cyniscus, Tychiades, Parrhesiades. Consequently, of the three ways in which Lucian identifies his characters, by an immediate exchange of names, by the substitution of a descriptive word or phrase for a name, and by a description arising during the course of the dialogue, the first is much the most common. In this way the audience is provided with a world of reference from the first words. Erasmus is much more concerned to identify types, because, with the odd exception, Irides, Misoponus, Eubulus, his names indicate very little, or are even the names of personal acquaintances unlikely to be recognized by the common reader. Immediate use of names is thus much less helpful in most cases. It happens in *The New Mother, The Cheating Horse-Dealer, Beggar Talk* and *A Pilgrimage for Religion's Sake,* but in the last two examples the names are descriptive in themselves, and are accompanied by further description. A variant is that of *A Fish Diet* where the characters address each other by their occupations, a directly functional approach. However, in many colloquies only one character is immediately identified, usually the *alazōn,* as in *The Well-to-do Beggars, Rash Vows* and *The Funeral,* sometimes the ironist, as in *The Sermon.* Quite frequently identification of rôle is merely allowed to arise out of the information given in the course of the colloquy, as in *The Abbot and the Learned Lady,* where the names are never used by the characters themselves, *The Ignoble Knight,* where Nestor is never identified by name, and *Cyclops,* in which only Polyphemus is named.

However, though Erasmus' use of Lucian's expository patterns is partial and limited, the way in which he expresses those patterns where he does use them is very close to that of his model. There are two Lucianic motifs which sometimes form part of the opening of a colloquy. The first is the 'unless my eyes deceive me that is X' motif, after the manner of *Menippus* 1, which is found in, for example, *In Pursuit of Benefices* and *The Old Men's Chat*. The other is a series of variations on the idea 'we thought you were in Hell', as used in *A Pilgrimage for Religion's Sake*, *Rash Vows* and *In Pursuit of Benefices*, which may also derive from *Menippus* 1 (though Menippus actually has been in Hades). More widely used is the description of physical appearance in the exposition to announce some important character trait or theme of the piece. This can be a description of manner, as in *The Cheating Horse-Dealer* or *The Seraphic Funeral:*

Philec. Where does our Theotimus come from with his new religious look?
Theot. New? How so?
Philec. Because of the stern brow, eyes glued to the ground, head inclined
    somewhat to the left shoulder, beads in your hands.[1]

Lucian opens *Hermotimus* in precisely this way. Alternatively, it can be a description of garb, as in *The Soldier and the Carthusian*, where both characters comment upon each other's dress, or as in *A Pilgrimage for Religion's Sake:*

Mened. . . . But what's this fancy outfit? You're ringed with scallop shells,
    choked with tin and leaden images on every side, decked out with
    straw necklaces, and you've snake eggs on your arms.[2]

Again, one might compare the response to Menippus' garb at the beginning of *Menippus*. Ogygius, we can tell, must have been on a pilgrimage, just as Menippus can only have been to Hades.

Finally, there are two important opening gambits used by Erasmus to establish that a certain character is the critical mouthpiece of a colloquy, both of which are modelled on Lucian's usage. There are two ways in which these writers launch a dialogue. *In medias res,* whether conversation or action; and at the beginning of a conversation or action. *The Shipwreck* and *Zeus Rants* would be respective examples of the first type, but both authors prefer the latter. The two gambits in question are both designed to get the ironist onto the stage 'in character'. The first introduces him laughing as he enters:

Pamph. Where have you come here from Lycinus, and what is the cause of
    your laughter? (*The Eunuch* 1)

[1] ibid., 503.
[2] ibid., 287.

The second shows the ironist talking to himself about some topic later revealed as central to the plot:

Menip. So it was three thousand stades from earth to the moon, that was my first staging-post, and from there about another 500 parasangs up to the sun; and from there to heaven itself and Zeus' citadel, the ascent would take about a day for a lightly-laden eagle.

Friend In the Graces' name, Menippus, what's all this astronomy and silent calculation? I've been following you for some time, listening to you taking in the strangest way about suns and moons and all that tiresome stuff about staging-posts and parasangs. (*Icaromenippus* 1)

Erasmus uses the 'laughter' motif in *Alchemy* and *Exorcism*:

Thomas What's the good news that makes you chuckle so merrily, as if you had stumbled upon a treasure?[1]

while *The Sermon* begins with the 'overhearing' motif:

Hilary Good God, what monsters the earth breeds and nourishes! So the seraphic gentlemen stop at nothing, eh! I expect they think they're talking to mushrooms, not men.

Lev. What's Hilary muttering to himself? Making verses, I dare say.[2]

These last examples lead us from dramatic effect pure and simple to their use as part of the satirical presentation, contributing to the manipulation of the reader's response to the vices satirized.

The satirical form of the colloquies is particularly interesting because it shows clearly both the similarities and divergencies between Erasmus and Lucian. One important category of colloquies uses a presentation which is not Lucianic at all; that in which both partners take a more or less equally active rôle in expressing the critical point at the heart of the colloquy. So in *Rash Vows*, the critique of pilgrimages is sustained by both Arnold and Cornelius, in *Charon* both Charon and Alastor contribute to the attack on war, equal contributions are made in *A Fish Diet* by the butcher and the fishmonger, in *Beggar Talk* by the beggar and the confidence-trickster. The last is an example of variety within the category; the other dialogues consist of exchanges of criticism by speakers with the same or equivalent standpoints, whereas *Beggar Talk* is a conversation between two *alazones* in which each unmasks himself. This type of exchange is quite different from the

[1] ibid., 231.
[2] ibid., 464.

genuinely dramatic presentation of *The Young Man and the Harlot,* where Erasmus has enlivened the mediaeval morality tale on which he draws for the plot by casting it in the mould of *Dialogues of the Courtesans.* In *Rash Vows, Charon* and the others, it is not a case of dramatic presentation, simply of an exchange of views.

A second group of colloquies uses the very common Lucianic form of a retrospective account given by a critical speaker to a passive listener. *The Shipwreck, The Sermon, The Funeral, Alchemy* and *Exorcism* are examples of this type, which follows the conventions of *The Eunuch.* The other three types of dialogue can all be categorized as ironic. They are variants on Lucianic techniques, without having precise equivalents. In the first, an uncritical speaker gives an account which is satirically received by his interlocutor. This is the technique in *A Pilgrimage for Religion's Sake* and *The Seraphic Funeral.* In the second, a self-conscious *alazōn* gives an account of himself to an openly critical interlocutor, as in *Cyclops, Military Affairs* and *The Dedicated Liar.* In the third, a mock encomium is delivered by the ironist to an uncritical speaker, who plays an equal but unintentional rôle in attacking the vices censured. This, a very elaborate form, is used in *The Ignoble Knight.* The first two of these are, in fact, simply variants on the same structure, since the uncritical speakers of *A Pilgrimage for Religion's Sake* and *The Seraphic Funeral* are unconscious *alazones* satirized for their credulity. The idea can be seen as an extension into dialogue form of the self-revelation of the villain in *A Professor of Public Speaking* or a more immediate version of the self-revelation of philosophers reported at second-hand in dialogues such as *The Lover of Lies* and *The Banquet.* *The Ignoble Knight* similarly takes the pamphlet style of *A Professor of Public Speaking* and re-distributes the rôles of the ironist, and of the trainer's speech as he records it, into a direct dialogue.

This remodelling of different elements to create a more varied range of satirical presentation is an understandable necessity for Erasmus, if we take into account the fact that he is committed to realistic subjects (only *Charon* is a fantasy) and to maintaining dialogue form. Most of Lucian's realistic subjects are handled as pamphlets or treatises, so that he is not obliged to repeat the techniques of *The Eunuch* or *The Lover of Lies* very often. The variation of satirical form in the dialogues occurs largely with the fantasy subjects, where a broad range of motifs such as the mock trial or the shift from earth to heaven could be brought in. This sort of material was hardly appropriate to Erasmus' purpose.

Hence the adaptation of a narrow range of Lucianic elements into new combinations.

This extension of dialogue types also involves greater variety in the rôle of the second speaker. I have already remarked that in the non-Lucianic form of *Rash Vows* et al. both speakers are given equal status as critical observers. In the form where the criticism is delivered directly by one speaker, the interlocutor retains the normative rôle that Pamphilus has in *The Eunuch*. This can vary, however, from the passive rôle of Thomas in *Exorcism*, who apart from a little corroborative sarcasm—'Clearly Polus behaved like a reverent and modest devil'—merely serves to prompt Anselm's story with appropriate questions, to the abusive interjections of Levinus in *The Sermon*, who denounces the wretched Merdardus with as much vigour as Hilary does. Erasmus also makes use, though more sparingly than Lucian, of the convention whereby the second speaker assumes the best about the villain, and has to be corrected. As with Pamphilus, and with Philocles (*The Lover of Lies*), Levinus shows a tendency to assume that the *alazōn*, in this case a Franciscan, must have the virtues to which his type lays claim. He assumes that he must be a learned man; he explains his vices by the incorrect supposition that he belongs to a slacker branch of the order. None the less, his rôle remains within the category of prompter to the main critic. Where the dialogue is centred on irony rather than invective, and the main speaker is the *alazōn*, the second speaker's rôle is quite different. It has something in common with the manner of Tychiades in *The Parasite*, but is more overtly subversive. The subversion can range from direct attack to the driest of irony. Cannius (*Cyclops*) and Philetymus (*The Dedicated Liar and The Man of Honour*) rely largely on invective, Menedemus (*A Pilgrimage for Religion's Sake*), says almost consistently the opposite of what he means, or deliberately supports an absurd position, as in the interchange following the reading of the Virgin's letter:

Mened. A dreadful, threatening letter indeed! Glaucoplutus will take warning, I imagine.
Ogyg. If he's wise.
Mened. Why didn't the excellent St James write to him on this same subject?
Ogyg. I don't know, except that he's rather far away, and all letters are intercepted nowadays.[1]

Finally, in *The Ignoble Knight* the rôle of the second speaker is raised to

[1] ibid., 291.

completely equal status with that of the ironist, while remaining totally different in kind. This is done in order to accommodate the two aspects of *A Professor of Public Speaking*, mock encomium and self-inculpation, on the same level. Here both speakers apparently subscribe to an entirely inverted set of values, leaving the reader to judge the true values from his own common sense, and with a little covert assistance from the ironist. Such a development is, in a sense, the logical effect of Erasmus' attempt to give as great a variety as possible to the secondary roles. It is Lucianic in spirit, but original in execution.

What Erasmus does in the *Colloquies*, then, is to focus on a narrow range of Lucianic techniques. Parody, pastiche, fantasy are largely ignored as not germane to the realistic genre. There are isolated examples of Lucian's purely rhetorical devices, the use of syncrisis in *The Funeral*, or the allegorical description of paintings in *The Godly Feast*, but it would be difficult to show that these are significantly Lucianic. The satirical presentation, on the other hand, represents a careful exploitation of a few techniques to give the greatest variety of effects.

If the *Colloquies* show the widest variety of Lucianic traits, the most sustained piece of Lucianic satire in the Erasmian corpus is undoubtedly the *Praise of Folly*. This should not be surprising. Written in 1509, published in 1511, and subject to minor revisions and additions right up to 1522, it belongs fairly and squarely to the period of the Lucianic translations and of several of the satirical colloquies. It is a mock encomium of Folly, spoken by herself, and constructed according to the rules of the genre.[1] The subject itself was closely connected with Lucian; the Aldine edition had printed at its head the epigram 'On his own book', whose opening couplet proclaims an expert knowledge of folly:

> This work is Lucian's, who well knew
> The foolishness of times gone by,
> For things the human race finds wise
> Are folly to th' unclouded eye.

The genre of the mock encomium was also very particularly associated with him. Though Erasmus' prefatory letter to his fellow Lucianist, Thomas More, lists many other precedents, among them only Lucian was the author of satirical parody cast in the form of pseudo-praise. The

[1] See W. J. Kaiser, *Praisers of Folly: Erasmus, Rabelais, Shakespeare*, London 1964.

closest parallel is not with *The Fly,* mentioned in the preface, which is merely praise of the trivial, or *Phalaris,* which Erasmus gives as an example in 3 of the text, where the inversion of normal values is simply ingenious. It is with *A Professor of Public Speaking* and *The Parasite*; the indefensible is praised in order to attack it.

Any such rapprochement is, however, an over-simplification. One of the notable features of *Praise of Folly* is the ambiguity of its meaning, and the close relationship of this to the ambiguities of its literary form. The encomium sets out as a light-hearted defence of folly as the chief benefactor of mankind. It plays with a number of conceits that bring to light the natural absurdity of essential aspects of existence—procreation, entertainment, friendship—and also touch upon genuine anomalies such as the attractiveness of childhood, the pre-rational state of man. As in *The Parasite,* leaps of logic encompassed by the assumption that if you prove something is not true, you have proved that the opposite *is* true, lead to charming absurdities of argument. Yet, at times, these leaps lead to the assertion by Folly of a perfectly acceptable statement speciously—or is it so speciously?—associated with her rule:

In short, no association or alliance can be happy or stable without me. People cannot long tolerate a ruler, nor can a master his servant, a maid her mistress, a teacher his pupil, a friend his friend, nor a wife her husband, a landlord his tenant, a soldier his comrade nor a party-goer his companion, unless they sometimes have illusions about each other, make use of flattery, and have the sense to turn a blind eye and sweeten life for themselves with the honey of folly. (21)[1]

From para. 31, the tone of the work gradually changes into one of direct attack on vices. At first, paradox remains uppermost, with the use of the innocent instinctiveness of the Golden Age as an argument for the benefits of ignorance. As Folly moves on to examine gamblers and the superstitious, the satire is more overt. Again, however, there are ambiguities, as in 45 on the advantages of being deceived; Folly employs potentially interesting ideas to the wrong ends just as much as she relies on openly absurd ideas. Eventually, at 48, the element of parody, and with it the ambiguity, disappears, to be replaced by an all-out diatribe against a series of followers of Folly: pedants, writers, lawyers, philosophers, theologians, monks, princes, courtiers, church

[1] Quotations from *Praise of Folly* are given in the translation by B. Radice, Penguin Classics, 1971.

dignitaries, even popes. Then, from 62, the element of paradox returns, as Folly expounds the Christian folly of St Paul. Here the interpretation of the piece is at its most difficult, since the rejection of worldly wisdom that is involved is an important part of Erasmus' own Christian ideals, yet Folly, in attacking 'Greek pedants', is scoffing at the humanist approach to the Bible which Erasmus himself worked so hard to promote.

The gradations of attitude which the reader is asked to assume towards Folly are wide, nor do they form the continuum which this analysis might suggest. The norm of common sense is a hard one to maintain in the face of so many areas in which, as on day-to-day human relations (21; see above), Folly seems to speak in a way that is pragmatically, if not ideally, acceptable. There Erasmus is toying with the problem of whether complete honesty between individuals is practicable or desirable; to get an answer by simply inverting the terms in which Folly speaks is impossible. But when the denunciatory voice of the pamphleteer speaks out on matters of religious malpractice, such that the true character of Folly as speaker disappears, then there is no difficulty in identifying the moral standpoint one is expected to take.

To achieve this shifting moral perspective Erasmus has grafted together several literary elements which are not strictly compatible. A large number of them come from Lucian, but from works whose methodology and type of satire are quite different from one another. It would be possible to see Lucian's influence in much the same terms as we looked at it for the *Colloquies*. There are textual references, particularly to *The Cock*, which Erasmus had recently translated (34, 45, 63, 68). There are passages broadly modelled on particular dialogues (*A Professor of Public Speaking, Menippus, The Lover of Lies*). And there are motifs and literary techniques which bear a general resemblance to those of Lucian. Perhaps, however, it is more important to see how these elements combine to create different effects in different parts of the encomium. Folly twice borrows her style of argument from *A Professor of Public Speaking*. The first time is in the opening sections, where she defends her speech and its delivery. Like the trainer, she has deployed the advantages of a style of dress. She is extravagant in her self-praise (cf. *A Professor of Public Speaking* 21) speaks extempore (cf. 20), says 'whatever was on the tip of my tongue' (a grammatically adjusted quotation, in Greek, from *A Professor of Public Speaking* 18), and takes no trouble to get things in the right order (also 18). At one point a passage of the same pamphlet is apparently used negatively.

Folly pours scorn on those who sprinkle their text with Greek and who 'dig four or five obsolete words out of mouldy manuscripts with which to cloud the meaning for the reader'; whereas the trainer speaks enthusiastically of throwing in obscure vocabulary. This is not in fact a negative use at all. For Folly herself uses Greek phrases liberally throughout the text, and is thus ridiculing her own practice. This instance highlights the complexity of the literary game that is being played. Folly, like the trainer, is delivering an encomium of herself in terms which (thus far) we are clearly meant to reject. Her description of her verbal manner is, however, the opposite of what it really is. It is not extempore, but precisely follows the normal rhetorical patterns. It uses Greek, but not in the inelegant or obscurantist way which she attacks.

Here Erasmus is using the inversion of values from *A Professor of Public Speaking* to confuse the reader's response to the text, though on a purely light-hearted level. The second time we meet material from that pamphlet, it is being quite differently used. This is in the diatribe against the followers of Folly, in the section on monks. Erasmus has already attributed to them the boorishness and shamelessness of behaviour that characterizes all Lucianic villains. Now he comments on their sermons, attacking in them what the trainer recommends in himself: slander (cf. 23), gesticulation, shouting and general histrionics (19–20), the irrelevance of the exordium (20), the elaborate honorific forms of address (19). This time Erasmus has eliminated the element of paradox, and invites the reader to take up a relationship to the material quite different from that exploited in the earlier instance.

A comparable manipulation of directly borrowed motifs occurs with the images of the world as a stage, and seen as from a great height. If we set these motifs as they occur in *Menippus* (16) against their use in *Praise* (29), it is clear that Lucian's direct denunciation of the human condition, in the Cynic mode, is irrevocable. Erasmus' paradoxical enunciation of life's shortcomings is given without a clear moral standpoint at all. For Folly is in fact pursuing the argument that, in judging the 'play' of life, there is such a thing as misplaced wisdom. Though unacceptable in the terms in which she formulates it, the argument is not simply to be rejected, or the truth to be perceived by inverting it. The same is true of the 'world seen from on high' in 31. But when the latter motif occurs again in 48, this time drawing on a direct reference to *Icaromenippus* 15–19, the presentation is completely different. The diatribe tone of the original is maintained without modulation, and marks the transition from a section of diluted paradox to one of direct attack:

> To sum up, if you could look down from the moon, as Menippus once did, on the countless hordes of mortals, you'd think you saw a swarm of flies or gnats quarrelling among themselves, fighting, plotting, stealing, playing, making love, being born, growing old and dying. It's hard to believe how much trouble and tragedy this tiny little creature can stir up, shortlived as he is, for sometimes a brief war or an outbreak of plague can carry off and destroy many thousands at once.

This double use of motifs borrowed from specific works is matched by double attitudes to more general themes held in common. Take, for example, the type of the philosopher as presented in *Praise*. All the sects are pilloried directly (52), after the manner of *Icaromenippus* 4–6, for their cosmologies, their abstract notions and their single-minded assertion of possessing the only key to the truth. The Stoics, Lucian's particular favourites as target, come in for ridicule in *Praise* too, on the familiar counts. When Folly is speaking slightingly of dialectical subtleties, it is the crocodile and the horns that she refers to (cf. *The Banquet* and *The Cock*). When dealing with pleasure, it is the hypocrisy of the Stoics, again as in *The Banquet*, that she instantly adduces:

> Even the Stoics don't despise pleasure, though they are careful to conceal their real feelings, and tear it to pieces in public with their incessant outcry, so that once they have frightened everyone else off, they can enjoy it more freely themselves.

These attacks occur in the paradoxical section of the piece, but we can hardly do other than take Folly's remarks at face value. The same would be true of her view of Plato, whose theory of ideas is sent up, along with later notions of a comparably abstract sort, in the same way that it frequently is in Lucian (e.g. *Icaromenippus* loc. cit., *Philosophers for Sale* 18):

> Though ignorant even of themselves, and sometimes not able to see the ditch or stone lying in the path, either because most of them are half-blind or their minds are far away, they still boast they can see ideas, universals, separate forms, prime matters, quiddities, ecceities, things which are all so insubstantial that I doubt if even Lynceus could perceive them.

Yet elsewhere Erasmus would seem to praise the Stoic concept of virtue, and the scorn for Plato in 27 redounds to his honour. He uses, in fact, philosophical ethics in certain parts of *Praise* as a positive quantity, while making, in other parts, metaphysics a negative quantity. But the precise relationship of the reader to the voice of Folly as she communicates this judgment has to be adjusted for each individual statement.

It would not be true to say, however, that all Lucianic parallels occurred in this double form. In general, one can see in all those who are directly attacked that they fall into the same Lucianic categories as the equivalent characters in the *Colloquies*. Erasmus is again dealing with hypocrisy, superstition and the exploitation of power. Superstition is introduced by the type of credulous man portrayed in *The Lover of Lies* and exemplified in the colloquy *Exorcism*. The uneasy joys of kingship are exposed in the manner of *The Ship* and *The Cock*. In presenting these themes, Erasmus limits himself more or less to one variety of Lucianic presentation, invective. Burlesque and other humorous elements are eliminated; indignation remains.

If one tries to make a summary of the Lucianic contribution to the structure, style and content of *Praise*, it goes some way, perhaps, towards explaining its inconsistencies. Erasmus is presenting a very complex case. Some of what Folly attacks is clearly meant to be seen as praised, some as dispraised. Some of what she praises is clearly to be rejected: some seems to have a potential positive quality, or, by the end of the piece, an almost entirely positive quality. That Folly should praise the right thing for the wrong reason, or be so foolish as to attack what she should be praising, is in character. It is not entirely un-Lucianic, either. When the first speaker in *A Professor of Public Speaking* rejects archaism, in the form of the study of Plato and Demosthenes, as a suitable training for the profession, we are meant to accept the criticism of archaism, but to reject the belief that Plato and Demosthenes are its representatives. The right thing is dispraised on the wrong grounds. But, beyond all this, Erasmus has to reconcile two quite different problems. The first is a moral one: though he knows the limitations of what he attacks, he also knows the limitations of what he defends. Hence the self-irony in the references to his own work and to the attitudes of humanism in general. There is no simple definition of wisdom; hence there is none of folly. The second problem is purely aesthetic. Since his subject is by no means straightforward, he has a lot of material to cover. Now, unlike the dialogue, mock encomium is a very restrictive form. It can be varied with anecdote, quotation and proverb (here the resemblance to Lucian is more significant than it is in the *Colloquies*), but you cannot alternate action and narration. The risk is that of monotony. As a solution to the double problem, Erasmus imports all the major Lucianic devices, but concentrates each in a different 'movement' of the piece. In this way the divergencies within the thought are deliberately emphasized by the divergencies within the form. Broadly speaking, the encomium passes from the ironic manner of *A Professor of Public Speaking*, considerably lightened by the burlesque of the pagan gods, to a mixture of irony and invective after the manner of the 'realistic' dialogues, and gradually arrives at the invective, barely alleviated even by sarcasm, of the treatises (there are even close textual parallels with *On Sacrifices* in 47) and the blacker pamphlets. Borrowed motifs will be presented according to the predominant tone of the section in which they appear, and not necessarily that of the Lucianic works from which they are borrowed. The result is that motifs which Lucian treats in different ways in different works, Erasmus treats variously within the same work, emphasizing the complexity of his subject by this variety of approach, and at the same time maintaining the literary interest.

The influence of Lucian on Erasmus' literary manner is clearly a fundamental one, in the works discussed. This is not to say that Erasmus took his concepts, or even the desire to use satire as a medium, from his model. He found in Lucian both positive and negative attitudes which accorded with his own, and which he thought applicable to both his private experience and to public events of his day. This encouraged him to adapt the literary methods of his forerunner to his own ends. Undoubtedly he met many of the same devices in Lucian's own sources, the dramatic method in Aristophanes, the ironic conduct of argument in Plato; but the prefaces to the translations show that it was to Lucian he instinctively looked when he thought of the vices of his age. Indeed, since he clearly believed that Lucian's work itself dealt with reality—even if it sometimes approached it via allusion and allegory—then in attacking Heinrich von Eppendorf under the guise of *The Ignoble Knight* or in denouncing the disgrace brought upon true religion by the excesses of certain monks, he was responding to the world about him in the same way that he supposed Lucian had done. Of course, many other influences, classical and mediaeval, contributed to the final shape of the *Praise of Folly* and the *Colloquies*, just as many contemporary events and people contributed to their content; but the spirit, form, and in some degree the matter, were all deeply Lucianic.

2. FIELDING

That Fielding knew Lucian, and knew him well, is not hard to establish.[1] An auctioneer's pamphlet, preserved in the British Museum, shows that Fielding owned no less than nine editions of Lucian's collected works. Two of the sets were in French, one was the four-volume 'Dryden' English translation, one was a reprint of the first Latin *Opera omnia*, edited by Jacob Moltzer, in which the stock sixteenth-century versions (by Erasmus, More et al.) were all collected, the other five were bilingual Greek-Latin editions with scholarly notes, ranging from an early seventeenth-century reprint of the Basel 1563 edition (the first bilingual *Opera omnia*) to the most up-to-date and elaborate edition available.[2] The reason for this proliferation, and for the fact that every single volume is in part or whole a translation, becomes obvious from the advertisement in the *Covent Garden Journal* no. 51 (Tuesday June 27, 1752) announcing a proposed (but apparently never started) translation by Fielding himself, in collaboration with William Young, of Lucian's complete works.

The interest in Lucian which such a proposal indicates is confirmed by the many references to him in Fielding's journalism. He puts great emphasis on his qualities as a moralist. In an early number of the *CGJ* (no. 10) he had named him, with Cervantes and Swift, as one of a triumvirate, whose satire he valued particularly highly: '. . . not indeed for that wit and humour alone which they all so eminently possess, but because they all endeavoured, with the utmost force of their wit and humour, to expose and extirpate those follies and vices which chiefly prevailed in their several countries.' Elsewhere he lays more stress on the comic manner itself. As he puts it in *CGJ* no. 60: 'It requires . . . the wit of Lucian or South to drag the philosophers or dissenters into almost every subject', an attitude confirmed by the passage in *Amelia* 8. v where Booth describes Lucian as 'a Greek wag, and in my opinion, the greatest in the humorous way that the world ever produced'. These two sides, humour and moral instruction, are brought together and balanced against one another in an extended eulogy in *CGJ* no. 52. The quality of the satire is in part attributed to

---

[1] The impetus for my study of Fielding was derived from the excellent discussion of Lucianic influence on the first book of the *Miscellanies* in H. K. Miller, *Essays on Fielding's 'Miscellanies': a commentary on volume 1*, Princeton 1961.

[2] See E. M. Thornbury, *Henry Fielding's Theory of the Comic Prose Epic*, Madison 1931, 10–11. The description of the volumes is confused, but it is possible to identify which editions are involved.

the material available to Lucian: 'What fund of pleasantry hath any age produced equal to that theology and to that philosophy which he hath exposed!' At the same time, his standing as a moralist is enhanced by attributing to him a positive moral position: Fielding agrees with Dryden in finding what the latter had called 'examples of a good life in the persons of the true philosophers'. None the less, it seems to be the comic manner which essentially attracts Fielding. He defines it in terms of 'the exquisite pleasantry of his humour . . . the neatness of his wit, and . . . the poignancy of his satire'. He stresses Lucian's attainments in this field, describing him as 'almost to be called the father of true humour', and trumpeting the superiority of genius which seems to him to appear in Lucian when he is compared with any other humorous writer (notably Aristophanes). The reading of him, he says, will be an exquisite pleasure for those who already have a true taste of humour, and for those who have not will be the only proper means of acquiring such a taste. Most important of all, he concludes the article by drawing our attention to the influence of Lucian on his own writing, calling himself a man 'who hath formed his style upon that very author'.

Though the panegyric is fulsome, and as vague as one would expect of the genre, the outlines of Fielding's attitudes are clear. He evidently took Lucian very seriously as a moralist, finding in particular a common ground in the attack on religious humbug. Equally he saw in him a positive standard of which he approved, the 'examples of a good life'. Thirdly he saw him as having developed the perfect satirical balance between humour and attack. And lastly he felt a significant stylistic indebtedness. Given that he considered that 'there is a strict analogy between the taste and morals of an age; and depravity in one always induces depravity in the other', he clearly felt that he and Lucian shared that balance of good taste and morality which was so lacking in their respective contemporaries.

Possibly the most direct imitation of Lucian in Fielding's works is an article written for the *Champion* for Saturday May 24, 1740. In the opening paragraph, Fielding paraphrases the plot of *Dialogues of the Dead* 20:

I took up the other day one of Lucian's dialogues in which that witty author introduces Charon addressing himself to several passengers, and representing to them the smallness of his boat, and the necessity of their leaving everything behind them for want of room. Then Mercury proceeds to examine into the baggage of each individual, and obliges one to lay aside his beauty, another his riches, his pride, his cruelty, a third his honours, a fourth his delicacy, and thus having stripped them of all their vices and follies, he admits them into his boat.

The rest of the article relates the substance of a dream modelled on this dialogue, in which Fielding substitutes for Lucian's types a succession of his own more appropriate to his age, including the politician, the prude, the Methodist and the patriot. In many ways he conforms to Lucian's pattern. The first three to enter the boat all fall into the category *beauty*, like the first person (after Menippus) to enter Lucian's boat, Charmoleos, the darling of Megara. But Fielding's attack on beauty concentrates on its contemporary aspect. His victims are satirized for their fashions: the lady's wig, the young girl's absurd dress, the beau's 'laced paduasoy'; whereas Lucian deals only with traditional physical beauty. The closest parallel among the voyagers is between Fielding's 'man with a very grave countenance, who . . . spoke very little to any of the company', and Lucian's philosopher:

This august personage, at least he looks to be one, with his head held high, his eyebrows superciliously raised, his meditative air, his thick beard—who is he? (8)

Fielding too has Mercury make him discard his grave countenance, but does not exploit the difference between outer gravity and inner corruption which is essential to Lucian's portrait. Nor does he reveal the show of wisdom to be a cloak for ignorance: the gentleman is allowed to keep his wisdom as genuine. Apart from these characters, Fielding's travellers are dealt with after the style of Lucian's, but not in their image. At some points motifs from other works are brought in to vary the presentation. The sinking of the boat which ends the dream matches both the idea contained in Charon's opening remarks of *Dialogues of the Dead* 20: 'As you can see, the boat you're getting is small, rotten and full of leaks; and if it tilts to one side, it will turn turtle and sink without trace', and the equivalent situation from *The Downward Journey* 18, where Menippus initially elects to swim for it, lest the boat should founder. Fielding's theme of attempting to bribe Charon, and similarly the expressed intention to bribe the devil, have a parallel in *The Downward Journey* 4 where Hermes announces that someone has tried to bribe him, the someone in question being the same Megapenthes who later (9) attempts to bribe Clotho to let him not enter the boat. The arrival of a group of officers, apparently signalling the occurrence of a battle, is similar to the presence of war dead in *The Downward Journey* 6, but here Fielding gains an amusing point by making his men dead of a cold (this idea of unexpected, and somehow irrelevant, death is a favourite Lucianic motif too). Thus what Fielding does is to take the basic situation from *Dialogues of the Dead* 20, particularly the notion of Hermes stripping his victims of abstract qualities and of the comic attempts of the victims to cling to these abstracts by concealing them about their person. At the same time he expands upon Lucian's idea that genuine and positive qualities may be retained:

Philosopher What about you, Menippus? Take off your liberty, your plain-speaking, your freedom from pain, your high-mindedness and your laughter. You are the only one who laughs.

Hermes Not at all; you keep them. For they are light and very easy to carry and useful on the voyage.

In Fielding's version several characters are allowed to retain positive qualities—the grave gentleman his wisdom, the young girl both her innocence and her beauty, the parsons their religion (in moderation). He is distinguishing closely between moderate or unaffected qualities and the cloak of social convention in a way that Lucian is not. As a result the work is quite distinctive in tone. It offers a more particular satire, because of the contemporary references, and a more positive picture of virtue, while using, with comic variations of Fielding's own, the structure of one Lucianic dialogue and a number of motifs from another.

Two of Fielding's plays, *Eurydice* (1737) and *The Author's Farce* (1730), contain material of a similar kind to the *Champion* article. Curiously enough, the Eurydice theme is linked by Fielding with that article, when he says in the preamble that the dream was inspired either by reading *Dialogues of the Dead* 20 or by attending a performance of *Orpheus and Eurydice*. The main theme of the play is not Lucianic; Fielding simply uses the Orpheus legend as an excuse for ridiculing the foibles of fashionable society. One little scene is, however, straight out of the *Dialogues of the Dead*. As it opens, Charon has ferried over the Styx an Irishman who is unable to pay his fare:

Charon You, Mr Maccahone, will you please to pay me my fare?
Macch. Ay, fet would I with all my shoule, but honey, I did die nor worth a sixpence, and that I did leave behind me.

It is the opening of *Dialogues of the Dead* 2.

Charon Pay me the fare, scoundrel.
Menipp. Shout away Charon, if it pleases you better.

Charon Pay me, I say, for ferrying you over.
Menipp. You can't take what I haven't got.
Charon Is there anyone without even a farthing?
Menipp. I can't speak for anyone else, but I certainly haven't got one.

Charon threatens to carry Maccahone back to the other side, which, in Lucian, is what Menippus suggests he do. Maccahone is represented as laughing at Charon, which only Menippus does, and his plan to annoy Charon by building a bridge across the Styx is represented as 'biting' the ferryman, a doggish image most appropriate to a Menippus-substitute. The rest of the play passes on again to its satire of marital infidelity, fops and prominent persons, isolating the literary reference of this single scene as almost a private literary joke.

The underworld scene in *The Author's Farce* has a variation on the same motif to open it—Lucian too uses it twice, for *The Downward Journey* 21 records the inability of the cobbler Micyllus to pay his farthing. This time Charon is ferrying across literary figures to the Court of Nonsense—a scene which we shall have cause to look at shortly in another context. But before these persons arrive, he has a series of more conventional encounters:

Charon Never tell me, sir. I expect my fare. I wonder what trade these authors drive in the other world: I would with as good a will see a soldier aboard my boat. A tattered red coat and a tattered black one bilked me so often that I am resolved never to take either of them up again—unless I am paid beforehand.
Poet What a wretched thing it is to be poor! My body lay a fortnight in the other world before it was buried. And this fellow has kept my spirit a month sunning himself on the other side of the river, because my pockets were empty.

The rest of the scene is more broadly in the manner of *Dialogues of the Dead* 20 and *The Downward Journey* with some of the motifs re-used in the *Champion* sketch. A rich man,[1] here a company director, tries to bribe Charon to let him take his wealth over:

Director Pshaw, pshaw! you shall go snacks with me and I warrant we cheat the devil . . .

just as Megapenthes tries to persuade Clotho not to put him on the boat: 'If you let me run off, I promise to give you a thousand talents of

---

[1] This episode was added in the revised edition of 1734 as a reference to the misconduct of officials of the Charitable Corporation.

gold newly minted' (9). As a result, the director is 'well-fettered and carried aboard', while Megapenthes has to be fastened to the mast. The pattern of Fielding's imitation is much the same as in the *Champion* article. He varies his range of types far more broadly than his model and indulges in more contemporary reference. When a crowd of spirits arrive together, they are not the victims of a war, but 'a waggon-load of ghosts arrived from England that were knocked on the head at a late election'. Similarly, the occasion of death is used, as in *Journey from This World to the Next*, for a little satire at the expense of the medical profession of the day:

2 sailor   Sir, a great number of passengers arrived from London, all bound to the Court of Nonsense.
Charon   Some plague, I suppose, or a fresh cargo of physicians come to town from the universities.

This is a motif sketched in by Lucian, e.g. *The Downward Journey* 6 '. . . and bring those who died from fever too, and their doctor, Aga-thocles, with them', but developed in terms of the comic type of the incompetent doctor consecrated by Molière and late seventeenth-century comedy.

So far I have spoken of deliberate imitation. In a broader sense, too, one can see a use of specific Lucianic motifs in works which do not, like the ones so far considered, have the general form—an underworld visit—of a Lucianic work. Take, for example, the auction scene in Fielding's scandalous political lampoon *The Historical Register for the Year 1736*. The name of the auctioneer in the play, Mr Hen, shows that Fielding had in mind a genuine auctioneer, one Christopher Cock, whose institution was patronized by the beau monde. But the idea of putting under the hammer a series of abstract qualities, and recording the buyers' response to them, is very reminiscent of the auction of philosophies (for that is what the work really portrays) in *Philosophers for Sale*. Fielding's lots include 'a most curious remnant of political honesty', 'a most delicate piece of patriotism', 'three grains of modesty', 'one bottle of courage', 'a very clear conscience which has been worn by a judge and a bishop' and 'a very considerable quantity of interest at court'. He uses them to poke fun at the buyers, which Lucian does not, but the revelations of roguery and hypocrisy are in the Lucianic man-ner. So too are the positive qualities which are so unenthusiastically received:

Hen   Lot 10 and Lot 11, a great deal of wit and a little commonsense.

Banter Why do you put these up together? They have no relation to each other.

Hen   Well, the sense by itself then: Lot 10, a little commonsense—I assure you gentlemen, this is a very valuable commodity; come, who puts in?

Medley You observe, as valuable as it is, nobody bids.

Some of the verbal devices are the same too, though Fielding is fonder of puns (to which English, in any case, lends itself much better). The straightforward recommendation by the auctioneer of somewhat ambiguous qualities is an example. Thus, Hermes, praising the accomplishments of the Pythagorean:

Hermes He knows arithmetic, astronomy, jugglery, geometry, music and quackery. It's a tiptop soothsayer you're looking at.

And Mr Hen, offering the bottle of courage:

. . . it has served a campaign or two in Hyde Park, since the alderman's death —it will never waste while you stay at home, but it evaporates immediately if carried abroad.

A piece in the *Champion* for Saturday December 15, 1739 transfers a similar Lucianic motif, the notion of fishing for philosophers in *The Dead Come to Life*, into the image of politicians fishing for supporters. The attractiveness of the bait is, of course, the important thing although, whereas Lucian's philosophers all bite at gold, Fielding's politicos are rather more various in their tastes. In practice, however, the distinctions are not so very fine. The greed of the dog-fish (i.e. the Cynic) who swallows fig and gold right down and has to be made to regurgitate them is similar in kind to both the pike of Scotland and Cornwall—'they all bite very greedily, and require little nicety in the baiting'—and the political chubb, who will 'bite at anything, either natural or artificial, indeed anything that is soft or sweet and will hang on the hook'. The satire of the article, which is openly a comparison, 'The art of politics is not unlike the art of fishing', and not a fantasy as *The Dead Come to Life* is, depends upon the ingenuity with which the central point is elaborated:

As the chief excellency of both consists in choosing proper baits, I shall lay down some instructions whereby the politician may know how to bait his hook as well as the fisherman.

An essential part of the humour comes from the device, highly Lucianic but not used in the same way in *The Dead Come to Life*, of using misplaced quotations for comic effect, since his descriptions of the various fish are drawn from a real fisherman's guide, the *Compleat Fisherman* of James Saunders (1724).

A somewhat different example of parallel motifs is the letter from the man-in-the-moon to Hercules Vinegar, in the *Champion* for May 10, 1740. Here Fielding takes two Lucianic devices, the letter from heaven, e.g. Cronos to Lucian in *Saturnalia,* and the speech of the moon to Menippus in *Icaromenippus.* Lucian's moon, who is a woman, devotes part of her complaint to her objections about philosophical speculation over her nature, but the second section of her speech (21) sets out in a simple way the same theme as Fielding's moon embroiders upon, i.e. the revelations of hypocrisy on earth that the moon could make. Fielding extends Lucian's general statement about adultery and thieving to a whole string of vices—the worship of wealth, social pretension, private tyranny—as well as embroidering on sexual misdemeanours. The second part of the letter introduces a theatrical metaphor entirely within Lucian's manner in passages of moral commentary; it is a Cynic device which he uses passim in *Nigrinus* (and cf. *Menippus* 16, *The Dead Come to Life* 31–5).

A final example of motif-borrowing is Nehemiah Vinegar's dream of the Palace of Wealth in the *Champion* for December 27 and 29, 1739. The moral of the articles is one dear to both Lucian and Fielding:

> As soon as I came to myself, I could not avoid some reflections on my vision which may possibly arise in the minds of most of my readers. It appeared to me that wealth is of all worldly blessings the most imaginary; that avarice is at once the greatest tyrant and the greatest object of compassions; and that the acquisition of overgrown fortunes seldom brings the acquirer more than the care of preserving them and the fear of losing them.

It is the theme of Lucian's *The Cock,* which Booth is made to admire so enthusiastically in *Amelia* 8.v; Micyllus also dreams about wealth, and the cock proves to him its overwhelming disadvantages. Perhaps this is hardly a significant connexion, given the general currency of such a moral stance in European literature: Fielding had himself written a play, *The Miser,* adapted from Plautus and Molière. However, the central image of the *Champion* articles, the Palace of Wealth itself, is after the style of Lucian's description of an imaginary allegorical painting of Wealth and her devotees at the end of *On Salaried Posts* (42). Lucian's 'high gilded gateway' is in Fielding 'a huge old fabric of the Gothic kind; its outside seemed all of pure gold'. In Lucian the palace is placed at the top of a steep and arduous hill. Those who actually reach its doorway are greeted with the sight of the very beautiful and desirable God of Wealth. But the approach to the god is illusory. Hope leads the would-be suitor on to a series of disillusioning encounters with Deceit, Servitude, Pain and Old Age, until finally, broken, old and naked, he is ejected 'from some concealed back exit'. Fielding makes the approach simpler: the palace is across a vast plain. The difficulty of ascent is transferred to within the palace. Wealth, here a young lady of great beauty 'whose person was set off with all the nicety of art and a vast profusion of shining ornaments', is equally unapproachable. The main occupation of those within the palace is avoiding falling into a huge pit, the equivalent of Lucian's back exit; people continuously attempt to scramble from the crowded gallery upward to positions of illusory safety. Fielding, however, balances his picture of the trials of wealth not with the total annihilation of *On Salaried Posts*, but with the glimpse of the pleasures of poverty:

I was alarmed with a very loud laugh ascending from the cave, upon which casting my eyes downwards, I could just perceive, by the dim light of a very small candle, several persons dancing to the sound of a scraping fiddle; and not far from them a set of the merriest countenances I had ever seen, sitting around a table, and feeding, as it appeared, very heartily on some dish which I could not at that distance distinguish.

Here we have poverty after the style of the cobbler Micyllus in *The Cock* (22):

When you have finished a sandal, you get your 7 farthings pay, get up from your work in the late afternoon, have a bath if you fancy one, buy a bit of rock salmon, or some sprats, or a few onions, and enjoy yourself, singing a lot and having a heart-to-heart with dear old Poverty.

For, in both *The Cock* and the *Champion* article the final irony is that within the limitations of their means the poor still have a capacity for enjoyment denied the rich. Simon the parvenu (29) is pale, thin as a rake from worry: in the gallery of the Palace of Wealth Vinegar notes 'the meagre aspects and wretched appearance of its inhabitants, most of whom were little better dressed than beggars'. The elaborate allegory of Fielding, with its contemporary touches—e.g. the great man whose fall brings down others, but who always seems to regain his own fortune—far outstrips Lucian in its variety of detail, though lacking the formal element of *ecphrasis* of *On Salaried Posts* or the lighter humour of *The Ship*. None the less, it seems to have been prompted, or at least assisted, by elements from both.

In a broader category of imitation are those works which take the form of a Lucianic genre in its entirety without approximating to any particular work. The first volume of Fielding's *Miscellanies* (1743) contains two pieces which fall into this category, *An Interlude between Jupiter, Juno, Apollo and Mercury* and *A Dialogue between Alexander the Great and Diogenes the Cynic*. The latter is a confrontation between two of Fielding's unfavourite characters, the 'great man' and the kill-joy, in which each unmasks the pretensions of the other. The substance is a discussion of power, honour and ambition, with a sideswipe at the hypocrisy of totally rejecting worldly values. It is not a dialogue of the dead, but a version of the famous meeting between general and philosopher which several ancient writers (though not Lucian) record. It is true that Lucian uses Alexander in two of the *Dialogues of the Dead* 12 and 13, of which the latter is between Alexander and Diogenes, but the subject of that dialogue is a playful account of Alexander's family tree, especially his claims to divine blood, a point which Fielding touches on only once. There is a more general connexion between *Dialogues of the Dead* 12, with its insistance on Alexander's pride in his military achievements, and the emphasis put on honour, glory and fame by Fielding's Alexander; but Lucian makes little play with the concept of power, a strong motif in the English dialogue, nor does he investigate the foundations of that power. For that aspect we must look to *Dialogues of the Dead* 25, the rivalry between Alexander, Hannibal and Scipio for the title of greatest general. Alexander's speech, in Fielding's dialogue, beginning: 'Thou dost speak vainly in contempt of a power which no other man yet arrived at' follows the tone and pattern of his self-encomium in Lucian (4). Both lay stress on the number of dead as some sort of achievement:

(Fielding) Are not the fields of Issus and Arbela still white with human bones?

(Lucian) . . . I reached Issus, where I was met by Darius, leading an army of many thousands of men. Minos, you know how many dead I sent down to you as a result of this in a single day.

But the details could as well come from Plutarch or Arrian, and the vision of Alexander as a mad butcher is a common eighteenth-century one. If there is a parallel between texts, it is perhaps with the wish formulated by Samippus in *The Ship*, which, despite the protestation

(28), 'My wish is to become a king, but not one like Alexander, son of Philip', is founded on Alexander's career. Lycinus plays the Diogenes, mentioning Samippus' victims, the oriental adoration to be paid to him, the danger to his troops, the obsession with going on to greater glory: all of them motifs used by Fielding. Diogenes' attack on the validity of Alexander's supposed happiness:

> For if the satisfaction of violent desires be happiness and a total failure of success in most eager pursuits, misery . . . what can be more miserable than to entertain desires which we know never can be satisfied

is close in attitude to Lycinus' rejection of Samippus' wish, which he bases on the insecurity of the attainments hoped for. Fielding also defines Alexander's weakness as the inability to identify what it is he really wants, a theme allied to the whole satirical presentation of wishing in *The Ship*, though not brought out *à propos* of Alexander. Lastly, it is worth noticing that Lycinus is not simply an *eirōn;* he has a killjoy aspect which makes him, like Diogenes, partly a butt of the story too. On the other hand, although Cynics are debunked as hypocrites in Lucian (e.g. Peregrinus and Theagenes in *Peregrinus*), there is no precise parallel for the way in which Alexander turns the tables on the philosopher in Fielding's dialogue. It is true, none the less, that the portrait of Diogenes in *Philosophers for Sale,* where he claims the life of a Cynic to be 'happier than the Great King's', is completed by a revelatory encomium of that life, preaching an hypocrisy and enjoyment of nastiness akin to that disclosed in Fielding's Diogenes.

On a broader plane the two types involved, the symbol of wealth and power (in Lucian usually a tyrant, but Alexander occurs often enough) and the hypocritical censurer of humanity, are certainly frequent in both authors. The technique of dialogue has something in common, too. Both authors take care that the essence of the character is conveyed through his words, neither troubles himself with place or setting, since the moral values (and in Lucian the literary reference) are the essentials, not the *pittoresque*. Fielding is the subtler, allowing his characters to identify their type by their opening words before the names are attached to them, and retaining a sense of physical drama— e.g. Diogenes' reminder to Alexander to 'stand a little more out of the sun, if you please'—which is present in only a very few of the *Dialogues of the Dead,* though it is important in *The Downward Journey* and in *Dialogues of the Courtesans*. In general one can say of Fielding's dialogue that it shows many influences, both contemporary and classical (much of his historical and moral material seems to come from the fourth oration of Dio), but that the impetus towards undertaking a work of this type may well have been his liking for Lucian.

Interlude is equally general in its Lucianic echoes. It presents four scenes of dialogue in heaven, linked loosely together by the idea of preparing for a visit to earth by Jupiter. In the first scene Juno attacks her husband about relations between the sexes in general, and his adulteries in particular. The second shows Jupiter describing his pleasure at the discovery, from the fulsome dedications to books, that men of outstanding merit do exist, while Apollo casts doubt on this, describing the sway held among men by the God of Wealth. The third is transitional, bringing together the themes of marital difficulty and human virtue; and the fourth is a comparison between thieves and poets. The dialogue form allows Fielding to maintain a dramatic structure while collecting together a small number of characters for the overt purpose of discussion. The themes of discussion themselves are largely contemporary, but among the motifs of presentation some are Lucianic. Hera's jealousy and Zeus's lechery are constantly referred to in the *Dialogues of the Gods*, Hera accuses Zeus of showering abuse on her in *Dialogues of the Gods* 6, Aphrodite is slighted by Hera in *Judgment of the Goddesses* (still classified among the *Dialogues of the Gods* in Fielding's day), where Athena also compares her with a whore. Some classic themes of both writers occur *en passant*. Hypocrisy, for example: Jupiter says, 'I hear at this instant several grave black gentlemen railing at riches and enjoying them, or at least coveting them, at the same time', just as in *Icaromenippus* 30 Zeus, addressing the other gods on the vices of philosophers observes: '. . . in front of their pupils they practice patience and moderation and spit upon wealth and pleasure, but when they are all alone, how could one describe how much they eat, how much they indulge their lusts, and how they lick all around their filthy coins.' But this is the common stock of much satire, and the references to the God of Wealth may as well be prompted by Aristophanes' *Plutus*, which Fielding translated, as by, say, *Timon*. There is a closer resemblance between *Interlude* and the *Dialogues of the Gods* in the part devoted to characterizing the gods themselves and their traditional activities, notably in the fourth scene with its play on the notion of Mercury as god of thieves, Apollo as god of poets, and the question of whether lying poets, being more thieves than writers, come within Mercury's domain. Much of the material, however, is really about the doings of men: sexual inequalities, literary fashions, abuse of parliamentary privilege. As such it is closer to the concern of the gods with human actions shown in *Timon* or *Zeus Rants*, than to the literary games of *Dialogues of the Gods*. The most one can say is that Fielding has been prompted by general traits in Lucian to adopt a particular version of ingénu satire, the world as observed by the gods, and to combine with it the comic possibilities of burlesque sketched in by the dialogue of the gods as a genre. It is true that Homer or Virgil could as well have been an authority for the burlesque, but it is Lucian who tends to be held responsible at Fielding's period. When Addison defined the distinction between comedy and burlesque in *The Spectator* (no. 249), it was Lucian's gods that he chose as the type of 'great persons acting and speaking like the basest among the people'. There was, too, a vogue for travesty, of which Charles Cotton's travesties of Lucian, *Burlesque upon burlesque* (1675), had been an early popular example. In fact the language of Fielding's burlesque is much more obviously low-style than his model's, where the human element derives from the situations and the emotions rather than the way the gods speak, although Ganymede's addressing of Zeus as *anthrōpe (fellow,* but literally *man)* has something of the comic manner of Fielding's 'Dear Mr Apollo, I am your humble servant'. The general example of Lucian seems to have encouraged Fielding to write this little series of *Dialogues of the Gods*, without his having any wish to observe its conventions too closely.

The third formal structure which Fielding borrows from Lucian to create independent satirical pieces is the mock-trial. As a magistrate he might well have been drawn to this format on his own account, but it is also popular with the Greek writer. Among the notable examples is Lucian's own arraignment by Oratory and Philosophy in *The Double Indictment*; the device is also central to *The Consonants at Law*, and is incorporated into some of the underworld scenes, particularly in *The Downward Journey*. Two of the best examples in Fielding are an article in the *Champion* for May 17, 1740, in which Cibber's *Apology* is arraigned for murdering the English language, and the trial of Amelia at the Bar on a charge of dullness (*Covent Garden Journal,* nos 7 and 8). In the *Champion* article, as in *The Double Indictment*, a number of cases are briefly introduced in order to bolster the court-room atmosphere, with the substantive one third on the agenda. In *CGJ* no. 7 a certain dramatic awareness of the physical circumstances of the court is included:

A great noise was now heard in the Court, and much female vociferation; when the Censor was informed that it was a married lady, one of the witnesses against Amelia, who was scolding at her husband for not making her way through the crowd

just as *The Double Indictment* 12–13 describes the hubbub of those rushing to litigation. In general the courtroom situation allows both writers freedom for some humour based on the forms and formulae of their respective legal situations (e.g. the clerk's indictment of *Col. Apol.* and the parliamentary formulae pronounced by Momus in *The Parliament of the Gods* 14). Some of the rhetorical manner of the trials is similar too. In the trial of Amelia, Fielding personifies the Town as prosecuting counsel, in the same way that Philosophy and Rhetoric prefer charges against Lucian. Ultimately, however, the Lucianic flavour of the court scenes depends largely on Fielding's adoption in them of elements which Lucian exploits in other contexts. Town's oratory against Amelia contains an excellent example of an inverted mock-encomium (i.e. a mock-*psogos*); the charges proffered against her redound to the book's credit:

Now the humour, or manners, of this age are to laugh at everything, and the only way to please them is to make them laugh; nor hath the prisoner any excuse, since it was so very easy to have done this in the present case; what, indeed, more was necessary than to have turned the ridicule the other way, and, in the characters of Dr Harrison and Amelia herself, to have made a jest of religion and the clergy, of virtue and innocence?

In a similar way, the principal humour of the trial of Col. Apol. comes from the way in which he is allowed to condemn himself, e.g. 'It is impossible I should have any enmity to the English language, with which I am so little acquainted.' Fielding has in fact taken a form used by Lucian for largely, though not exclusively, ingenious purposes of rhetorical display, and has developed it as a vehicle for specific satire by importing into it ironic verbal devices which he shares with the Lucian of other writings.

The longest and most substantial of Fielding's experiments in a Lucianic genre is *Journey from This World to the Next*, which was first published in vol. 2 of the *Miscellanies*. As the name implies, the work belongs to the 'underworld visit' tradition, which goes right back to Homer. However, since all Fielding's characters are spirits of the dead, the closest Lucianic parallels are not *A True Story II* or *Menippus*, in which, as in the *Odyssey*, a live hero visits Hades and returns to tell the tale, but *The Downward Journey* and *Dialogues of the Dead* 20. *Journey* is very loosely constructed. Chs 1–9 form one unit, describing the soul's journey to the underworld, a judgment scene, and some glimpses of life in Elysium. Chs 10–25 introduce the shade of Julian the Apostate, who proceeds to recount the many reincarnations to which he was subjected before his admission to paradise. A separate chapter, whimsically numbered Book 19, ch. 7, gives a life of Anne Boleyn (probably written by Fielding's sister). And the work concludes on the reiteration of the 'partial manuscript' motif used in its introduction. Only chs 1–9 are significantly attached to the underworld theme, since the Julian section is merely an excuse for a series of anecdotes whose connexion with each other and with the earlier chapters is moral rather than aesthetic. The recounting of a series of reincarnations provides the theme of *The Cock* (15–21), but there it is very tightly executed within another narrative structure. A succession of anecdotes within a loose narrative framework is also not un-Lucianic; *Toxaris* and *The Lover of Lies* spring to mind. But in the former the element of syncrisis gives a shape to the work; in the latter there is a sketchily contrived climax, the arrival of the Pythagorean, Arignotos. Fielding's stories are just that—a collection of tales; they throw some light on his attitude to history in general and the byways of Byzantine history in particular, but they have no shaping principle at all.

The literary tradition within which the work is constructed is in some respects Augustan. Like several works by members of the Scriblerus Club (including Swift and Pope) *Journey* has a little fun at the expense of academic scholarship and the learned edition. Notes on the history of the ms. occur at beginning and end, and bk. 1 contains pompous 'editorial' material on such matters as the propriety of referring to the eyes and heart of a shade. The mockery is very light, and can barely be called parody; it has no apparent aim but to amuse. However, these points apart, the bulk of the first nine chapters can fairly be called Lucianic. A series of details could be conscious reminiscences. As the work opens, the soul observes the world around it, but cannot act, because the body is already cold and stiff, like the soul of Megapenthes in *The Downward Journey* 12. Off-stage it hears quarrelling over the will, an implicit part of *Dialogues of the Dead* 19. 3–4. When escaped from the corpse, the soul finds as his guide, inevitably, Mercury (as passim in Lucian), who arranges for souls to proceed to the ironically named 'upper' world in parties; cf. the opening of *The Downward Journey*. Having crossed the Cocytus by boat (a motif evidently exploited enough in the *Champion* article and the plays, for here it is dismissed in a line), the souls go on toward Elysium on foot, as in *Dialogues of the Dead* 20. 12. Ch. 7 presents a judgment scene, of which there are several in Lucian, though only in *Menippus* are the judgments given, as in Fielding, by Minos—elsewhere always by Rhadamanthus. Finally, in ch. 8, there is a meeting with famous authors which recalls *A True Story II*. 20, though it may just as well come via Swift, who uses the theme in *Gulliver's Travels* 3. vii–viii. Lucian's narrator asks Homer about his birthplace, is told that the Alexandrian commentators Zenodotus and Aristarchus were quite wrong to bracket certain lines as spurious, that the *Odyssey* was written after the Iliad, and other points all relating to famous scholarly controversies. Fielding's Homer is also asked his birthplace (though he does not give so outrageous an answer), and is faced with a comparable scholarly enquiry, referring to the theory that the Homeric epics were patched together from a series of folk ballads:

> I had the curiosity to enquire whether he had really writ that poem in detached pieces and sung it about as ballads all over Greece, according to the report which went of him. He smiled at my question, and asked me whether there appeared any connexion in the poem; for if there did, he thought I might answer it myself.

The more pointed aspects of the attack on pedantry are transferred to the interview with Shakespeare. The question of variant readings is dealt with in a hilarious discussion of Othello's 'Put out the light and then put out the light', while the whole question of such analysis is disposed of very sharply by Shakespeare's observation:

> Certes the greatest and most pregnant beauties are ever the plainest and most evidently striking; and when two meanings of a passage can in the least balance our judgment which to prefer, I hold it matter of unquestionable certainty that neither of them is worth a farthing.

There are, within this general structure of Lucianic motifs, certain details which also have parallels. From the list of the chief messengers of death given in *Charon* 17, chills, fevers, consumption, and the sword are all represented in Fielding's account. One fair spirit announces: 'I caught cold by overdancing myself at a ball, and last night died of a violent fever'; another 'died of honour' having been killed in a duel. Consumption accounts for another traveller, and has a prominent house in the City of Diseases through which the party travels on its way to Hell. The death of the man so busy protecting himself from smallpox that he fell victim to a surfeit of mussels, touches on a theme, death from one cause while the attention is fixed elsewhere, which Lucian uses more than once, e.g. *Dialogues of the Dead* 16. 4. Mitigating circumstances, which Minos allows to offset past crime, are also admitted in *Menippus* 13; the flowers of Elysium occur twice in the description of the Isles of the Blest, *A True Story II.* 5, 13; as for the vices attacked, they include hypocrisy, avarice, and pride among the foremost, and as in the *Champion* article their embodiments are a mixture of classical and contemporary types—the dead in battle *en masse* as usual, but also the beau, the prude, the patriot.

In the main, however, the creative influence on the work does not lie in these possible parallels, many of which may have been absorbed through the post-Lucianic tradition, or have grown spontaneously out of Fielding's own vision of the subject. What is more important is that Fielding contributes new motifs to enhance the old traditions. The City of Diseases and the Palace of Death allow an updated version of the *ecphrasis*, a Lucianic device at which Fielding excels, though the descriptions are less virtuoso on their own count than part of a structure of argument. Thus the external description of the Palace of Death is deliberately at odds with the mood of gaiety within:

Its outside, indeed, appeared extremely magnificent. Its structure was of the Gothic order; vast beyond imagination, the whole pile consisting of black marble. Rows of immense yews form an amphitheatre round it of such height and thickness that no ray of the sun ever perforates this grove, where black eternal darkness would reign, was it not excluded by innumerable lamps which are placed in pyramids round the grove; so that the distant reflection they cast on the palace, which is plentifully gilt with gold on the outside, is inconceivably solemn.

Motifs are brought in from later traditions, such as the Wheel of Fortune, and the idea of the souls preparing for reincarnation. And, above all, a positive moral, extending well beyond the Cynic commonplaces of Lucian's Hades, informs all the values of *Journey*, whether it be in the presentation of the various souls within the coach, the attack on greatness (particularly military greatness), or the formal exposition of the ethical attitudes of Minos. Chapter 7 is really the core of the work in this respect. Minos is given St Peter's rôle as porter, at the gates of a pagan Paradise, rather than sitting in his formal court of judgment. There is certainly an area of common ethical ground between the two writers, which can be summed up in the words of Menippus' description in *Menippus* 12:

Minos would examine each man with care, then despatch him to the place of the impious to undergo a punishment proportionate to the evil of his deeds. He was hardest on those who were obsessed with wealth and power and all but expecting men to worship them. He was disgusted by their pretensions and arrogance over such ephemeral things.

His assessment of souls is, however, based on much subtler principles than is Lucian's, and his range of punishment is wider. The irredeemable are cast into the bottomless pit, those who meet with his approval pass through the gates, but the rest are all sent back to another life-cycle. The criteria by which these fates are allotted are clear. Minos rejects both the show of virtue and the rigid observance of virtue for its own sake. A man who vaunts his regular church-going and 'the great animosity he had shewn to vice in others' is rejected because he disinherited his son for begetting a bastard. Another who spent his whole life collecting and studying butterflies and 'had done neither good nor evil in the world' is pushed back with scorn. But a playwright who clearly suffers from inordinate pride in the moral value of his works is none the less admitted when it is discovered that 'he once lent the whole profits of a benefit-night to a friend, and by that means had saved him and his family from destruction'. In other words, goodness is the essential qualification: a beau, a politician, a prude are excluded by definition, whereas a poor wretch hanged for the theft of eighteen pence, but a very tender husband and kind father, is admitted with a friendly slap on the back from Minos. In addition to this distinctive, positive ethical message, the scene is marked by the great ingenuity with which Fielding varies his presentation. The captain and his troops are almost admitted, until Minos discovers that they were the aggressors in their war. A patriot who has gained admittance talks himself out of it, in his quest for general approval, by revealing himself a double-dealer. A parson intervenes to confirm the case of a poor family, but in the process proves himself to have lacked charity, is caught and pulled back from the gate. This last is a good example of the degree of physical activity with which Fielding invests an essentially static situation:

. . . the parson was stepping forwards with a staitly gait before them; but Minos caught hold of him and pulled him back, saying 'Not so fast, doctor—you must take one step more into the other world first; for no man enters that gate without charity'.

Similarly the poet is pushed in, the Duke kicked away, the patriot seized by Minos' guards and conducted back.

Although Fielding shows far more literary sophistication than Lucian in his elaboration of the same or like motifs, the comic and satirical manner of the two writers has much in common. Some of the humour is, obviously, situational, deriving from the failure or refusal of characters to acknowledge that they are no longer alive—the assumption that worldly greatness or success carries weight below (cf. *Dialogues of the Dead* passim), or the panic of the shade who for a moment fears he may catch smallpox (cf. the dead Protesilaus trying to murder the dead Helen, *Dialogues of the Dead* 27). A variant of this is the insistence of the author himself, or of his narrator, on the reality of his fictional world. The problem of how to accommodate Micyllus in Charon's boat when it is already full—with insubstantial shades—is solemnly solved by his sitting on the tyrant's shoulders (*The Downward Journey* 19). In like manner the narrator of *Journey* records (ch. 1) his problem in boarding the coach that will take the dead to the 'upper' world:

... the coachman told me his horses were to, but that he had no place left; however, though they were already six, the passengers offered to make room for me. I thanked them, and ascended without much ceremony. We immediately began our journey, being seven in number; for, as the women wore no hoops, three of them were but equal to two men.

Other humour relies on the presentation of the material. Both authors pompously adduce an authority for what is clearly only a fictional device. The cock in *The Cock* produces an impressive list of references to epic poetry to prove that talking animals are a frequent phenomenon. Likewise Fielding footnotes the information that most of the shades in the coach were asleep (ch. 2) with the observation: 'Those who have read of the gods sleeping in Homer will not be surprised at this happening to spirits.' A satirical variant of this is the solemn discussion of an absurd point, with suitable authority adduced. At the opening of chapter 2, the narrator observes:

It is the common opinion that spirits, like owls, can see in the dark; nay, and can then most easily be perceived by others. For which reason, many persons of good understanding, to prevent being terrified with such objects, usually keep a candle burning by them, that the light may prevent them from seeing. Mr Locke, in direct opposition to this, hath not doubted to assert that you may see a spirit in open daylight full as well as in the darkest night.

On a similar topic, Tychiades in *The Lover of Lies* (16) comments upon Ion's account of spirits he has seen:

'It is no great thing,' I said, 'for you to see such things, Ion, given that you can perceive the ideal forms of which your father Plato teaches, but which are very dimly visible to the rest of us with our weak eyes.'

These two examples provide an interesting contrast; one sees how Fielding's humour benefits from the unexpected. For Lucian to use Plato to ironize Ion the Platonist, and for him to pick on the theory of ideas as his particular weapon, is an almost inevitable consequence of his literary method. Whereas the introduction of Locke, and the phrase 'in direct opposition to this' suggests that a denial of the visibility of spirits will follow. Our expectations are overthrown dramatically by the still more absurd belief with which the philosopher shows himself as superstitious as the ordinary man.

Finally, the two writers not unnaturally share many tricks of verbal irony. In the simplest, what is said is shown by the context to be the opposite of what is meant. Just as the ignorant book-collector is said to have acquired perfect wisdom and an unparalleled knowledge of literature and language from the books we know he has not read (*The Ignorant Book-collector* 26), so Minos, on hearing the Patriot praising his Vicar-of-Bray career, observes:

On second consideration, Mr Patriot, I think a man of your great virtues and abilities will be so much missed by your country, that, if I might advise you, you should take a journey back again. I am sure you will not decline it; for I am certain you will, with great readiness, sacrifice your own happiness to the public good.

A less transparent technique is the insertion of an absurd explanatory or concessive phrase. The narrator of *Journey,* explaining why his soul was obliged to hop, on leaving his corpse, notes '. . . I had not the gift of flying (owing probably to my having neither feathers nor wings)'. Lucian uses the same device for satirical purpose in *Zeus Rants* (37), when Damis pretends to explain the failure of the gods to intervene in human affairs: 'Clearly they are out of town—perhaps on the other side of the Ocean visiting the noble Ethiopians.' More subtle still is the use of understatement or concession to soften a direct inversion of meaning. A modest doubt is made the vehicle for an ironical certainty. Cyniscus closes *Zeus Catechized* (19) by mocking Zeus for the knots in which he has tied himself, but affects a humble awareness of the difficulties involved:

But if it is not easy for you to give me an answer on these points, Zeus, we shall be contented with what you have already said, for you have thrown enough light on the concepts of Fate and Providence. Perhaps I was not destined to hear any more.

Similarly Fielding, in the introduction to *Journey*, says of those complacent about the world as it is:

There are some indeed who, from the vivacity of their temper and the happiness of their station, are willing to consider its blessings as more substantial, and the whole to be a scene of more consequence than it is here represented; but, without controverting their opinions at present, the number of wise and good men who have thought with our author are sufficient to keep him in countenance . . .

The sustained recreation of Lucian represented by *Journey* makes it clear, as the occasional pieces perhaps do not, that Fielding's debt to Lucian is a complex mixture in which the rôle of direct borrowings is much less than that of general satirical parallels. Evidently many of the stereotyped concepts and characters on which Lucian based his literary comedy were identical with people and ideas that aroused a genuine strong moral response in Fielding. Hypocrisy, arrogance and greed, with their natural representatives the philosopher or cleric, the man of power and the man of wealth, provide the bulk of the cast list in Lucian and are well represented in the major works of Fielding. For example, the delightful scene in *Tom Jones* 5. 5, where the philosopher Square is discovered in a compromising situation, is fully in the Lucianic tradition of stressing the sexual weaknesses of the would-be sage; and Fielding's commentary upon it is what one would expect of a moralist's reading of, say, *The Eunuch*:

Philosophers are composed of flesh and blood as well as other human creatures; and however sublimated and refined the theory of these may be, a little practical frailty is as incident to them as to other mortals. It is indeed in theory only and not in practice, as we have before hinted, that consists the difference; for though such great beings think much better and more wisely, they always act exactly like other men.

Given that such characters and such vices are the staple of most satirical representations of society from Aristophanes to Flaubert, it may seem inevitable that both our authors should concentrate upon them. More interesting, perhaps, is the overlap between Fielding and Lucian on the matter of language itself. Both authors show respect for literary tradition, despite the novelty of the forms they use: the imitation of certain classics is widely canvassed by Lucian, and Fielding makes Tragedio in *The Author's Farce* (Act III) damn himself by saying:

> To Shakespeare, Jonson, Dryden, Lee, or Rowe
> I not a line, no, not a thought do owe.
> Me, for my novelty, let all adore,
> For as I wrote none ever wrote before.

This similarity in their attitude to literature is closely connected with their attitudes to convention and moderation in its medium, language. Lucian presents language as the formal subject of certain works, notably *The Consonants at Law, Lexiphanes, A Slip of the Tongue in Greeting*. In addition he introduces professional users of language as his satirical butts, both in extended satire of rhetoricians, *A Professor of Public Speaking* and *The Mistaken Critic*, and in the incidental references to grammarians and orators in other works. Lastly, he selects the misuse of language, in the form of jargon, as one of his charges against philosophers. There are two distinct areas of linguistic satire here. One is ridicule of the form of language itself, the other of the uses to which it is put. The parody of pretentious diction in *Lexiphanes* is only a more sustained version of the burlesque tragic quotations that open *Menippus* and *Zeus Rants*. In the latter the characters give us the nudge that the verbal play is merely for amusement, by their conscious pursuit of parody, as when Zeus criticizes Hermes for the prosaic tone of his proclamation:

Herm. How do you think I should do it then, Zeus?
Zeus How do I think you should do it? Give the proclamation some style, put it into verse with some high-flown poetic words. I'd say that's more likely to get them together.

In *Lexiphanes*, though the later part of the dialogue purports to give a serious critique, we easily recognize, even without the aid of internal hints, that the bulk of the humorous part is simply the exploitation for comic effect of excess in language, here the excess of archaism:

Then said Hellanicus; 'I look askew, for my dollies are obfuscate, I nictitate full oft, and I am lachrymose; mine eyes want drugging, I require some scion of Aesculapius, sage in opthalmotherapy, who will compound and decant a specific for me, and so effect that my ruddy optics may be de-coloured, and no longer be rheumatic or have a humorous cast.'[1]

[1] Para. 4, trans. A. M. Harmon, Loeb vol. v, 301.

It is the forerunner of that same joy in pretentious gibberish with which Rabelais paints the francolatin of his sixteenth-century undergraduate:

> We transfretate the Sequence at dilucule and crepuscule; we ambulate along the urban compitals and quadrivials; we despumate Latian verbocination, and as verisimilar amorosos we captate the omnijugous, omniform and omnigenous feminine sex (etc).[1]

The satire of the uses to which language is put has a much more serious air. As with the attack on the jargon of philosophers, or indeed on the pretensions of contemporary historians in *How to Write History*, Lucian derides the use of language as a screen, a way of giving the user status, which at the same time degrades his medium. In pursuit of fame the would-be rhetorician is advised:

> Hunt up obscure, unfamiliar words, rarely used by the ancients, and have a heap of these in readiness to launch at your audience. The many-headed crowd will look up to you and think you amazing, and far beyond themselves in education, if you call rubbing down 'destrigillation', taking a sunbath 'insolation', advance payments 'hansel' and daybreak 'crepuscule'.[2]

He should indulge in neologism, defend solecism, and above all subordinate the content of his speeches to the manner of his delivery. None of this is strictly an attack on the art of the sophist; it is a parody of an inadequate version of that art. But read in the context of, for example, Menippus' denunciation of philosophical word-chopping (*Menippus* 4) it has the air of being part of a consistent defence of plain speaking.

Fielding must certainly have read it in such a way. It would, of course, be quite false to represent his view of language as in any sense deriving from Lucian. It belongs to the tradition of Swift and Pope, a parentage which he directly acknowledged when he attributed the linguistic satire in his preface to *The Tragedy of Tragedies* to the pen of one H. Scriblerus Secundus. But both Fielding and Lucian appear to treat the debasement of language and the debasement of values in tandem, as though moral decline and linguistic abuse were interrelated phenomena. In this respect perhaps their satire of language should be seen as falling not into the categories 'usage' and 'users', but as dividing up between the ridicule of the preposterous use of language that derives

---

[1] *Pantagruel*, ch. 6.
[2] *A Professor of Public Speaking* 17, trans. A. M. Harmon, Loeb vol. IV, 15.

from ignorance and insensitivity, and the attack on those who know-
ingly debase language for their own personal gain. Fielding's gibes
against Cibber in *The Champion* and his caricature of him as Sir
Farcical Comic in *The Author's Farce* employ the same range of
accusations, ignorance, negligence, pretension, indifference to meaning
which Lucian levels against the effusions of a Lexiphanes. Fielding
seems almost to be amusing himself at the expense of a brand of
language-despoiling which he sees as relatively harmless. Elsewhere, in
his attacks on the language of journalism, politics and polite society,
he is much more engaged against what he sees as the cultivation of the
lie—a pet theme of Lucian's too, but here the lie is less the misrepre-
sentation of fact than the distortions of speech fashions. Another figure
from *The Author's Farce*, Dr Orator (standing for the notorious John
Henley), is the type of the willing corruptor of language, the mani-
pulator of the lie. He boasts that loudness is important and sense
irrelevant, delivers a ridiculous oration on a fiddle and a fiddlestick,
and hymns his own quality as the greatest of all contemporary de-
ceivers:

> The lawyer wrangling at the bar
> While the reverend bench is dozing,
> The scribbler in a pamphlet war,
> Or Grub Street bard composing,
> The trudging quack in scarlet cloak
> Or coffeehouse politic prater,
> Can none come up to what I have spoke
> When I was a bold orator.
>
> The well-bred courtier telling lies
> Or levee-hunter believing,
> The vain coquette that rolls her eyes,
> More empty fops deceiving,
> The parson of dissenting gang
> Or flattering dedicator,
> Could none of them like me harangue
> When I was a bold orator.

Dr Orator's entire performance at the Court of Nonsense is indeed,
highly reminiscent of the trainer's instruction in *A Professor of
Public Speaking* 19:

If it ever seems appropriate to go into a chant, then chant it all and let it
turn into a song. And if you do not know what to sing, just say 'gentlemen

of the jury' in time to the beat, and be satisfied that the musical requirements
are being fulfilled. Let there be plenty of 'alas, alack!' and thigh-slapping,
bellow, clear your throat noisily and walk up and down wiggling your arse.

This affinity between Lucian and Fielding in the matter of language
is emphasized by the form in which the latter presents some of his
linguistic satire. I have already mentioned that the ridiculing of Cibber's
Apology is conducted via a mock-trial (see above p. 210). In *The
Author's Farce* the various suitors for the hand of the Goddess of
Nonsense are brought to Hell, and are allowed, after the manner of the
philosophers in *Philosophers for Sale,* to condemn themselves out of
their own mouths. There is also a parallel between the positive views
on language held by the two authors, if we relate the behaviour of
those characters in his novels of whom Fielding clearly approves, e.g.
Parson Adams in *Joseph Andrews,* to the injunctions set out by Lucian
at the close of *How to Write History* to write in such a way that posterity will say of you: 'He was a free man, full of frankness, with nothing
fawning or servile about him, but truthful in all things.' Taken together, these three aspects, the attacks on misuse, the form in which the
attacks are expressed, and the positive course approved, constitute a
significant correspondence of manner and matter.

We have looked at some length into the negative approaches which
Lucian and Fielding share. Language is an area in which, in the most
general of senses, they have a positive approach in common. What of
morality? How far are Fielding's positive moral views congruent with
anything he might have found in Lucian? The message which permeates Fielding's writings is that you should judge a man by what he
does, not by what he says, that his actions should be disinterested, and
that he should avoid any sort of excess. It follows from this that he,
like Voltaire, prefers ethics to metaphysics, as being the philosophy of
action. There is, underlying these qualities, a positive vision of goodness which is entirely alien to anything in Lucian. It is defined thus
in *The Champion* for March 27, 1740:

... a delight in the happiness of mankind, and a concern at their misery,
with a desire, as much as possible, to procure the former, and avert the latter;
and this with a constant regard to desert.

But the rejection of excess entirely reflects Lucian's adoption of the
standpoint of the common man as the norm against which the activities
of his *alazones* are to be measured. And the praise of action as the measure of a man is in accord with the doctrine preached by Tiresias to

Menippus at the end of *Menippus* as well as being the understood basis for the rejection of the many hypocrites with whom Lucian peoples his works. This coincidence of views, an entirely general one, cannot, again, be accounted an influence of the one writer upon the other, but it is additional evidence for the affinity between them.

If one can, in fact, meaningfully talk of *influence*, it is, as Fielding himself indicates, a stylistic influence. By style, I do not think he means sentence balance, choice of vocabulary and the like; for despite the strictures that he makes upon translators who resort to French versions as an intermediary (a criticism placed in the mouth of Booth in *Amelia* 8. v), the evidence of the version of Aristophanes' *Plutus* on which he collaborated with Young suggests that, though his Greek was good, it was not good enough to stand unassisted, which makes it seem unlikely that he would have felt sufficient linguistic sensitivity to Lucian's original to model his own verbal structures upon it. He more probably means his affection for certain formal ironic devices which he uses not only in his occasional satire, but also in his major works. Some of them can be called presentational devices: the juxtaposition of actions and speech such that the former give the lie to the latter, the use of speech which itself runs counter to what the character speaking purports to be, the genuine naïveté or assumption of ignorance on the part of a narrator, the varieties of mock encomium. The others are verbal conventions: the pretence of doubt over the validity of material, the ironic use of pedantry, and a wide-ranging use of quotation, anecdote and proverb.

The character who unwittingly unmasks himself we have already come across in Fielding: the suitors at the Court of Nonsense (*The Author's Farce*), for example. In Lucian they are everywhere: the Cynic advertising his brashness in *Philosophers for Sale*, the trainer recommending effrontery in *A Professor of Public Speaking*, the philosophers of *The Banquet* brawling, stealing, quarrelling over food. Fielding introduces them into his novels too: Parson Trulliber discoursing on his charity but violently dismissing Adams when he seeks a loan (*JA* 2. 14), Thwackum's disingenuous letter to Squire Allworthy coupling criticism of Tom with a barely concealed request for the gift of a benefice (*TJ* 18. 4). Even Parson Adams himself is subjected to a little of the treatment:

He said he searched after a sermon, which he thought his masterpiece, against vanity. 'Fie upon it, fie upon it!' cries he; 'why do I ever leave that sermon out of my pocket? I wish it was within five miles; I would willingly fetch it, to read it to you . . . for I am confident you would admire it; indeed, I have never been a greater enemy to any passion than that silly one of vanity.' (*JA* 3. 3)

The ingénu or pretended ingénu occurs in Lucian in several forms. Menippus in *Icaromenippus* and *Menippus* appears to take the philosophers seriously only to be disillusioned by them. Lycinus in *Hermotimus* only feigns acceptance of Hermotimus' trust in philosophy. Then there are the genuine naifs, like Pamphilus in *The Eunuch*, who seem honestly to expect a philosopher to be the moral and intellectual paragon that the title suggests. Fielding, too, uses both approaches. Although the primary debt is doubtless to Cervantes and the picaresque tradition, the relationship between the persona of the narrator and his ingénu characters is a more complex one than can be explained in terms of that tradition alone. The narrator of *Jonathan Wild* accepts, and expects his readers to share, the inversion of natural values on which the whole book is based. The narrator of *Joseph Andrews* begins as an innocent, admiring Cibber's *Apology* and the moral value of Richardson's *Pamela*, defending Lady Booby's motives: gradually the mask is dropped to be replaced by a more directly ironical approach. Equally, there are characters within the narrative who throughout their respective books are the unconscious vehicles for the criticism of the world around them: Joseph, Parson Andrews, Tom, Amelia.

Mock encomium, both in a technical sense, and also in the form of any passage of praise intended to damn, is a device which Fielding uses widely. Among his occasional pieces, some, like the *Essay on Nothing* derive from later stages of the tradition than the Lucianic, but his article on how to become a successful villain by manipulation of the lie (*The Champion* 29 January, 1739/40) has many parallels with *A Professor of Public Speaking*. The 'correspondent' who masks the authorial voice, writes:

The first quality which every man ought to be possessed of, who promises himself to make any figure in this hemisphere, is the art of lying. This word, as it regards out interest . . . comprehends flattery and scandal, a false defence of ourselves and a false accusation of other people.

He particularly praises the infallible resources of the *lie panegyrical*. It is the echo of the trainer of orators' dictum:

Effrontery and shamelessness, a ready lie and your lips ever prepared to swear to its truth, indiscriminate jealousy and hatred, abuse and plausible slanders—these are the qualities which will overnight make you renowned and admired.

The only distinction, as this parallel demonstrates, between mock encomium and allowing a character to reveal himself in speech, is that of voice. The mock encomium proper, as in the *Champion* article, is delivered by a person not involved in what he describes. It is a posture which Fielding's narrators often adopt. In *Joseph Andrews*, for example, while making a serious point about biography as an insight into human nature (3. 1), the narrator inserts a little ironic praise of fashionable fiction:

> I would by no means be thought to comprehend those persons of surprising genius, the authors of immense romances, or the modern novel and Atlantis writers; who, without any assistance from nature or history, record persons who never were, or will be, and facts which never did, nor possibly can, happen; whose heroes are of their own creation, and their brains the chaos whence all their materials are selected. Not that such persons deserve no honour; for what can be nobler than to be as an example of the wonderful extent of human genius? One may apply to them what Balzac says of Aristotle, that they are a second nature (for they have no communication with the first, by which authors of an inferior class, who cannot stand alone, are obliged to support themselves as with crutches); but these of whom I am now speaking seem to be possessed of those stilts which the excellent Voltaire tells us, in his letters, 'carry the genius far off, but with a regular pace'. Indeed, far out of sight of the reader.

Here we are fully in the style of the passages of ironic commendation by which Lucian pillories historians in *How to Write History*. The technique is to start with exaggerated praise, 'of surprising genius', sometimes, as in that phrase, with a hint of ambiguity—is *surprising* to be read in a positive way? So Lucian, mocking a would-be eyewitness account of the Parthian War (29) refers to 'so wonderful an author'— a source of admiration or merely amazement? Against this is set praise of qualities which clearly provoke the reader to observe that they are faults. Fielding insists on the originality and imaginative qualities of his writers in such a way as to show that he means their sheer absurdity. Into this he inserts a phrase indicating that he knows which way the reader will have interpreted him: 'Not that such persons deserve no honour.' So Lucian puts the pursuit of rhetoric into its proper perspective (*A Professor of Public Speaking* 4): 'Is it impossible to become an orator—which is well below the inflated style of poetry—overnight, if one can discover the quickest way?' Lastly, Fielding uses the trick of giving authority to his argument by a quotation (twisted), which is then deflated by the use of its metaphor to make an adverse point: Voltaire's stilts carry the fantasist out of sight of the reader. So (*A Professor of Public Speaking* 26) Plato's phrase from the *Phaedrus* about surging forward in a winged chariot is first applied to the orator; then its implications are turned against him: 'Just remember this; it is not by your speed that you have beaten us . . . but by turning down the easy down-hill road.'

In analysing presentational devices of irony I have necessarily encroached upon verbal conventions. The pretence of doubt over the validity of material described, which Lucian himself parodies from Herodotus, is common to both writers. In *A True Story I*, the narrator runs the whole gamut of variations on the motif, declining to record what he has not seen as an eye-witness (13), recounting the absurd with scientific precision (26), disingenuously admitting that what is about to be said will sound implausible (41). To take examples from *Journey* alone, we constantly find in Fielding this same affectation of an anxiety for scholarly accuracy and credibility. 'I was at too great a distance to hear any of the conversation,' says the dead narrator, as he observes Charles XII and Alexander the Great. A beautiful young female who has thrown away the Nousphoric decoction that regulates her intellectual faculties in her next reincarnation, receives from the Wheel of Fortune a coronet, which to the narrator's regret 'she clapped up so eagerly that I could not distinguish the degree'. In both writers the irrelevance of such precision is both comic in itself, and a way of emphasizing the transparency of the satirical point made. The ironic use of pedantry is similar in kind. I have already mentioned Fielding's adhesion to the Scriblerian tradition of footnotes; but he also, like Lucian, enjoys mock etymology and pun. There is a particularly outrageous example in an article on names in *The Champion*, for June 7, 1740, in which William is derived from violin, 'which might probably typify some nonsensical talkative fellow, who abounded much in sound, or might allude to someone who might not improperly be played upon with a good stick'. In the same way (though with slightly more etymological justification) Lucian insists on the element of 'dog' in Cynic or of 'gold' in Chrysippus for satirical effect in *The Dead Come to Life*.

Most important of all is the wealth of anecdote and quotation in both writers. It is one of the rhetorical hallmarks of Lucian's narrative manner to pepper his prose with proverbs, exempla, anecdotes and quotations. The proverbs are a way of obtaining general assent to an idea, and of raising the tone of the context, though they can also be used insultingly or ironically. Fielding has relatively few proverbs, though he sometimes uses proverbial quotations, akin to Lucian's quotations from Hesiod, such as Sir Roger L'Estrange's 'If we shut nature out at the door, she will come in at the window' (*TJ* 12. 2), with the same aim of giving general value to a particular context. Exempla in Lucian are usually extended allusions to familiar stories, particularly historical or mythical, in which some parallel with an aspect of the text is drawn. Fielding's exempla, which are usually cast in the form of a comparison, fall into the same categories: historical—e.g. in *TJ* 10. 9 Sophia's fortitude is compared with that of Arria as related by Pliny; mythical— e.g. in *TJ* 17. 3 Squire Western comically compares his fate with that of 'Acton' (i.e. Actaeon). It is also noticeable that both writers are fond of examples from the history of art, in Fielding's case with particular reference to Hogarth.

It is, however, in his use of anecdote and quotation that Fielding especially resembles Lucian. Anecdote in Lucian falls into several different categories, particularly, historical, erotic and fantastic; the sources of his material were manuals in which such stories were classified under such rubrics for use in rhetorical exercises. His anecdotes are really extensions of the *exemplum*, but they are more often fictional. They have three functions. To confirm a general or a specific truth, as with the illustrations of friendship in *Toxaris*, to act as stylistic decoration, or to be developed into full-blown entertainments in their own right. This last is particularly true of the fantastic tales of *The Ship* and *The Lover of Lies*. Fielding's anecdotes fall less obviously into categories, but they fulfil much the same functions. The many inserted tales which are a feature of his narrative style, e.g. the story of Leonora in *Joseph Andrews* or that of the Man of the Hill in *Tom Jones*, are examples of the anecdote which takes on a semi-independent fictional life within the main structure. Sometimes, as with Leonora, the tale reveals something about either the teller or the audience—the same is true of the stories in *The Lover of Lies*. But in itself it is told for the joy of telling it. There are also ornamental anecdotes: a historical example would be the story of Cleostratus with which Tom's extreme drunkenness is illustrated (*TJ* 5. 10). But the bulk of the anecdotes demonstrate a truth. This can be of a personal kind. In *JA* 3. 7 the bogus anecdote about Socrates recounted by the doctor as part of the roasting scene is a way of mocking parson Adams' vanity, i.e. the illustration of a private truth. The fictional tale of Mr Fisher who kills his benefactor (*TJ* 8. 1) demonstrates the general point that it is very easy to illustrate a negative moral. It is in just this fashion that Lucian uses anecdotes in the *prolaliai* or *Toxaris*.

In his use of quotation Fielding comes still closer to Lucian. There are two main types of quotation in Lucian; the ornamental is simply a restatement of an idea in a more beautiful way: the authoritative gives backing to a linguistic or literary usage, or to a moral point. An ornamental quotation can be used to heighten the style of a passage, particularly in panegyric (e.g. *Essays in Portraiture*). There is also an important use of ornamental quotations in which they are integrated into the narrative. Part of what the author has to say is conveyed exclusively in the words of the quotation. As for the form of the quotations, they are sometimes textual, sometimes in paraphrase, 'textual' being a loose classification, for the wording is often fairly approximate. Slight modification may be (apparently) accidental, or it may be for deliberate effect; the quotation may be a contamination of references (e.g. a cento); or the phrase may be absorbed into the grammar of the passage. All these nuances of use and form occur in Fielding. The same division can be made between ornament and authority. Partridge in *TJ* 16. 5 quotes Juvenal (*Sat.* ii. 8) for authority (with a characteristic, apparently unmotivated, slight alteration to the text):

'Well,' said he, 'how people may be deceived by faces! *Nulla fides fronti* is, I find, a true saying.'

But some of this character's quotations are purely ornamental: e.g. *TJ* 15. 12:

'Well sir, as I was saying, it was a long time before he could recollect me: for indeed I am very much altered since I saw him. *Non sum qualis eram.*'[1]

Such pure ornament is, as in *Essays in Portraiture*, used among other things to heighten the tone of panegyric, as with the quotations from Suckling, Donne and Horace which are incorporated into the portrait of Sophia Western in *TJ* 4. 2. More frequent are the examples of inte-grated ornament. In *TJ* 3. 6, the narrator intervenes in an ironical vein to comment upon the actions of two rascals:

---

[1] Fielding, of course, is also dealing in characterization in a way that Lucian is not. This quotation is more than ornamental in the sense that by quoting Latin at all, Partridge shows himself, ironically, to *be* essentially what he was before. The act of quotation itself belies the terms of the quotation.

We would not, however, have our reader imagine that persons of such characters as were supported by Thwackum and Square would undertake a matter of this kind, which hath been a little censured by some rigid moralists, before they had thoroughly examined it, and considered whether it was (as Shakespeare phrases it) 'stuff o' th' conscience' or no?

The point about the quotation from *Othello* (II. i) is that Iago, like Thwackum and Square, is being hypocritical. Our understanding of the characters is thus advanced through our appreciation of the function of Shakespeare's words in their original context.

Finally, the form of the quotation can be as varied as in Lucian. We have seen Fielding quoting Juvenal with an emendation which, having no other apparent function, is perhaps just a slip of the memory. He also uses contamination for comic effect. In *TJ* 8. 9, Partridge observes: 'And to forsake such a house, and go rambling about the country the Lord knows whither, *per devia rura viarum*', where the garbling of two tags, like the centos given to Zeus or Menippus, makes a comic point about the speaker. Fielding also exploits the humorous possibilities of the gross misapplication of a quotation. Thus Tom Jones and Mrs Walters (*TJ* 9. 5):

Many other weapons did she assay; but the God of Eating (if there be any such deity, for I do not confidently assert it) preserved his votary; or perhaps it may not be *dignus vindice nodus* and the present security of Jones may be accounted for by natural means . . .

The highly technical reference to dénouement from Horace's *Ars poetica* 191 is put to a purely frivolous mock-heroic use.

As a final example of the way in which Fielding can use quotation as thickly and with as much variety as Lucian, let us look at a short passage from *TJ* 12. 10:

Jones, who in the compliance of his disposition (tho' not in his prudence) a little resembled his lively Sophia, was easily prevailed on to satisfy Mr Dowling's curiosity, by relating the history of his birth and education, which he did like Othello,

—even from his boyish years
to th' very moment he was bade to tell;

the which to hear, Dowling, like Desdemona, did *seriously incline;*

He swore 'twas strange, 'twas passing strange;
'Twas pitiful, 'twas wondrous pitiful.

In all three cases the Othello quotations (I. iii, 131–2, 146, 159–60) are strictly ornamental, but they are integrated in that they are essential to the narrative progress of the text. 'Seriously inclined' is worked into the grammar of the passage, the other two quotations are introduced, as are so many ornamental quotations in Lucian, in the form of comparisons. The slight misquotation in the first has no apparent deliberate purpose, whereas the alterations in the last, emphasizing the absurdly inapposite substitution of Dowling for Desdemona, enhance the humour.

The effect of this coincidence of satirical effects and verbal manner is to make Fielding's claim that his style is modelled on Lucian's seem, taken in its broadest meaning, hardly an exaggeration. When reading the major novels, however, one's awareness of this aspect of his writing is rightly subordinated to an appreciation of elements of the novelist's art which are quite alien to anything Lucian wrote, if only because of the very nature of the novel as a fictional form. It is when one comes to *Jonathan Wild* that the concentration of Lucianic effects instantly makes the parallel between the two writers seem the result of an important creative influence. *The History of the Life of the Late Mr Jonathan Wild the Great* is, in its major lines, Fielding's *Alexander or the False Prophet*. The two works are both biographies of villains,[1] with a number of themes in common: the denigration of the hero's background and upbringing, the hero's indifference to normal moral and sexual standards, his apprenticeship to another villain whose talents are rapidly outstripped, and the rake's progress towards an eventual 'apotheosis'. But there are more fundamental links. Lucian's opening paragraph reveals the implicit comparison with Alexander the Great on which the moral of his work is structured:

Perhaps, my dear Celsus, you think you are asking me to do something slight and easy, when you command me to write down in book form, and send you, the life of Alexander, the charlatan of Abonuteichus, with all his schemes, deeds of daring and pieces of trickery. But if one wanted to go over each point in accurate detail, it would be no less a task than to write up the deeds of Alexander, son of Philip. The one was as great in villainy as the other in valour.

The title of Fielding's book, with its use of 'the Great' as a qualification of the hero's name, the comparison with the deeds of Alexander and of Julius Caesar in the opening chapter, and the emphasis on the young

---

[1] The background to Fielding's work is set out in W. R. Irwin, *The Making of 'Jonathan Wild'*, New York 1941.

Wild's interest in Alexander (ch. 3), make the same parallel, with the exception that Lucian's last sentence would, for Fielding, have to read: 'The one was as great in villainy as the other', Alexander of Macedon being, as we have seen from both the *Dialogue* and *Journey*, one of his bugbears. Both writers are in fact dealing in abstract studies of certain qualities, of which a high degree of intelligence combined with a complete absence of moral scruple are the foremost. Consummate hypocrisy is a constant feature of the conduct of both heroes: Alexander is false priest, Wild is both thief and thief-taker; both men build up a full-scale industry designed to fleece the public; both show indifference to human life (although Alexander merely tries to dispose of his enemies, whereas Wild is to have his own gang hanged if they cross him in any way). Fielding carries the abstract meaning of his work over into a whole new field by making the contrastive study of greatness (in the worldly sense) and goodness an allegory for the English political scene. Wild and his methods had, since before his death, been used as a basis for satire against the Prime Minister, Walpole (cf. the parallel arch-rogue/politician in Gay's *The Beggar's Opera*); it is Walpole's cult of the individual in politics, and his pursuit of the interests of party over nation which Fielding here attacks. The effect of this primary interest in elements other than the purely biographical is to produce a relationship between text and reality similar in the case of *Jonathan Wild* to Lucian's reworking of the life of Alexander of Abonuteichus. In each case the hero as a historical entity means far less to the author than the hero as symbol. Consequently, in writing their works, the two authors make only a restricted use of whatever biographical material was available to them. They adopt a conventional characterization for their central figure, with enough biographical detail to make him recognizable, and add characteristics and incidents of their own invention. This is, I think, a clear case of Fielding arriving naturally, through his own interest in political satire and the moral issue of greatness versus goodness, at a subject which he instinctively approaches in the manner of a Lucianic pamphlet. There is no question of conscious imitation of Lucian, with the exception of a section of Mrs Heartfree's voyage (ch. 9, pp. 346–54 in the 1743 edition, but omitted from later editions) which contains motifs from *A True Story*. In this original version Mrs Heartfree's tribulations were extended into a fantastic traveller's tale. It opened with an encounter with an elephant comparable in size with Windsor Castle, and the killing of this monster by a sailor who walks inside it and shoots it through the heart. The travellers later see a snake a quarter mile long, shoot a lark weighing thirty stone, find a phoenix expiring in flames, and finally hit upon 'something resembling the famous Stonehenge in Wiltshire, and which we found to be a bed of pumpkins', one of which they scoop out and rest inside it from the heat of the sun. Here we see the familiar Lucianic motifs of ludicrously large monsters (1. 30), the comparison of monsters with architectural features (1. 18), and the idea of killing a monster from the inside (2. 1). The pumpkins, in particular, are probably a direct borrowing from 2. 37, where hollowed out giant pumpkins are used as boats. Entertaining though this piece of light literary satire may be, it is out of tune with the general tone of the work, and detracts from the reader's sympathy with Mrs Heartfree. It is Lucianic in a way irrelevant to its context.

Fielding's approach to his material is, in general, Lucianic in a way entirely germane to his main theses. For though he attacks Wild as a villain, he does it not with the largely direct attack of *Alexander*, but with the indirect mock-encomium of *A Professor of Public Speaking*. Throughout the work natural values are inverted, just as they are by both narrator and orator in Lucian's work. This applies not just to the portrait of the negative characters, Wild and his gang, the count, Laetitia, but to the positive ones too. The Heartfrees, for all they show the same gullibility as Rutilianus (*Alexander*), are ridiculed for the purpose of praise, and not, as Rutilianus is, because they have any glaring faults. At the same time, as in *A Professor of Public Speaking*, certain verbal elements intrude into the praise of villainy in such a way as to stabilize the reader's moral sense. Thus in ch. 1 the narrator, attacking Alexander and Caesar for such 'sneaking qualities' as clemency which detract from their glory, brings us up short by leading his definition of the function of greatness to a climax on a word entirely at odds with his apparent meaning:

Now, who doth not see that such sneaking qualities as these are rather to be bewailed as imperfections than admired as ornaments in these great men rather obscuring their glory, and holding them back in their race to greatness, indeed unworthy the end for which they seem to have come into the world, viz of perpetrating vast and mighty mischief?

This kind of verbal surprise prepares the reader for that eventual stage in Wild's career when true values will begin to reassert themselves. For example, in 4. 6, Heartfree's innocence is discovered by a justice in terms which the narrator makes no attempt to invert: 'The justice having thus luckily and timely discovered this scene of villainy, alias greatness (etc).'

An inevitable consequence of the inverted presentation of values is to allow the characters to unmask themselves, as well as for them to be commented upon ironically via the narrator. That Wild should betray his character in deed and word during the normal conduct of the narrative is a natural consequence of the way that character is created in a novel. But Fielding is also fond of allowing him set-piece orations in which the abstractions for which Wild is symbol can be allowed to betray themselves through his oratory, just as in the second half of *A Professor of Public Speaking* the trainer condemns himself. The rhetorical *syncrisis* between prig and statesman which is Wild's contribution to the dialogue on greatness held with the count (1. 5), the speech on villainy delivered to the warring factions of prigs ('On hats', 2. 6), the soliloquy in Newgate marking his response to the arrival of Heartfree's death warrant (4. 4) are all examples of this. The first two have a political function; the last-named is part of the wider moral issues, restating the parallel with Alexander: 'I ought rather to weep with Alexander that I have ruined no more, than to regret the little I have done.' On the reverse of the coin, Heartfree reveals the nature of goodness by his soliloquy in 2. 2, where, with minimal insistence, the narrator proposes the speech as self-condemnatory, 'full of low and base ideas, without a syllable of GREATNESS', the reader naturally understanding it in the opposite sense.

As well as the parallels between overall themes and between general ways of exploiting an ironic mode, it is also possible to find innumerable parallels in the detailed treatment of greatness as a theme in *Jonathan Wild* and in Lucian's satires. For example, the fear and inner discomfort which dog the achievement of greatness are analysed at the end of 3. 13 in terms which occur wherever Lucian treats the idea, e.g. *The Ship* 39. Stylistic devices are held in common too. As well as those mentioned above (i.e. mock-encomium and self-condemnation), there are common rhetorical flourishes, such as extended theatrical metaphor, the Cynic device favoured by Lucian when expounding the theme of life as an empty mask, and of which Fielding makes subtle use in 3. 9 (cf. his use in another context; see above, p. 205). It is an instance of the highly mannered commentary by which Fielding fastens the reader's attention on the meaning of his novelistic world, deliberately subordinating realism to the artificiality of allegory. That is not how the same element functions in Lucian, but Fielding may have read it in such a way. There are, too, of course, plentiful examples of devices such as anecdote and quotation which I have adequately illustrated from other works. Let one further example of integrated ornamental quotation in a totally inappropriate context suffice. In his absurd mock-panegyric of Laetitia Snap, the narrator brings Ovid to his aid in describing her underclothes:

> . . . beneath this appeared another petticoat stiffened with whale-bone, vulgarly called a hoop, which hung six inches at least below the other, and under this again appeared an undergarment of that colour which Ovid intends when he says:

> *Qui color albus erat nunc est contrarius albo.*

The full range of Lucianic verbal mannerisms is just as much present in *Jonathan Wild* as in the major novels.

To say that the satirical manner and much of the matter of *Jonathan Wild* make it Fielding's most sustainedly Lucianic work is naturally not to deny its relationship with Defoe's *True and Genuine Account of the Life and Actions of the late Jonathan Wild* (1725), in which hypocrisy and cruel egoism are the elements emphasized, or with the ironic presentation of the same subject in the anonymous *The Life and Glorious Actions of the most Heroick and Magnanimous Jonathan Wild.* The book's moral position must also be related to the whole eighteenth-century ethical controversy on greatness and goodness, and to the tradition of political satire equating statesman and rogue of which *The Beggar's Opera* was also a product. *Jonathan Wild* is Lucianic simply because Fielding had absorbed so much of the satirical manner (according to his own interpretation of the texts) of that writer that, on approaching a subject which echoed ideas broached by Lucian, he could write in no other way.

Fielding's debt to Lucian is evidently as considerable as he himself makes it out to be. It ranges from a few direct borrowings of scenes, particularly from *Dialogues of the Dead*, through interest in specific satirical genres, to the development of certain presentational and verbal ironic devices, which are central to Fielding's style. The final effect is not one of imitation, but of an independent literary manner nurtured on a particular style of satire. It has to be admitted that much of the similarity, thematic and stylistic, concerns elements that can be traced individually in other eighteenth-century writers, notably Swift, or in other foreign writers of earlier periods, for whom Fielding had considerable esteem, particularly Cervantes, but also Rabelais and Aristophanes. But Fielding seems to have been drawn to Lucian by a process of elective affinity. In his work he found united the many elements which he appreciated individually elsewhere. In that sense he would, I think, have identified as Lucianic in his own works the aspects here indicated, however much their presence also owed to his affection for later writers themselves influenced by Lucian, or for Aristophanes, on whose work Lucian himself had so much drawn.

Epilogue

LUCIAN did not pass into total obscurity in the nineteenth century, for there are traces of his influence in the work of major writers, such as Leopardi, and examples of conscious imitation in individual works, e.g. the 'Conversation not imaginary' in Pater's *Marius the Epicurean* (ch. 24). He simply ceased to provide an important general creative stimulus. None the less, the length of time for which his influence exercised itself in Europe and the variety of forms in which that influence was felt are perhaps unparalleled in literary history. Varied as were the interpretations placed on Lucian's text in the eight hundred years from Leon the Philosopher to Wieland, most of them have certain common features which seem odd to the modern eye. Almost consistently from the early fifteenth to the close of the eighteenth centuries, Lucian was read as a moralist, sometimes positive as with Alberti, Erasmus and Fielding, sometimes negative as with Cyrano de Bergerac and Fénelon. Although my account of Lucianic satirical dialogue in the northern Renaissance barely scratches the surface of the available material, it highlights the ambiguity of an author who could appeal to reformers (Hutten), Catholics (Argensola and the author of *El Crótalon*) and agnostics (Des Periers) alike. The curious fact is that although so many authors felt that the essential Lucian they were imitating was the moralist or satirist, the qualities which they consistently transferred into their works were the purely literary ones. It is significant that one thinks of Lucian in the context of certain genres, the imaginary voyage, the dialogue of the dead, and more particularly of certain techniques, the use of irony and burlesque. The closer one looks at the parallels between the work of Lucian and that of his most fervent admirers, the more clearly one sees that they have not, in fact, borrowed their way of seeing the world from him. They have adapted to a critical purpose forms and techniques designed purely to entertain. How to construct an armchair dialogue vividly, how to use burlesque to reduce characters to absurdity, how to present the ridiculous with assumed gravity and the grave ridiculously, how to vary the comedy of a passage with pastiche, anecdote, misquotation, these are the arts upon which such writers as Erasmus and Fielding instinctively fastened, and which are more important to the best examples of the Lucianic genres—Boileau's *Les Héros du roman*, Swift's *Gulliver*—than the mere mechanics of *Dialogues of the Dead* or *A True Story*. Though Lucian the travelling entertainer was not recognized as a literary phenomenon until the twentieth century, the skills on which his art depended still contrived to convey themselves to European writers setting out, as they thought, to emulate a very different image of their master.

Appendix

(i) LIST OF WORKS COMMONLY ATTRIBUTED TO LUCIAN

The works are arranged in the traditional order, as found in Ms. Vaticanus 90. Those marked * are possibly spurious, those marked ** definitely so. The English titles (mostly as in the Loeb translation) are those I have used in the text, the Latin ones those in more or less standard use since the sixteenth century. Where the title is the same almost to the letter in all three languages I have given only the English.

> Phalaris I and II
> Hippias (Hippias ē balaneion, Hippias sive Balneum)
> Bacchus (Dionusos, Bacchus)
> Hercules (Hēraklēs, Hercules Gallicus)
> Amber (Peri tou ēlektrou ē tōn kuknōn, Electrum)
> The Fly (Muias enkōmion, Muscae encomium)
> Nigrinus
> *Demonax (Dēmōnaktos bios, Demonax)
> The Hall (Peri tou oikou, De domo)
> *In Praise of my Country (Patridos enkōmion, Patriae encomium)
> **Octogenarians (Makrobioi, Longaevi)
> A True Story I and II (Alēthōn diēgēmatōn, Vera historia)
> Slander (Peri tou mē radiōs pisteuein diabolēi, De calumnia)
> *The Consonants at Law (Dikē phōnēentōn, Iudicium vocalium)
> The Banquet (Sumposion ē Lapithai, Convivium seu Lapithae)
> **The Sham Sophist (Pseudosophistēs ē soloikistēs, Soloecista)
> The Downward Journey (Kataplous ē turannos, Cataplus sive Tyrannus)
> Zeus Catechized (Zeus elenchomenos, Iuppiter confutatus)
> Zeus Rants (Zeus tragōdos, Iuppiter tragoedus)
> The Cock (Oneiros ē alektruōn, Somnium sive Gallus)
> Prometheus
> Icaromenippus (Ikaromenippos ē hupernephelos, Icaromenippus)
> Timon (Timōn ē misanthrōpos, Timon)
> Charon (Charōn ē episkopountes, Charon sive contemplantes)
> Philosophers for Sale (Biōn prasis, Vitarum auctio)

The Dead Come to Life (Anabiountes ē halieus, Piscator)

The Double Indictment (Dis katēgoroumenos, Bis accusatus)

On Sacrifices (Peri thusiōn, De sacrificiis)

The Ignorant Book-collector (Pros ton apaideuton kai polla biblia ōnoumenon, Adversus indoctum)

Lucian's Career (Peri tou enupniou ētoi bios Loukianou, Somnium sive vita)

The Parasite (Peri parasitou, De parasito)

The Lover of Lies (Philopseudēs ē apistōn, Philopseudes)[1]

The Judgment of the Goddesses (Theōn krisis, Dearum iudicium)

On Salaried Posts (Peri tōn epi misthōi sunontōn, De mercede conductis)

Anacharsis (Anacharsis ē peri gumnasiōn, Anacharsis)

Menippus (Menippos ē nekuomanteia, Menippus)

*The Ass (Loukios ē onos, Lucius sive asinus)

On Funerals (Peri penthous, De luctu)

A Professor of Public Speaking (Rhētorōn didaskalos, Rhetorum praeceptor)

Alexander (Alexandros ē pseudomantis, Alexander)

Essays in Portraiture (Eikones, Imagines)

*The Syrian Goddess (Peri tēs Suriēs theou, De dea Syria)

On the Dance (Peri orchēseōs, De saltatione)

Lexiphanes

The Eunuch (Eunuchos, Eunuchus)

*Astrology (Peri tēs astrologias, De astrologia)

**Affairs of the Heart (Erōtes, Amores)

Essays in Portraiture Defended (Huper tōn eikonōn, Pro imaginibus)

The Mistaken Critic (Pseudologistēs ē peri tēs apophrados, Pseudologista)

The Parliament of the Gods (Theōn ekklēsia, Deorum concilium)

The Tyrannicide (Turannoktonos, Tyrannicida)

Disowned (Apokēruttomenos, Abdicatus)

Peregrinus (Peri tēs Peregrinou teleutēs, De morte Peregrini)

The Runaways (Drapetai, Fugitivi)

Toxaris (Toxaris ē philia, Toxaris sive de amicitia)

---

[1] As the Mss. all contain the title in the singular, i.e. *Philopseudēs*, I have retained the traditional form, although logic requires the plural (as conjectured by Rothstein), since the action of the story involves several 'lovers of lies'.

**In Praise of Demosthenes (Dēmosthenous enkōmion, Demosthenis encomium)

How to Write History (Pōs dei historian sungraphein, Quomodo historia conscribenda sit)

The Dipsads (Peri tōn dipsadōn, Dipsades)

Saturnalia (The Greek uses only the individual titles for the three sections: (i) Ta pros Kronon (ii) Kronosolon (iii) Epistolai Kronikai)

Herodotus (Hērodotos ē Aetiōn, Herodotus)

Zeuxis (Zeuxis ē Antiochos, Zeuxis)

A Slip of the Tongue in Greeting (Huper tou en tēi prosagoreusei ptaismatos, De lapsu inter salutandum)

Apology for 'On Salaried Posts' (Apologia, Apologia pro mercede conductis)

Harmonides

A Conversation with Hesiod (Dialogos pros Hēsiodon, Hesiodus)

The Scythian (Skuthēs ē proxenos, Scytha)

*Gout (Podagra, Tragoedopodagra)

Hermotimus (Hermotimos ē peri haireseōn, Hermotimus)

A Prometheus in Words (Pros ton eiponta Promētheus ei en logois, Prometheus es in verbis)

**Halcyon (Halkuōn ē peri metamorphōseōn, Halcyon)

The Ship (Ploion ē euchai, Navigium seu vota)

**Swift o'foot (Okupous, Ocypus)

**The Cynic (Kunikos, Cynicus)

Dialogues of the Dead (Nekrikoi dialogoi, Dialogi mortuorum)[1]

Dialogues of the Sea Gods (Enalioi dialogoi, Dialogi marini)

Dialogues of the Gods (Theōn dialogoi, Dialogi deorum)

Dialogues of the Courtesans (Hetairikoi dialogoi, Dialogi meretricii)

Also included in Mss. are the following indubitably spurious works, with their provenance indicated in brackets:

Philopatris (Byzantine)

Charidemus (possibly early Byzantine)

---

[1] In the text I have numbered all four sets of short dialogues (the *Dead*, the *Sea-gods*, the *Gods*, the *Courtesans*) as they are numbered by M. D. Macleod in Loeb vol. VII, i.e. according to the order in Ms. Vaticanus 90. A table giving the equivalent numbers in the traditional order appears on p. x of that volume.

Nero (perhaps a work of the first Philostratus, see M. D. Macleod
Loeb Lucian vol. VIII, 505–7)
The Epigrams (various hands)

(ii) A BIBLIOGRAPHICAL NOTE ON LUCIAN

The only complete edition is still that of C. Jacobitz, in four volumes,
Leipzig 1836–41 and 1851 (reprinted in three volumes in Teubner
1896–7). However, two out of a planned four volumes have now
appeared in *O.C.T.*, edited by M. D. Macleod. The standard translation is the eight volume Loeb, variously translated by A. D. Harmon,
K. Kilburn and M. D. Macleod, but a good deal can be said for the
literary qualities of the version by H. W. and F. G. Fowler, Oxford
1905. Useful bibliographies are to be found in J. Bompaire, *Lucien
écrivain, imitation et création*, Paris 1958 and H. Betz, *Lukian von
Samosata und Das Neue Testament*, Berlin 1961.

(iii) LIST OF ERASMUS' COLLOQUIES

The works are listed in order of date of publication. The English titles
used are those given by C. R. Thompson in *The Colloquies of Erasmus*,
Chicago 1965. An asterisk against a word indicates that it is a trans-
literation.

Rash Vows (*De votis temere susceptis*), 1522
In Pursuit of Benefices (*De captandis sacerdotiis*), 1522
Military Affairs (*Confessio militis*), 1522
The Master's Bidding (*Herilia*), 1522
A Lesson in Manners (*Monita paedagogica*), 1522
Sport (*De lusu*), 1522
The Whole Duty of Youth (*Confabulatio pia*), 1522
Hunting (*Venatio*), 1522
Off to School (*Euntes in ludum litterarium*), 1522
The Godly Feast (*Convivium religiosum*), 1522
The Apotheosis of That Incomparable Worthy, John Reuchlin (*De
incomparabili heroe Ioanne Reuchlino in divorum numerum relato*),
1522
Courtship (*Proci et puellae*), 1523
The Girl with No Interest in Marriage (*Virgo misogamos**), 1523
The Repentant Girl (*Virgo poenitens*), 1523
Marriage (*Coniugium*), 1523

The Soldier and the Carthusian (*Militis et Cartusiani*), 1523

Pseudocheus and Philetymus: the Dedicated Liar and the Man of Honour (*Pseudochei et Philetymi*), 1523

The Shipwreck (*Naufragium, Nauagion**), 1523

Inns (*Diversoria*), 1523

The Young Man and the Harlot (*Adolescentis et scorti*), 1523

The Poetic Feast (*Convivium poeticum*), 1523

An Examination Concerning Faith (*Inquisitio de fide*), 1524

The Old Men's Chat, *or* The Carriage (*Gerontologia*, sive Ochēma**), 1524

The Well-to-do Beggars (*Ptōchoplousioi**), 1524

The Abbot and the Learned Lady (*Abbatis et eruditae*), 1524

The Epithalamium of Peter Gilles (*Epithalamium Petri Aegidii*), 1524

Exorcism, *or* The Spectre (*Exorcismus, sive Spectrum*), 1524

Alchemy (*Alcumistica*), 1524

The Cheating Horse-Dealer (*Hippoplanus*), 1524

Beggar Talk (*Ptōchologia**), 1524

The Fabulous Feast (*Convivium fabulosum*), 1524

The New Mother (*Puerpera*), 1526

A Pilgrimage for Religion's Sake (*Peregrinatio religionis ergo*), 1526

A Fish Diet (*Ichthuophagia**), 1526

The Funeral (*Funus*), 1526

Echo (*Echo*), 1526

A Feast of Many Courses (*Poludaitia**), 1527

Things and Names (*De rebus ac vocabulis*), 1527

Charon (*Charon*), 1529

A Meeting of the Philological Society (*Synodus grammaticorum*), 1529

A Marriage in Name Only, *or* The Unequal Match (*Agamos* gamos* sive Coniugium impar*), 1529

The Imposture (*Impostura*), 1529

Cyclops, *or* The Gospel Bearer (*Cyclops, sive Evangeliophorus*), 1529

Non-sequiturs (*Aprosdionusa* sive Absurda*), 1529

The Ignoble Knight, *or* Faked Nobility (*Hippeus* anhippos*, sive Ementita nobilitas*), 1529

Knucklebones, *or* The Game of Tali (*Astragalismos*, sive Talorum lusus*), 1529

The Lower House, *or* The Council of Women (*Senatulus, sive Gunaikosunedrion**), 1529

Early to Rise (*Diluculum*), 1529
The Sober Feast (*Nēphalion* sumposion**), 1529
The Art of Learning (*Ars notoria*), 1529
The Sermon, *or* Merdardus (*Concio, sive Merdardus*), 1531
The Lover of Glory (*Philodoxus*), 1531
Penny-Pinching (*Opulentia sordida*), 1531
The Seraphic Funeral (*Exequiae seraphicae*), 1531
Sympathy (*Amicitia*), 1531
A Problem (*Problema*), 1532
The Epicurean (*Epicureus*), 1533

Index